RURAL DEVELOPMENT: TOWARDS SUSTAINABILITY

RURAL DEVELOPMENT: TOWARDS SUSTAINABILITY

(In 3 Volumes)

(Rural Sustainable Development)

Volume 2

Editor

B.K. Pandey

ISHA

ISHA BOOKS

Delhi-110033

Rural Development: Towards Sustainability
(Rural Sustainable Development)

Rs. 2500 (Set)
Rs. 835 (Each Volume)

ISBN : 81-8205-209-2 (Set)
ISBN : 81-8205-311-0 (Vol. 2)

Published in 2005 in India by
Isha Books
D-43, Prithviraj Road,
Adarsh Nagar, Delhi - 110033
e-mail : ishabooks@hotmail.com

Laser Typesetting at : Global Printers, New Delhi
Printed at :
Rajdhani Printers, Ph. : 011-23215190

Contents

Preface

Rural development is the process of helping rural people to set the priorities in their own communities through effective and democratic bodies, by providing the local capacity; investment in basic infrastructure and social services; justice, equity and security; dealing with the injustices of the past and ensuring safety and security of the rural population.

In recent years, rural development is getting increased attention in countries around the world. It is one of the most important item in the development agenda of all countries. It contributes greatly to the development of disadvantaged (rural) regions through its various structural funds. A reason for the heightened attention is the deep structural change in rural areas, which includes not only changes in the rural economy, but also serious demographic, social and cultural transitions.

The sustainability of rural development initiatives depends greatly on the capacities of the stake-holders involved, the relationships among them and their relative power. A strategy to foster pluralistic approaches to rural development should focus on building the capacities of those who have been marginalised by development strategies as well as on developing relationships that allow more effective, efficient and equal interactions and greater accountability among all participants. Therefore, the types of changes that are needed to promote substantive and sustainable community-based development are closely associated with more general processes of promoting pluralism and democratisation. Without political space it is exceedingly difficult for local people to organise or have an impact on policy-making processes.

Rural Development: Towards Sustainability is a compilation of three volumes: *Rural Empowerment, Rural Sustainable Development* and *Rural Diversity and Community Development*. Each volume describes the issues and concerns related to its title. It is hoped that this work will address the needs of a wide range of audiences like students, teachers, researchers, policymakers, governmental and non-governamental organisations and all who are directly or indirectly related with rural development.

Editor

1 Introduction

Sustainable rural development is necessary to have an adequate supply of land which is available for development. Without an adequate quantity and quality of land for development, the ability of the planning system to help maintain viable communities and economies within the countryside is likely to be constrained. Inadequate land supply can also have a negative effect on the market in some areas, with high demand for sites which are in short supply pushing up prices and reducing accessibility. However, providing an adequate supply of land for development is much more complex than some of the more quantitatively focused debates which focus on population modelling etc. might suggest.

Rural Land Development

A number of factors influence the availability of land for various activities. Of particular concern to planners and indeed many rural communities, is the availability of land for housing. Business and Industry provides policy on land supply, which specifies that the planning system needs to ensure that appropriate site choices of size, location and environmental amenity are available to the market. This emphasises the importance of not only ensuring that enough land is provided for development, but also that the provision of land takes into account the type and quality of those sites. The planning system therefore has an important role to play in working with the market to help balance disparities between supply and demand within the context of wider environmental, social and economic characteristics. It is therefore important that this evaluation focuses on the applicability of this advice, particularly in terms of the extent to which it is regarded as appropriate by different stakeholders at different levels in the process.

There are a number of factors which influence the extent to which land is available for development in rural areas. Migration is a key factor in some areas, this exerts the greatest pressure in the constrained housing markets lying within commuting distance from larger cities. This is also viewed by Findlay et al as a long term trend which requires greater consideration on the part of policy makers for rural areas, requiring action in relation to rural space, housing, transport systems and social services.

The structure plans for lowland regions have recognised that the demand for housing in rural areas may outweigh the availability of suitable sites, and therefore encourage development towards 'preferred building groups' or by the conversion of existing buildings to residential use. This represents a policy move to increase the available land supply by looking to alternative sites.

Closely related to land supply is the supply of affordable housing. Affordable housing is an issue owing to a combination of high development costs, low incomes and in some areas competition from in-migrants. Restrictive planning policies may exacerbate problems of affordable housing provision. The continuing growth of second home owners also has the potential to compound these problems. A number of steps have been taken in different areas to address the issue associated with land supply and affordable housing.

Many councils have introduced rural exceptions policies, enabling them to grant planning permission for land in and around villages which would not normally be released, to provide affordable housing to meet local needs. The policies were not being used to their full potential. This may have been due to a number of factors such as poor communications between the planning authority and potential developers, or it may have been due to local resistance to the implementation of the policy.

Issues in Rural Land Supply

A number of distinct issues relating to rural land supply emerged during the course of the study, including:

- the extent to which local authorities are able to provide land for different types of development;
- the ways in which the recommendations on partnership working to achieve land supply are being taken forward at a local level;
- whether the recommendations on the use of CPOs are being followed by planning authorities.

The first question relating to the supply of land in rural areas therefore relates to the extent to which the policy has facilitated this process. Representatives of the housing sector in particular, felt that more radical solutions were required, including taking forward the concept of new settlements. They were also concerned that planners have continued to maintain a defensive approach to land allocation, assuming that house builders do not have the best interests of the environment in mind when in fact this is an integral part of achieving high quality and therefore marketable developments.

However, this is clearly a much more complex picture than one where planners are reluctant to clearly define land for development for environmental reasons alone. In some of the case study areas, pressure for residential development tends to overshadow the need for economic investment. In both East Lothian and Fife in Scotland, for example, there is concern that the high values associated with residential development land reduces the scope for earmarking sites for economic development — in these areas it is possible to sell land for more money than a business would generate over a number of years. In East Lothian, the protection of prime land was also considered to limit opportunities.

Highland Council noted that some rural settlements have already reached capacity, with topographic constraints limiting the extent to which existing communities can be expanded as an alternative to development in the open countryside. Stirling Council also felt that the high levels of demand for housing developments in some areas had raised land prices in some areas to the extent that it would be very difficult to viably provide land for other types of proposal.

In addition, where sites have been identified through the planning process for industrial development, there has been considerable pressure to reallocate that which has not been taken up for housing development. The Council has aimed to respond to this situation by identifying 'rural development areas' — this avoids identifying specific sites and therefore focusing the pressure, but nevertheless helps to promote a positive climate for other types of development.

Detailed proposals for each development area/ housing site will be the subject of advice from the District

Valuer to ensure that the pro rata financial burden is comparable and cost-neutral with the base case. This appraisal will take into account any public sector grant or asset contributions made which shall be entirely offset from the balance sheet.

In Stirling, policy focuses on restricting mainstream residential developments and allowing affordable housing within rural areas. However, the impact of this approach will be closely monitored by the Council, as it could have the impact of pushing up the price of land and also overlooks the potential demand for housing which migration associated with the desired increased in economic investment in the area might stimulate.

Public Pressure

In addition, in both East Lothian and Fife concerns were raised about the difficulties that arise where existing local communities are strongly resistant to the release of land for development. In contrast, some of the more 'remote' case study authorities felt that the issue of community rights to buy land. In particular, land purchase may be reliant on securing development on land in community ownership. In addition, crofting legislation and grant mechanisms aim to stimulate the repopulation of some more remote rural areas, providing crofters with a right to build on their land. Indeed, some consultees emphasised that this is potentially a much more significant issue than local authority land acquisition, given the limited resources available to the public sector to achieve this.

Rural Economic Investment

In some countries, significant areas of land have been designated for development, but have not been taken up for a number of reasons. For example, a site in Duns makes up a significant part of the area's housing land allocation. However, the supply is currently ineffective as a result of a lack of sufficient infrastructure to support any future proposals for its use in a cost effective way. Market demand was also previously considered to have limited the take up of the land, although it was also noted that this has decreased as a factor as the commuting zone for Edinburgh has grown more extensive over the years.

In Highland, there appears to be a wide range of sites which could accommodate economic uses, but much of the supply has not been taken up as a result of a lack of market demand or infrastructure. This is also the situation in Argyll and Bute where land supply in itself is not regarded as being as significant an issue as market demand. As a result, the planning system feels that it is important to focus on attracting and accommodating development in the area. The Council argues strongly against the high investment approach of building industrial capacity ahead of demand as experience has shown that this can overlook market needs.

The example of the business and industrial estate at Kilmory which is not yet fully occupied was used to illustrate the way in which a top down approach to land supply can be less effective than a more flexible approach. Area Capacity Evaluation is being used to define the development capacity of an area, with conclusions in turn being used to inform the assessment of development proposals. The methodology is currently being developed, but will include an assessment of infrastructural, other environmental capacity and social capacity. Most of the case study representatives would clearly benefit from more advice, or at least an exchange of experience, on the ways in which some of the contradictions of identifying land for development can be overcome through these different methodologies.

Partnership

Partnership is increasingly important in rural planning, though the extent of such working varies considerably. In East Lothian planners have had difficulty in working with the LEC, as the latter does not recognise a need for investment to support more rural areas, regarding East Lothian as part of a wider urban market. In contrast, planners in South Lanarkshire Council have benefited from working with partners to assemble land and funding to help encourage investment. However, they also acknowledge the difficulties in securing land to meet a range of needs for different types and scales of development. Highland Council reported a willingness to work with the housebuilding industry, but difficult in maintaining a useful working relationship with relevant bodies. This contrasts with the positive role played by Highlands and Islands Enterprise.

The use of compulsory purchase orders (CPOs) in rural development states that: Planning authorities and the other agencies involved in rural development should adopt a more positive and proactive approach to providing development opportunities in rural areas. Development plans should clearly set out where development will be encouraged, identify sites, help with site assembly and if appropriate, promote the use of compulsory purchase powers. This suggests that CPOs should be used as part of a positive approach to development in rural areas. CPOs are a means for the state and other appropriate bodies to acquire property by compulsion, where it can be demonstrated that it is for the benefit of society.

Procedural problems have been blamed for the low level of use of CPOs, although this initial hurdle may mask other disincentives to the use of the system. In other words, if the system is not in common use because it is a complex and lengthy process, users may not be familiar with other difficulties or benefits associated with the process. CPOs have not been used in rural areas and that planners are reluctant to use the system due to a number of inherent issues associated with the process. The orders were overwhelmingly used as instruments to promote urban regeneration on brownfield sites rather than urban expansion onto greenfield sites. This fails to reflect the fact that regeneration and development are as important issues in rural areas as they are within their more urban counterparts.

However, a number of examples of the use of CPO in a more rural context in other parts of the UK have been identified and reported on. For example, the Waterways Trust, which works to restore and promote greater public enjoyment and awareness of the UK's canals and rivers, used a CPO to achieve the full restoration of the Rochdale Canal. The canal had been severed by the M62 and the use of the CPO allowed the restoration to be completed with a new route passing through an existing underpass.

The use of CPOs may increase in the future partly due to current planning policies supporting the redevelopment of brownfield sites in town centre locations and an increase in infrastructure projects. Additional pressures for the increased use of CPOs may come about as a result of changes in planning policy and alterations in the available land supply. There also is some wider consensus that CPO powers for local authorities will be strengthened. However, unless the procedural problems highlighted by recent research are clarified, increased use of CPOs may not become a practical reality.

There are other mechanisms that can be used by local authorities to help adopt a more positive and proactive approach to providing development opportunities in rural areas such as through identifying sites and helping with site assembly, before suggesting the use of CPOs. Providing greater guidance on how to facilitate these processes may provide a more amenable and facilitative approach to promoting rural development than the use of CPOs. Land acquisition was much less of a problem in rural as opposed to urban settings. In general, CPOs themselves were regarded as an unwieldy tool which would only be used as a last resort.

Although land use planning is only one part of the rural and supply jigsaw, there is scope for policy and development control to be undertaken in a more imaginative way to address issues such as the availability of infrastructure. Whilst it may seem to be sufficient to designate land, the type and quality of the sites are more likely to influence their development than the fact that it is supported in the local plan. In addition, the competing pressures for development within commuter areas and the lack of market flexibility or interest in remote areas, means that emerging zonal approaches may prove more effective than allocating sites which could either be ignored by investors or be put under pressure to accommodate demand for residential development.

The advice on partnership working has been regarded as useful by some local authorities, but could be taken much further. The emphasis on traditional tools such as CPOs is potentially less relevant for rural areas where other issues are more prevalent than land ownership concerns. The need to consider rural land supply in relation to market demand and land prices is clearly central to this process.

2

Development Trends

The high rate of economic growth has been accompanied by a reduction in poverty. There has been an appreciable decline in the percentage of population below the poverty line from over 50 per cent in the 1970s to less than 30 per cent in the late 1990s. There have been improvements in the social indicators as well. The literary rate has increased from less than 20 per cent in 1951 to 65 per cent in 2001. According to the recent Human Development Reports (HDRs) of United Nations Development Programme (UNDP), India has been moving up steadily in the international comparative ranking of human development.

The adoption of planning and a strategy of State-led industrialisation was intended to lead to a more balanced growth in the country. It was expected that, over time, inter-State disparities would be minimised. Plans and policies were designed to facilitate more investments in the relatively backward areas. Nevertheless, socioeconomic variations across States continue to exist even today.

Economic Indicators

The major economic indicators used here to capture long term development trends of States are income growth, structural composition of income and employment, poverty, agricultural productivity and population.

Growth of State Domestic Product (SDP) is the single most important indicator of development for a State. Ideally, the SDP series of each State should be fully consistent with the national accounts estimates of GDP. However, this is not the case. Information on SDP compiled by the State Governments is collected by the Central Statistical Organisation (CSO) and is used as one of the inputs of national accounts estimation. In this process, the CSO takes notes of the differences in methods of estimating the SDP in different States, but it does not refine the series to make them statistically comparable with each other and with the national accounts.

Accordingly, we restrict the use of the data to comparison of the trends in growth rate only in order to reduce the error margin inherent in the data and avoid direct inter-State comparison of data as far as possible. We look at the trend rates of growth for State domestic product from 1960s to 1990s of major States only, as comparable data are not available for smaller States and new States created during this period. With the exception of Assam, Haryana, Himachal Pradesh and Punjab, the State income data from 1960-61 is available for all of the other major States. For Assam, Haryana and Punjab, data for 1960-61 and from 1965-66 onwards is available. For Himachal Pradesh the data set begins from 1967-68. Base years taken for arriving at the trend real rates of decadal growth are 1960-61, 1970-71, 1980-81 and 1993-94 for the four decades respectively.

Although the first data series continues through 1984-85, we have taken 1960-61 to 1979-80 to be the first period. This is because with effect from 1980-81 a second data series came into existence, incorporating improvements in method and extension of coverage. The

1980- 81 series was in use till 1997-98. A third series with 1993-94 as the base year was introduced in 1999, with changes in the coverage of economic activities. In the analysis of the growth experience of individual States, we will thus be making use of these three distinct data series. The source of the data is the Central Statistical Organisation.

In the nineteen sixties, the highest growth rates were recorded by the erstwhile unified Punjab and adjoining areas (now Himachal Pradesh, Punjab and Haryana). In this decade, Bihar was the slowest growing State economy recording less than 1 per cent growth, which implied a decline in per capita income. Uttar Pradesh, Rajasthan, Madhya Pradesh and Andhra Pradesh recorded less than 2 per cent growth.

In the seventies, the pattern of rates of growth remained largely unchanged. Along with Punjab, Haryana, Jammu & Kashmir, the western States of Maharashtra and Gujarat, and the southern States of Karnataka and Tamil Nadu began to register higher rates of growth. Madhya Pradesh and Kerala were at the bottom with negative real per capita income growth in this period.

The national average of economic growth picked up from the 3.6 per cent of the previous decade to 5.6 per cent in the eighties. Individual States showed the greatest consistency in their growth record during this decade as reflected in the decrease of measure of inter-State disparity from 2.20 to 1.39. The difference between the highest and the lowest values for the rates of growth across States was 4.0 percentage points. Haryana, Rajasthan, Punjab, Maharashtra, Karnataka and Tamil Nadu recorded the highest growth.

The new series of GSDP data was released by the CSO in August 2000 and subsequently updated in

November, 2001. The national average rate of economic growth picked up by more than 1 percentage point to 6.8 per cent in the nineties. The growth record shows an increase in the divergence of individual States (Standard deviation increased from 1.19 in the eighties to 1.60 in the nineties), broadly along the pattern that had come to be established in the decade of the seventies, with some notable differences, however. The difference between the highest and the lowest values for rates of growth across States was 5.5 percentage points, indicating widening of the spread over the preceeding decade.

There was one major difference in the growth experience of the nineties from that of the eighties. Punjab and Haryana registered slower rates of growth as compared to the earlier decades, whereas Karnataka, Gujarat, Tamil Nadu, Maharastra, Rajasthan and West Bengal recorded much higher growth. Karnataka had the highest GDP growth of 8.2 per cent. Assam registered the lowest rate of growth among major States.

The overall disparity in inter-State growth of NSDP and per capita NSDP of States has increased considerably during the nineties as compared to the eighties and the seventies. In recent decades, the decade of the eighties seems to be a period in which horizontal inequity across States was a minimum compared to other periods. In the nineties the magnitude of disparities was the maximum

The growth experience of the nineties has two alternative interpretations. One, that the faster growth experienced in some States is at the expense of others and is an outcome of a lessening of the equalising role of Centralised planning. Alternatively, it could be argued that the reformed economic climate allowed some individual States to harness more of their true economic potential; this was not at the expense of other States. The national average growth stepped up by 1 percentage point in the nineties, and most States experienced improved growth in this decade.

Changes in Income and Employment

The economy of the States have been experiencing major structural changes (Table 1), as would be expected in the structure of a developing economy. There has been a shift from the primary sector to secondary and tertiary sectors. Figures for all the 23 States taken together suggest major structural changes away from the predominantly agriculture-based economy that the country has traditionally had.

Comparable data regarding net State domestic product at current Prices available for 23 States indicate that in the last three plan periods, the percentage share of the primary sector marginally increased between 1987-88 and 1993- 94 and declined to a low of 30.83 per cent in 1999- 2000. The trend for the secondary sector is exactly the opposite, as it should be, and it stood at 14.02 per cent in 1999-2000. However, the share of tertiary sector has been steadily increasing from 49.14 per cent in 1987-88 to an all time high of 55.14 per cent in 1999-2001.

Table 1. Percentage Change in Percentage Share in Net State Domestic Product (1987-88 to 1999-2000)

Sl.	States	Change in Percentage Share		
No.		Primary	Secondary	Tertiary
1	2	3	4	5
1	Andhra Pradesh	-11.97	5.02	7.93
2	Arunachal Pradesh	-29.07	-52.96	41.87
3	Assam	-11.25	9.40	12.03
4	Bihar	-23.55	-10.43	34.64
5	Gujarat	-21.69	12.52	4.65
6	Haryana	-15.18	10.85	9.45
7	Himachal Pradesh	-24.96	48.23	11.81
8	Jammu & Kashmir	-11.38	-17.23	10.42
9	Karnataka	-25.42	10.51	18.50

10	Kerala	-28.01	-23.21	24.25
11	Madhya Pradesh	-16.40	21.05	13.36
12	Maharashtra	-32.48	-4.72	18.52
13	Manipur	-28.13	56.89	20.98
14	Meghalaya	-15.24	-33.22	10.19
15	Orissa	-4.91	-66.27	22.62
16	Punjab	-5.00	-5.03	7.33
17	Rajasthan	-18.15	0.85	15.66
18	Tamil Nadu	-26.15	-13.74	18.73
19	Tripura	-23.94	175.97	10.31
20	Uttar Pradesh	-10.78	27.11	2.96
21	West Bengal	16.72	-38.15	3.74
22	Delhi	-54.37	-43.14	12.07
23	Pondicherry	-56.55	164.88	-27.51

Against the normal pattern of development, there were significant falls in the share of the secondary sector in income in the case of Arunachal Pradesh, Orissa, West Bengal. On the whole, employment trends are consistent with the structural trends in income. Exceptions are, West Bengal, which witnessed a decrease in the growth of employment in the agriculture sector in spite of a sharp increase in the growth of the sectoral income; and Delhi, which experienced an increase in the growth of employment share of agriculture in spite of a sharp decrease in the growth of income from the sector.

Poverty

The growth performance of States has crucial implications in poverty reduction, which is a important objective of our economic policy. Prima facie, poverty may be expected to decline more rapidly in faster growing States.

The only available estimates of poverty in individual states for 1973-74 and 1977-78 are those estimated by NSS every five years. Large sample surveys were conducted in 1983, 1987-88, 1993- 94 and 1999-2000 and state specific poverty estimates were made by Planning Commission.

The percentage of population below the poverty line has declined from 54.88 per cent in 1973-74 to 26.1 percent in 1999-2000 for India as a whole. Nineteen States and Union Territories have lesser percentage of population below poverty line than the national average. Wide variations may however be noticed in the poverty ratios of different States. The poverty ratio in Orissa at 47.15 per cent is about eight times that in Punjab (6.16 per cent). Almost half the population in Orissa and Bihar are below the poverty line. On the other hand, there are 14 States which have less than 20 per cent of population below the poverty line.

States like West Bengal and Kerala have seen tremendous improvements in poverty levels over this period. Haryana, Himachal Pradesh and Punjab have also experienced significant gains in poverty reduction. The poverty ratios have fallen to less than 10 per cent in these States. An analysis of these data suggests that the pointwise compound rate of decrease in poverty ratios across these six years was around -13 per cent and the decrease was considerably uniform in both rural and urban areas for the country as a whole.

The different levels of poverty in the States have, however, shown varying rates of decline. The percentage of rural population below poverty line was 56.44 in 1973-74. The urban population in poverty for the same period was around 49 per cent. West Bengal had more than 70 per cent rural poor, while Orissa, Bihar and Madhya Pradesh also had more than 60 per cent of rural population in poverty. In 1973-74, Kerala was among the five poorest States, with nearly 60 per cent rural and 62 per cent urban poverty.

Among the States with lower levels of rural poverty in that period were Haryana, Punjab and Himachal Pradesh where rural poverty was 34, 28 and 27 per cent respectively. Ten States and Union Territories had

Table 2. Percentage of Population Below Poverty Line (Arranged in Decreasing Order of 1999-2000)

S. No.	States	1973-74	1977-78	1983	1987-88	1993-94	1999-2000
1	Jammu & Kashmir	40.83	38.97	24.24	23.82	25.17	3.48
2	Goa	44.26	37.23	18.90	24.52	14.92	4.40
3	Chandigarh	27.96	27.32	23.79	14.67	11.35	5.75
4	Punjab	28.15	19.27	16.18	13.20	11.77	6.16
5	Himachal Pradesh	26.39	32.45	16.40	15.45	28.44	7.63
6	Delhi	49.61	33.23	26.22	12.41	14.69	8.23
7	Haryana	35.36	29.55	21.37	16.64	25.05	8.74
8	Kerala	59.79	52.22	40.42	31.79	25.43	12.72
9	Gujarat	48.15	41.23	32.79	310.54	24.21	14.07
10	Rajasthan	46.14	37.42	34.46	35.15	27.41	15.28
11	Lakshadweep	59.68	52.79	42.36	34.95	25.04	15.60
12	Andhra48.86 Pradesh	39.31	28.91	25.86	22.19	15.77	
13	Dadra & Nagar Haveli	46.55	37.20	15.67	67.11	50. 84	17.14
14	Mizoram	50.32	54.38	36.00	27.52	25.66	19.47
15	Karnataka	54.47	48.78	38.24	37.53	33.16	20.04
16	Andaman & Nicobar Islands	55.56	55.42	52.13	43.89	34.47	20.99
17	Tamil Nadu	54.94	54.79	51.66	43.39	35.03	21.12

18	Pondicherry	53.82	53.25	50.06	41.46	37.40	21.67
19	Maharashtra	53.24	55.88	43.44	40.41	36.86	25.02
20	All India	54.88	51.32	44.48	38.86	35.97	26.10
21	West Bengal	63.43	60.52	54.85	44.72	35.66	27.02
22	Manipur	49.96	53.72	37.02	31.35	33.78	28.54
23	Uttar Pradesh	57.07	49.05	47.07	41.46	40.85	31.15
24	Nagaland	50.81	56.04	39.25	34.43	37.92	32.67
25	Arunachal	51.93	58.32	40.88	36.22	39.35	33.47
26	Meghalaya	50.20	55.19	38.81	33.92	37.92	33.87
27	Tripura	51.00	56.88	40.03	35.23	39.01	34.44
28	Assam	51.21	57.15	40.47	36.21	40.86	36.09
29	Sikkim	50.86	55.89	39.71	36.06	41.43	36.55
30	Madhya Pradesh	61.78	61.78	49.78	43.07	42.52	37.43
31	Bihar	61.91	61.55	62.22	52.13	54.96	42.60
32	Orissa	66.18	70.07	65.29	55.58	48.56	47.15

poverty ratios less than the national average, and 21 above it. The rural poverty ratios were higher than urban poverty ratios for all States except Uttar Pradesh, Andhra Pradesh, Gujarat Haryana, Kerala and Rajasthan. An encouraging trend that emerged between 1993-94 and 1999-2000 is that rural poverty decreased much faster than that of urban poverty for most States.

According to latest estimates, Orissa now has the maximum rural poverty, followed by Bihar. West Bengal registered a steep decline in both rural and urban poverty. The north eastern States have also recorded improvement in urban poverty ratios, which have declined from 36.92 per cent to 7.47 per cent. However, the rural ratios continue to be high at 40.04 percent. Among the States with the relatively lower levels of rural poverty ratios in 1999-2000 are Haryana (8.27 per cent), Himachal Pradesh (7.94 per cent), Punjab (6.25 per cent) and Goa (1.35 per cent). Chandigarh and Delhi have also registered low poverty ratios.

In the long run trends of selected States there does appear to be a positive linkage between growth and poverty reduction in the case of some States. Significant declines in rural poverty as a whole (between 33 and 40 percentage points) have been recorded in the period in question by the faster growing States of Maharashtra, Tamil Nadu, Karnataka, Gujarat and Andhra Pradesh. In the case of Madhya Pradesh, moderate growth has been accompanied by moderate declines in poverty over a long period. Both Bihar and Orissa have recorded relatively poor economic growth, and there seems to have been correspondingly little impact on poverty reduction.

The growth-poverty reduction linkage does not have such a good fit in the case of West Bengal and Kerala. Both States have recorded significant declines in the rural poverty ratio over the last three decades. However Kerala had a relatively weak to moderate growth till the eighties, with the per capita income growth ranging from negative to less than 2 per cent per annum. The reduction in the rural poverty ratio of almost 50 percentage points in less than three decades is, therefore, much more than for States that have been recording a strong growth performance.

Kerala is widely acknowledged as a success story of human development. The priorities which have guided public policy in the State have led to expansion in social opportunities, and a high level of human development in relation to the rest of the country. These policies have been followed over a long period, and it may be argued that the achievements in human development created a conducive environment for a significant decline in rural poverty and eventually also an increase in growth rates.

In the case of West Bengal too, economic growth has been very weak in the first two decades, rising significantly only in the nineties to a per capita income increase of 5 per cent per annum. However, this could not have been a contributory factor to the significant decline of 41 percentage points in the rural poverty ratio, most of which seems to have occurred in the period before the nineties. What may have set apart West Bengal is the different direction of public policy that it has followed since the seventies. The policy of increasing the access of the rural poor to assets, i.e., agricultural land, through a programme of asset redistribution (land reforms) may have helped spread income earning opportunities more evenly and contributed to a major decline in rural poverty in this period without having a noticeable impact on the growth rate of the economy.

Growth of Agircultural

The agriculture sector in the country employs over 69 per cent of the population. It is, accordingly, an important sector of the economy that has a direct bearing on overall growth, income levels and well being of the people. Changes in agricultural productivity over time in various States of the country is good index of the progress made in this vital sector by the States, and the consequent fallout on the States' economy. In order to measure agricultural productivity, we use growth in three-year average land yield for different States between the time period 1962-65 and 1992-95. In the initial period, 1962-65, the yield levels were high for the deltaic coastal States of Kerala, Tamil Nadu and West Bengal, with Kerala recording the highest yield. This was mainly due to development of irrigation.

At the all India level, land yield increased at a rate of 1.64 per cent per annum during the period 1962-65 to 1970-73. Jammu and Kashmir, Rajasthan, Karnataka, Punjab and Haryana recorded very high rates of growth. Uttar Pradesh, Gujarat and Tamil Nadu registered moderate growth rates.

By 1970-73, the relative positions underwent significant change with the introduction of new technology. With the extension of wheat and rice technology to eastern Uttar Pradesh and Andhra Pradesh during the period 1970-73 to 1980-83, these areas also started recording gains in productivity levels. In this period, Gujarat, Maharashtra, Andhra Pradesh and Punjab recorded very high rates of growth.

During 1980-83 and 1992-95, a very high rate of growth of productivity, of 3.15 per cent per annum was recorded. This growth was, more or less equally experienced by all the regions. The eastern region made a significant surge in productivity levels in this period. It registered a high growth of 3.32 per cent per annum as compared to a rate of only 0.57 per cent during the preceding period. West Bengal had the highest rate of growth of 4.39 per cent per annum. The distinguishing feature of this time period was that the improved growth rates were shared by all the States except for Jammu and Kashmir.

Looking at the entire period of three decades, it is seen that the rate of growth of agricultural productivity during the period 1962- 65 to 1992-95 was 2.30 per cent per annum for the country as a whole. The States also experienced moderate rates of growth in agricultural productivity during this period. Punjab and West Bengal recorded high growth rates in agricultural production and registered above average growth rates in agricultural productivity. The eastern States of Assam, Bihar and Orissa registered a relatively lower rate of growth during this period. The trend in increase in agricultural productivity of the States corresponds fairly closely to the trend of rapid decrease in population below the poverty line of the States. States in which agricultural production has increased significantly are the States in which there has been a rapid decline in poverty.

Growth of Population

India is the second largest country in the world, after China, to cross the billion mark in population. The population of India in 2001 has almost tripled since 1941. The growth rate of population peaked at 2.24 per cent per annum in the decade of the seventies, and has been gradually declining thereafter, though in absolute numbers population continues to grow at an alarming rate. The rate of growth has been less than 2 per cent per annum in the period 1991-2001.

During the decade 1991-2001, the highest growth rate in population among the States was that of Nagaland at an extraordinary 4.97 per cent. This was followed by Manipur at 2.63 per cent and Meghalaya at 2.62 per cent. The growth rates continue to be high for the heartland

States of Bihar, Uttar Pradesh, Madhya Pradesh and Rajasthan. The population situation in these States calls for urgent attention.

Union territories of Dadra and Nagar Haveli and Daman and Diu had rates of growth of over 4 per cent. These however could be attributed largely to substantial in migration. States like Kerala, Tamil Nadu and Goa have registered a substantial decline in the growth rate in the decade 1991-2001. These States also recorded rates much lower than the national average. The lowest rate was that of Kerala at 0.90 per cent, followed by Tamil Nadu at 1.06 per cent.

A total fertility rate (TFR) = 2.1 is considered to be the replacement level of fertility, which needs to be achieved in all States for population stabilsation. Looking ahead, it is instructive to compare the total fertility rates for 1998 and projections of TFRs for the States and Union territories for the year 2007, (Table 3)

Table 3. Total Fertility Rates, 1998 and Projected Total Fertility Rates, 2007

Sl No	States/Union Territorries	TFR 1998	TFR 2007
1	Kerala	1.8	n.a
2	Tamil Nadu	2.0	n.a
3	Andhra Pradesh	2.4	n.a
4	Karnataka	2.4	2.3
5	West Bengal	2.4	n.a
6	Punjab	2.6	n.a
7	Maharashtra	2.7	2.3
8	Orissa	2.9	2.4
9	Gujarat	3.0	n.a
10	All India	3.2	2.7
11	Assam	3.2	2.5
12	Haryana	3.3	2.1
13	Madhya Pradesh	3.9	3.4
14	Rajasthan	4.1	3.8
15	Bihar	4.3	3.3
16	Uttar Pradesh	4.6	4.4
17	Goa	1.77	n.a

18	Himachal Pradesh	2.14	n.a
19	Delhi	2.40	n.a
20	Arunachal Pradesh	2.52	n.a
21	Jammu & Kashmir	2.71	n.a
22	Sikkim	2.75	n.a
23	Mizoram	2.89	n.a
24	Manipur	3.04	n.a
25	Nagaland	3.77	n.a
26	Meghalaya	4.57	n.a

Note : n.a. : Projections for these States were not made.

It can be seen from the Table that all States will have TFRs less than three by 2007 except the newly formed States of Chhattisgarh and Jharkhand. Fifteen States and Union territories have achieved TFR of 2.1 or below, but the population of a large number of States would still be growing with TFRs more than 2.1, and these States have to be the focus of policy interventions during the Tenth Plan.

Human Development

Human development is a process of enlarging people's choices. In principle, these choices can be infinite and change over time. But at all levels of development, three essential ones are for people to lead long and healthy life, to acquire knowledge and to have access to resources needed for a better standard of living. If these essential choices are not available, many other opportunities remain inaccessible. Human development has two sides: the formation of human capabilities - such as improved health, knowledge and skills - and the use people make of their acquired capabilities. Development must, therefore, be more than just an expansion of income and wealth. Its focus must be people.

Education

Education is important in the development process for

two reasons. First, because education can be viewed as an end in itself as it improves the perception and quality of life of people. Secondly, education leads to formation of human capital and is an important investment for the development process.

Though the level and quality of education can be measured in a number of ways, literacy figures are essential in any measurement of educational attainment. The level of literacy is an important and the most basic index of the educational achievements of an economy. Besides overall education, female education has a special role in the development process; therefore, we also take a separate look at female literacy as an important determinant of development.

There has been a continuous rise in the literacy rates in India. The overall literacy rate has increased from 16.6 per cent in 1951 to 65.38 per cent in 2001. Amongst States, Kerala had the highest literacy rate of 90.92, followed by Mizoram, which had a literacy rate of 88.49 per cent in 2001. Pondicherry, Goa and Delhi had literacy rates above 80 per cent. Some of the traditional educationally backward States too have shown considerable improvements in recent times, especially in the last decade. Literacy in Rajasthan and Madhya Pradesh went up by around 20 percentage points in a single decade. The literacy rate increased from 38.50 per cent in 1991 in Rajasthan to 61.03 per cent in 2001. Madhya Pradesh registered an increase from 44.2 per cent in 1991 to 64.11 per cent in 2001.

Literacy in Bihar, which was at par with Rajasthan in 1991, has fallen far behind in just one decade. As against 61 per cent in Rajasthan in 2001, the literacy rate has gone up to only 47.53 per cent in Bihar. There are gender disparities in literacy at all-India level, as also within individual States. The gap was narrowest in

Mizoram where male literacy is recorded at 90.69 per cent and female literacy at 86.13 per cent in 2001.

For Kerala, the two rates were 94.2 and 87.86 per cent respectively in 2001. The gap is widest in the low literacy States. In Bihar, 60.32 per cent males were recorded to be literate in 2001 as against 33.57 per cent females. The rates were 70.23 and 42.98 per cent respectively in Uttar Pradesh and 76.46 and 44.34 per cent in Rajasthan. At the same time, it should be recognised that these States, as also Jammu & Kashmir and Madhya Pardesh, have come a long way since 1961, when female literacy rates were in single digits. The exception is Meghalaya where in spite of low overall literacy rate, the differential between male and female rate is small.

Sex ratio, (measured in terms of the number of women per 1000 men), is representative of gender inequality in India. Biologically, the sex ratio should be in favour of women, and it is so, in almost all countries of the world. However, a pronounced skew in sex ratios in favour of men has been a feature of most States in India. This is largely attributed to lower status of women in Indian society, which contributes to early marriages, lower literacy levels, higher fertility and mortality levels, and affects adversely progress in human development.

In 1951, there were as many as ten States and Union Territories in India that had sex ratios in favour of women. By 2001, only Kerala and Pondicherry have a sex ratio in favour of females. The ratio has also fallen considerably in some of the States which were better placed in 1951, eg., Orissa, where it declined from 1022 in 1951 to 972 in 2001, and Tamil Nadu which registered a decline in the ratio from 1007 to 986 in the same period. Bihar has shown the sharpest decline, from 1000 in 1951 to 921 in 2001. Rajasthan has registered a marginal improvement in the last decade from 910 to 922, which is significant in view of its low starting point. Of concern is the decline during the last decade, in particular in the relatively better off States like Haryana and Punjab. Kerala remained the only State in the postindependence period where the ratio remained in favour of females throughout.

Health

Improvement in the health status of the population has been one of the major thrust areas in social development programmes of the country. This was to be achieved through improving the access to health services with special focus on under-developed and under-privileged sections of the society. The infant mortality rate (IMR), measured in terms of death per thousand of children below 6 years, is considered to be a sensitive indicator of not only the health status of the population but also the level of human development in the context of education, economic conditions, nutrition etc. Poverty, malnutrition, a decline in breast- feeding, and inadequacy or lack of sanitation are all associated with high infant mortality.

High infant mortality and high fertility are related concepts. There is evidence that in the short run infant mortality reduces overall population growth, other things remaining constant. However, the indirect and long run effect of reduced mortality is probably to reduce fertility by more than a compensating amount - as, with greater certainty about child survival, parents reduce "insurance births" and shift to child quality investments.

Almost all the States in India have registered declining infant mortality rates over the period 1971 to 1998, yet some States have done better than the others. In 1981, Madhya Pradesh had the highest IMR at 150 followed by Uttar Pradesh at 130. Haryana, Orissa and

Arunachal Pradesh also recorded high IMRs. Manipur recorded the lowest IMR at 32.

By 1991, the IMR had fallen for almost all the States. But the fall in IMR for males was much higher than for females unlike in 1981, when female IMR was lower. The fall was faster between 1991 and 1998. IMR for all India for 1998 was 71. States with relatively high IMR today are Orissa, Madhya Pradesh, Uttar Pradesh and Rajasthan. The north eastern States of Mizoram at 23 and Manipur at 25 recorded the lowest IMRs amongst all States. There is cause for concern over the higher IMR for females than males in some of the States like Punjab, Uttar Pradesh, Haryana and Bihar, as the status of the female child is considered to be low in these States. Life expectancy at birth or longevity is an overall indicator of the economic and social well being of the people. As a society advances, the life expectancy of its people also increases.

Expenditure

A look at the sectoral composition of Plan expenditure in the last two decades reveals that the allocation to agriculture and irrigation has shown a downward trend for most of the bigger agricultural States between 1981-82 and 1997-98. The percentage declined from 30.17 to 19.05 in Uttar Pradesh and from 25.24 per cent 12.75 per cent in Punjab. Haryana and Madhya Pradesh have also registered falling shares of public expenditure going to agriculture. Karnataka, Gujarat and Maharashtra are the only States in which the share of Plan expenditure going towards agriculture have gone up in this period.

In the case of social sectors, many States have registered increases in percentage of expenditure over this period. Even in less developed States like Orissa and Madhya Pradesh the share of social sectors in Plan expenditure has risen. The trends are similar for Uttar Pradesh, Rajasthan, Assam and Haryana. Kerala,

Maharashtra and Jammu and Kashmir however registered a fall in this percentage. An interesting point to note is the high expenditure in the north eastern States in the year 1997-98. All these States spend more than 40 per cent on the social sector.

In order to see the expenditure undertaken specifically for human development, we look at the education and health ratios. These show the education and health expenditures as a ratio of total public expenditure. Since a large component of public expenditures in these sectors would fall outside the Plan, these ratios may provide a better comparative indicator. It can be seen that most of the States have registered increases in the education expenditure ratios. This implies that they are spending a higher proportion of public spending on education.

The education expenditure ratio has increased from 12.76 in 1980-81 to 26.34 in 1998-99 for Assam. It increased from 13.19 to 21.16 in Bihar in the same period. However, this increase does not get reflected in corresponding improvements in educational achievements for Bihar, perhaps because of the low absolute levels of Plan expenditure. Kerala, on the other hand, registered a fall in this ratio in spite of the fact that it had registered the highest literacy rate.

The expenditure ratio for health has shown a decline for most of the States. The highest fall was registered for Meghalaya where the ratio fell from 15.34 to 7.22 between the two time periods considered. It has also shown a significant decline for Haryana and Madhya Pradesh. The highest ratio in 1998-99 was for Tamil Nadu at 8.34 per cent. There is probably a case for strengthening relative budgetary support to the health sector in many States.

The fact that some States spend a higher proportion than the others on social sectors like health and education should also get reflected in the social sector indicators. States devoting a larger share to education should also register higher literacy rates and those spending higher share on health should have better health indicators. To the extent this outcome is not seen as in the case of Bihar & Assam for Education, it would suggest that the impact of proportionately higher expenditures also depends on the absolute levels per capita of such expenditures, and effective implementation and follow-up on the ground.

The first ever National Human Development Report (NHDR), 2001 brought out by the Planning Commission estimated the value of Human Development Index (HDI) for the States and the Union territories for 1981, 1991 and 2001. Although the estimation of HDI for 2001 does not cover all the States, NHDR has estimated that the HDI for the country as a whole has improved from 0.302 in 1981 to 0.472 in 2001. Kerala - albeit a middle-income State- an increase from 0.500 in 1981. West Bengal, which had an index of 0.305 in 1981, improved to 0.404 in 1991 and 0.472 in 2001. Orissa is almost at the bottom of the list, with an index of 0.267 in 1981, 0.345 in 1991 and 0.404 in 2001. The HDI for Bihar registered the lowest value of 0.367 in 2001, which however is an improvement over the earlier years. Amongst the north eastern States, Mizoram has the highest HDI and Arunachal Pradesh the lowest.

The States which have done well in terms of HDI, are Punjab (0.537), Tamil Nadu (0.531) and Maharashtra (0.523). The HDI of Karnataka, the Centre of the information technology revolution, has still a long way to go, however, with an index of 0.478 in 2001. So far as the urban - rural gap is concerned, the report shows that the national index for the rural areas has gone up from 0.263 to 0.340 and for urban areas from 0.442 to 0.511.

The rural-urban gap was at the minimum in the case of Kerala and the maximum for Madhya Pradesh. The picture as a whole is a mixed one and shows that different States have performed differently depending on the focus accorded to human development. The southern States generally have done better. Differences in treatment and status of women may perhaps explain their better performance in education, health and infant mortality. The gender development index of the NHDR is also definitely better for the southern States of India.

Infrastructure

Infrastructure is generally defined as the physical framework of facilities through which goods and services are provided to the public. Its linkages to the economy are multiple and complex, because it affects production and consumption directly, creates positive and negative spillover effects and involves large inflow of expenditure. Good infrastructure raises productivity and lowers production costs. But it has to expand fast enough to accommodate growth. Infrastructure capacity grows with economic output. As countries develop, infrastructure must adapt to changing patterns of demand. Infrastructure also determines the effect of growth on poverty reduction. The Infrastructure Index devised by the Eleventh Finance Commission is also considered.

Power

The availability of cheap, abundant and regular power supply is an essential condition for development. While generation capacity directly influences power production and hence availability, it may not always be a good indicator of power availability in the States of the country as sharing of power generated in a particular State is possible through the National Power Grid. A more reliable indicator of availability of power is the per capita consumption of power.

About three decades ago, in 1974-75, all the north eastern States had per capita consumption figures below the national level. The Union territories of Chandigarh consumed power the most (363.7 KwH), followed by Delhi (299.2 KwH) and Pondicherry (214.4 KwH). Among the States, Maharashtra recorded the highest per capita consumption at 172.6 KwH. On an average Punjab consumed 154.2 KwH. States that recorded the lowest per capita power consumption are Mizoram (4.3 KwH), and Arunachal Pradesh (3.4 KwH).

By 1999-2000, per capita consumption of power for the country as a whole increased to 354.75 KwH. The Union territories of Dadra and Nagar Haveli and Daman and Diu registered the highest per capita consumption of over 3800 KwH, more than four times the consumption of the next highest. Gujarat and Goa were the States with the highest per capita consumption in 1999-2000. Although States like Mizoram experienced significant growth in per capita consumption of power, the north eastern States continued to have the lowest per capita consumption figures in the country. Amongst the larger States, Bihar, Uttar Pradesh and West Bengal had the lowest per capita consumption levels.

The inter-State differences in per capita consumption of power have been widening over the years in spite of efforts made to streamline the availability of power. The inter-State variation, measured in terms of standard deviation in absolute terms, was only 87 in 1974-75 and it steadily increased to a level of 549 by the year 1996-97.

Growth of Road and Transport

Road transport has emerged over the past decades as the major mode of transporting freight and passenger traffic in India. It is the main mechanised means of transport in hilly and rural areas, not served by railways. The share of roads in the movement of goods and passengers has increased significantly over the years. In 1950-51, roads carried only 12 per cent of freight and 26 per cent of passenger traffic. By 1991-92, they carried 53 per cent of freight and 80 per cent of passenger traffic. Road network has expanded seven times, from four lakh km roads in 1951 to 24 lakh km in 1996.

A standard indicator of road density is road length per thousand square kilometres. In the nineteen seventies, Jammu and Kashmir had the lowest road density of 40 km. This was followed by Mizoram where road density was 43 km; it was also low in Andaman & Nicobar Islands and Arunachal Pradesh where it was 82 km and 125 km respectively. Among the States, Kerala had the highest density of 3106 km, followed by Goa at 1581 km.

During the year 1996-97, among the States Kerala had the highest density of 3749 per 1000 Sq.km of area, Goa had 2245 km and Orissa too had a high road density of 1687 km. The State with the lowest road density in 1997 was Jammu and Kashmir, which had a density of 96 km per 1000 sq. km area, followed by Arunachal Pradesh at 168 km. While road density for the country as a whole more than doubled in this period, for the poorest served State of Aurnachal Pradesh, it only went up by 34 per cent. Hilly States have a negligible network of railway lines, and roads are the mainstay of the transport system. However, the road density in these States is among the lowest of all. Arunachal Pradesh has a density of 168 km, Mizoram has 229 km and Sikkim has 258 km of density per 1000 Sq. Kms of area.

Railways

Railways have traditionally been the principal mode of

transportation in India, and though it no longer carries the lion's share of surface transport traffic, it remains, even now the backbone of the country's transport system. About 85 per cent of the railway network was inherited from the British. After Independence, the railway network has expanded at a very slow pace. The total route length has increased from 53,596 km in 1950-51 to 62,725 km in 1996-97. The rate of increase in the railway network was as low as 0.5 - 0.6 per cent per annum in the 1950s and the 1960s. This rate further dropped to 0.2 per cent per annum in the 70s and 80s. The total growth in the network between 1980-81 and 1996-97 has been only 2.5 per cent.

Rail density, which indicates availability of this critical infrastructure in a particular State, is expressed in terms of the route length per thousand square km of area. In 2000-01, the highest rail density among States was in Punjab at 41.73 km with West Bengal almost at par at 41.26 km. Bihar is well served by rail with a density of 36.55 km as also and Uttar Pradesh with 35.93 km. In the south, rail density was highest in Tamil Nadu at 32.21 km followed by Kerala where the rail density was 27.02 km. In the North East, Assam had the greatest concentration of rail lines, as compared to other States of the region. Amongst major States served by rail lines (32.08), Madhya Pradesh, Karnataka, Orissa, Chattisgarh have the lowest density of rail routes.

Telecommunications

Telecommunications is a crucial part of infrastructure and one that is becoming increasingly important, given the trend of globalisation and because of the enormous growth of information technology and its potential impact on the rest of the economy. In order to measure the extent of network in the States, we look at the spread of telephone network in terms of the increase in telephone lines and telephone density. Telephone density is the number of phones per hundred persons. Tele density is not only a function of growth of the network but equally dependent on the growth in demand, which in turn depends upon the overall economic development.

The nineties have witnessed a phenomenal growth of telecom network. The growth was faster during the Ninth Plan. During 1999-00, there were 2.85 telephone lines per 100 persons in the country as compared to only 0.59 in 1987-88 and 0.78 in 1991-92. However, the ratio is still low as compared to other developing countries, where it is around 5-6 and the world average, which is 11 telephones per 100 persons.

Amongst the States, the tele density was lowest for West Bengal at 0.10 in 1987-88, followed closely by Bihar, where the density was at 0.12. Gujarat had the highest density at 1.04, followed by Punjab at 0.88. By 2000, Kerala had the highest teledensity at 5.55, followed by Maharashtra at 5.33. The other high telephone density States were Tamil Nadu, Himachal Pradesh and Gujarat where the density was at 4.52, 4.32 and 4.22 respectively. Tele density continued to be relatively low for the north eastern States at 1.69.

In West Bengal it improved significantly to 2.06 over these three Plan periods, but Bihar had the lowest tele density at 0.65 in 2000 as well. Jammu & Kashmir recorded the lowest rate of growth of 2.8 per cent in this period. Among the metropolitan cities, Mumbai and Delhi had 13.26 and 10.29 telephones per 100 persons respectively in 1996, Chennai and Calcutta had 8.4 and 8.8 of density respectively.

Postal Sector

The Indian postal system is the largest in the world, having a network of 1.53 lakh post offices. Besides providing a variety of postal services, the Indian postal system is playing a vital role in the resource mobilisation efforts, especially in the rural areas. The importance of these functions is illustrated by the deposits to the tune of Rs.91,795 crore in 160.5 million accounts mobilised under the Post Office Saving Banks Scheme (POSBs) as on March 31,1996 3.95 Since the 1960s, however, the spread of post offices has been steadily declining.

The area covered by a post office in rural areas has come down substantially. In the beginning of the 1980s, 25.9 km of the rural area was served by one post office, while the urban post office served 3.8 km. By 1994-94, the rural post office covered an area of 23.8 km as compared to an urban post office that covered an area of 3.2 km.

In order to measure the spread of post offices in the States, we look at two indicators of their spread: population and area under one post office. Population under one post office reflects the burden on these post office branches. Area under one post office shows the accessibility of a post office in an area. These two indicators should register a fall in the growth of postal network is fast. However, the area under one post office will fall as more and more post offices are opened but population under one post office is also a function of the growth of population. This would fall only if the growth of post offices is higher than the growth of population in each State.

The growth of post offices has slowed down considerably after the 1970s. Almost all the States registered an increase in the number of persons per post office. This was a result of the fact that the growth of post offices was not able to keep pace with the growth of population. There was an increase in the population served by one post office by 1993-94. For all-India, the figure increased to 5,740. The relative position of the

States had also not changed much between the two periods.

West Bengal had the highest number of people to be served by one post office at 8,301. This was followed by Bihar where the figure was 7,658 and Uttar Pradesh 7,232. The lowest figure was for Sikkim where population per office was 1,880. An interesting feature to note is that some of the north eastern States registered a decline in population per office against the general trend of an increase in this number, indicating a significant improvement in coverage of services in the region. Population per office declined from 1,968 in 1980-81 to 1,724 in 1999-2000 for Mizoram, from 2,655 to 1989 for Sikkim, from 3,292 to 2,856 for Arunachal Pradesh and from 2,924 to 2,648 in Manipur.

Although in consideration of area under a post office hilly areas cannot be readily compared with equivalent areas in plains, area remains a good indicator of postal density. Area per post office registered a decline for all the States between 1980-81 and 1999-2000. The area to be served was highest in Arunachal Pradesh, followed by Jammu and Kashmir and Andaman and Nicobar Islands. The best postal density in the country in 2000 was in the Union Territory of Chandigarh and amongst States, Kerala at 7.72 sq. km. Tamil Nadu and West Bengal were also among the better-placed States.

Banking

The development of banking facilities in India has been significant especially after the nationalisation of banks in 1969. The commercial banks, most of which are in the public sector have gained prominence in the financial intermediation process. These banks have made significant strides in expanding geographical coverage, mobilising savings and promoting investments, especially in the backward areas.

The credit-deposit ratio provides an insight into the spread of banking facilities, credit opportunities, trend and pace of development taking place in the States of the country. The credit-deposit (C-D) ratios of bank branches in the eastern region were above 50 per cent in March 1993, declining to 37 per cent in March 2001. In Bihar, the ratio declined from 35.25 in March 1994 to 21.3 in March 2001. During the same period it declined from 60.08 to 41.5 in Orissa. The C-D ratio of the Central region fell from 42 per cent to 33 per cent, and that of the north eastern region from 39 per cent to 28 per cent in the same period. It declined from 37.22 to 28.8 in Uttar Pradesh and from 54.9 to 28.8 in Madhya Pradesh. The ratios increased mainly in the southern States. The C-D Ratios rose from 56.36 to 85.4 in Maharashtra and from 82.45 to 90.6 in Tamil Nadu for the same period.

There has been a steady fall in the C-D ratios of rural bank branches in underdeveloped regions compared to the all India levels. While the all India rural C-D ratios have fallen from about 55 per cent to 40 per cent, the corresponding ratios for the Central, eastern and north eastern regions have slipped from a range of 50-55 per cent to 26-33 per cent. Of note is the phenomenally faster growth of bank deposits in the rural areas of these regions than the growth of bank credit. Low C - D ratios in States are usually due to the perception of banks of either inadequate opportunities for lending, or an unsatisfactory environment for safe lending.

Amongst all the States existing in 1999, Goa had the highest index for infrastructure. This means that Goa was the best-placed State in terms of infrastructure facilities. The other States with a high infrastructure index were Kerala, Punjab, Gujarat and Haryana. Arunachal Pradesh, as also most of the other north eastern States, had the lowest Index. Amongst the major States, Rajasthan and Madhya Pradesh were weakest in infrastructure endowments in 1999. Infrastructural endowments of States are significant since they are important determinants in private sector investment decisions and consequently capital flows to States.

In the early plans, capital flows, whether public or private, were largely regulated and directed in nature. However, post-liberalization, and in particular during the last two plans, private, institutional and external capital flows have tended to become more and more market determined. The pattern of distribution of these flows is a subject of increasing interest. An attempt is made in this section to look at the direction of capital flows in five broad categories, i.e., Plan outlays, public and private investment, institutional investment, credit utilization and externally aided projects (EAPs).

Information on these categories is in itself not directly comparable. Information presented here for a particular category varies from giving the picture at a point of time, for a year, to the average of a five year period. There are also overlaps between public and private investment, Plan outlays and EAPs. Categories such as credit utilisation and investment may be linked. However, it is possible to draw inferences from relative rankings of States falling in a given category. All figures have been reduced to per capita terms for standardization and ease of comparison. The figures are for the latest available information, covering the years 1999 to 2001, except in the case of EAPs for which the Ninth Five Year Plan average annual flows are taken.

The general perception about private, institutional and external capital flows in the postliberalization era is that they would tend to be concentrated in the more prosperous States and those with better infrastructure. To test this presumption, we take a look at the ranking of the States in terms of per capita income, and the infrastructure index. If we relate the States identified as those which attract relatively larger per capita capital flows with the more prosperous and better endowed in infrastructure index, it is seen that there is a very high level of congruence, with the possible exception of Orissa. Amongst the non special category States which figure in at least one of the lists, Haryana and Kerala also figure in the high income/ infrastructure lists, while Andhra Pradesh and Rajasthan are among the lower income States which make it to at least one list.

In the case of Orissa, it is possible that relatively high level of external aid due to assistance received from multi-lateral institutions, as well as higher levels of private investment linked to power sector reforms of recent years have brought capital flows to the State at least temporarily at par with capital flows received by more developed States. In the case of Andhra Pradesh, it is essentially the outstanding success it has attained in attracting EAPs that enables it to be a leading State in one list (EAPs).

Of the various kinds of capital flows considered above, there is need for a special mention of flows arising out of disbursement from externally aided projects. This is because in the present era of rèsource constraints, it is imperative for the State Governments to maximize additionalities to their domestic resources to the extent possible. The single most important potential source of augmenting the State's resources is through EAPs because, typically, 70 - 90 per cent of expenditures on EAPs are reimbursed to the State in the form of additional Central assistance (ACA), and there is no ceiling on the amount a State can receive as ACA.

The amount of ACA received by a State by way of external assistance depends only on the efforts made by the State, primarily in terms of (i) efficiency of project implementation, (ii) preparation of project proposals keeping in view donor agency requirements, (iii) aggressive follow up of proposals, and (iv) projection of a positive perception of the State, specially relating to governance and reforms. This appears to be the only window in which it is possible for less developed States to attract financing for the development efforts, even if they are not so well off or well endowed in terms of infrastructure.

Both Andhra Pradesh and Orissa, in the list of top five States receiving highest levels of per capita per annum assistance during the Ninth Plan, are cases in point. In absolute terms, over the Ninth Plan period, States like Uttar Pradesh, West Bengal to a large extent, and Madhya Pradesh to a lesser extent, have also done well. The linkage of EAPs with high income/ infrastructure levels seems to be the weakest amongst all categories of capital flows, and this indicates considerable scope for State initiative.

3

Macroeconomic Dimensions

The Tenth Five Year Plan aims at achieving an average growth rate of the Gross Domestic Product (GDP) of 8 per cent per annum over the period 2002 to 2007. It also seeks to create the conditions for a further acceleration in the growth rate over the Eleventh Plan period in order to achieve a doubling of per capita income of the country over the next ten years. These are no doubt ambitious targets, but the Tenth Plan is predicated on the belief that the country has the potential to meet these expectations, provided that the appropriate policy measures and institutional changes are implemented expeditiously and effectively.

Economic growth should not be seen as an end in itself. Its true importance lies in the central role that it plays in realising the core objectives of all planning and public policy, such as providing adequate and decent work opportunities, eradicating poverty, reducing disparities and, in general, improving the quality of life of the people. Therefore, the growth strategy needs to embed these concerns and wherever trade-offs are involved, to explicitly indicate the preferred choice. Seen in this light, the growth rate is both a target and an instrument. However, it must also be recognised that the growth rate of the economy is probably the most important summary measure of the degree of success of the development strategy and macroeconomic management, and of the extent to which the recommended measures have been implemented.

The 8 per cent average growth target set for the Tenth Plan period appears ambitious when juxtaposed with the growth performance of the economy in the very recent past. However, a more optimistic picture emerges if a longer historical context is considered. Table 1 gives the growth performance of the Indian economy, relative to the targets set in the various Plans right since the inception of planning in India. As can be seen, the economy has performed better than the target in five of the nine previous plans, and even in the Second Plan, the gap was not large.

As far as the Third and Fourth Plans were concerned, the shortfalls were largely due to severe exogenous shocks that could not possibly have been predicted. The Third Plan witnessed the drought years of 1965 and 1966, which were possibly the worst droughts in recent history, and also the Indo-Pakistan War of 1965. The Fourth Plan experienced three consecutive years of drought and the first oil-price shock of 1973. More importantly, it may be noted that since the Fourth Plan, the growth rate of the economy had improved steadily until the Ninth Plan, when it received a set-back. Thus, there is evidence that the track record of planning in India is reasonably good, and indeed tends to err on the side of caution. Moreover, the evidence also suggests that there has been a steady improvement in the growth potential of the economy, and no reason to believe that this trend has actually reversed of late.

Nevertheless, the set-back suffered during the Ninth Plan period needs to be addressed right at the outset. During the Ninth Plan, the rate of growth has declined particularly in the agriculture and manufacturing sectors, as compared to the Eighth Plan; whereas in the services sector there has been marginal increase in the growth rate. Insofar as agriculture is concerned, three of the five years of the Ninth Plan witnessed poor performance as a result of weather-related shocks. In this respect, the Eighth Plan had been more fortunate. Following the Asian crisis in 1997 and subsequent reduction in the growth rates in the other parts of the world, there was a slow-down in the Indian economy as well.

The slow-down in the world economy also affected the level of exports. This, coupled with lower than expected public investment as well as the relatively poor performance in Agriculture sector in three of the five years of the Ninth Plan, led to a reduced demand for industrial goods and consequent reduction in the growth rate in the industrial sector. Some other developments, e.g. cyclone in Orissa, earthquake in Gujarat, Kargil war, etc., also resulted in diversion of resources from investment and consequent decline in the growth rates. The rate of investment in the economy during the Ninth Plan was 24.2 per cent of GDP at market prices.

The rate of savings in the economy during the Ninth Plan works out to 23.3 per cent of GDP. The bulk of the savings was accounted for by the private sector. In fact, there were dissavings in the public sector to the tune of (-)0.8 per cent. Within the private sector, the household sector and private corporate sector accounted for 80 per cent and 20 per cent of the savings respectively. On the other hand, within the public sector, the savings of the public sector undertakings (PSUs) were 3.5 per cent of GDP while government savings were (-) 4.3 per cent of GDP. The excess of investment over savings resulted in a current account deficit of 0.9 per cent for the Ninth Plan. This deficit was met from external sources.

Table 1: Growth Performance in The Five Year Plans

(per cent per annum)

		Target	Actual
1	First Plan (1951-56)	2.1	3.60
2	Second plan (1956-61)	4.5	4.21
3	Third Plan (1961-66)	5.6	2.72
4	Fourth plan (1969-74)	5.7	2.05
5	Fifth Plan (1974-79)	4.4	4.83
6	Sixth Plan (1980-85)	5.2	5.54
7	Seventh Plan (1985-90)	5.0	6.02
8	Eighth Plan (1992-97)	5.6	6.68
9	Ninth Plan (1997-02)	6.5	5.35

For the Ninth Plan as a whole, gross investment was targeted at Rs. 2,171 thousand crore (at 1996-97 prices) and public sector investment was targeted at Rs. 726 thousand crore. It is estimated that for the Ninth Plan, while the actual total investment was Rs. 2,050 crore, i.e. a shortfall of around 5.5 per cent, the private sector exceeded the targeted investment by 2.7 per cent, but public investment fell short of the targeted investment by nearly 22 per cent. Part of the investment requirement of the public sector was to be met from own savings, which were targeted at Rs. 127 thousand crore, while the rest of the investment requirement was to be met from borrowings.

However, actual public savings missed the target by a substantial margin. Instead of positive savings, the public sector ended up with dissavings or negative savings to the tune of nearly Rs. 67 thousand crore during the Ninth Plan, the indications of which were mentioned in the Mid-term Appraisal of the Ninth Plan. The fiscal position of both Central and State Governments worsened on account of the lower than expected generation of internal resources by the public sector as well as a decline in the tax-GDP ratio. With very little scope for reducing government expenditure, there was an increase in government borrowings.

The tax-GDP ratio declined from around 14.7 per cent in the Eighth Five Year Plan to 14.2 per cent in the first four years of the Ninth Plan. On the other hand, the government expenditure to GDP ratio was 23.5 per cent in 1996-97. Even for the Eighth Plan as a whole, it was 24.8 per cent. It was expected to be 26.7 per cent during the Ninth plan, with 28.5 per cent projected for the year 2001-02. The combined fiscal deficit of Central and State Governments increased from 6.3 per cent of the GDPmp in 1996-97 to 8.7 per cent of GDPmp in 2001-02 (as per the Budget Estimates).

It may also be noted that while public expenditure (including larger burden of subsidies) as a ratio of GDP has increased, there has been a cutback in public capital formation, especially in infrastructure, in order to control the fiscal deficit. The presence of growing food-stocks along with rising foreign exchange reserves also point towards a demand deficiency in the system. Furthermore, there has been a decline in bank credit to the commercial sector and banks have been holding SLR securities in excess of the stipulated minimum requirement. In addition, there has been a failure of the capital market, more so in the latter half of 1990s, to provide finance for domestic capital formation.

It is thus clear that in the Ninth Plan the economy achieved a much lower growth rate of 5.35 per cent despite higher levels of investment, i.e. 24.2 per cent, as compared to the Eighth Plan, when the investment ratio and the growth rate were 22.4 per cent and 6.5 per cent respectively. This implied that the incremental capital output ratios (ICOR) for the Eighth and Ninth Plans were 3.43 and 4.53 respectively. This increase in ICOR is not necessarily a reflection of the greater inefficiency in the economy, but could be on account of a slowdown in the demand, thus resulting in the existence of excess capacity in the economy.

The deficit in demand was seen not only in the domestic sector but also in the performance of the external sector. It may be noted that during the Ninth Plan, exports had increased by 5.6 per cent as against the target of 11.8 per cent. On the other hand, imports had increased by 4.1 per cent as against the target of 10.8 per cent. The trade deficit for the Plan as a whole was US$ 74 billion, or an average annual trade deficit of around US$ 15 billion. However, despite trade deficits of such magnitude, the foreign exchange reserves increased from US$ 26.4 billion in 1996-97 (i.e. the base year of the Ninth Plan) to US$ 54.2 billion in 2001-02, i.e. the base year of the Tenth Plan. This has been on account of large net inflow of invisibles and foreign investment. The Ninth Plan ended with a surplus in the current account, to the tune of nearly US$ 1.35 billion, or around 0.3 per cent of the GDPmp.

The Tenth Plan has been prepared against the backdrop of the performance of the Indian economy during the Eighth and Ninth Plan periods, during which many of the commonly held beliefs regarding the potentialities and constraints governing the operation of the economic system have been brought into question. Although much of this has been covered in some detail in the Ninth Five Year Plan document and the Mid-term Appraisal of the Ninth Plan, it is nevertheless useful aid agencies, such as the World Bank and the Asian Development Bank, or bilateral donors are almost always determined ex-ante and therefore cannot be treated as involuntary or as being for balance of payments purposes.

On the other hand, since the Indian government does not directly engage in sovereign external debt, some part of its extraordinary financing can be, and sometimes is, carried out through public sector entities, particularly the banks. During the 1990s, such financing was carried out in the early years, in order to restore the heavily depleted foreign exchange reserves after the 1991 crisis. In addition, the Resurgent India Bonds (RIBs) of 1997 and Millennium Deposit Bonds (MDBs) of 1999 could also possibly be classified in this category. Since 1993, by which time the level of foreign exchange reserves was adequate, 'voluntary' external inflows have consistently exceeded the CAD in all years except one, and often by a large magnitude.

To further underscore this point, it may be noted that foreign investment flows alone exceeded the CAD in six of the nine years. Thus, it can be unequivocally stated that during the Eighth and the Ninth Plan periods, availability of investible resources was not the primary constraint to growth and investment in India, and that the reasons would have to be sought elsewhere.

The literature offers a number of alternative constraints to growth and investment. In brief, there are six : (a) the foreign exchange constraint, or the adequate availability of foreign exchange for ensuring balance of payments (BOP) sustainability ; (b) the agricultural constraint, which arises from the insufficiency of 'wage goods', on one hand, and the lack of a widely dispersed distribution of purchasing power, on the other; © the fiscal constraint, or the availability of sufficient resources with the government to meet the development objectives in a fiscally sustainable manner; (d) the infrastructural constraint, which arises from the lack of adequate infrastructure for sustaining a high level of capacity utilisation in the rest of the economy; (e) the financial intermediation constraint, where weaknesses in the financial system prevents savings from being translated into investment; and of course (f) the general aggregate demand constraint in which there is a basic imbalance between the productive capacity of the economy and the level of aggregate demand.

Although each of these constraints is conceptually distinct, it is difficult to identify what exactly is the binding constraint with any degree of quantitative precision on the basis of ex-post data. The reason for this is that most of these constraints eventually manifest themselves either as an investment rate lower than the total savings rate (inclusive of foreign savings) or a rising rate of inflation. Nevertheless, it is important to identify at least which are the proximate constraints, since it has a crucial bearing on the macroeconomic strategy and conduct of policy.

From the recent economic experience it is evident that neither the foreign exchange constraint nor the agricultural constraint provides an adequate explanation, since both foreign exchange reserves and food-stocks have been rising steadily and the rate of inflation has come down significantly. All the other four are, however, candidates, and none can be excluded on a-priori grounds. Therefore, the strategy has to address the likelihood of each of them being a contributory factor to the lower than potential growth performance.

The second issue that needs to be highlighted is the fact that the growth rate of the economy is no longer being driven entirely by the level of investment activity in the country. The most compelling proof of this assertion is available from the observed growth rates during the Eighth and Ninth Plan periods. The real investment rate has been consistently higher during the Ninth Plan period as compared to the Eighth, with the exception of one year (1995-96). On the average, the Ninth Plan recorded a real investment rate of 26.3 per cent of GDP as compared to 24.9 per cent during the

Eighth Plan. Nevertheless, the rate of growth during the Eighth Plan was significantly higher at 6.7 per cent per annum on the average as against 5.3 per cent during the Ninth Plan.

Although it is tempting to infer a dramatic fall in the efficiency of capital from these figures, the real explanation lies elsewhere. The inference that can be drawn from the differential behaviour of the investment rate when measured in real terms and in nominal terms is that while the pace of capacity creation in the economy actually rose during the Ninth Plan period, the role of investment as a component of aggregate demand actually declined. As a consequence, the evidence suggests that the Ninth Plan period was characterised by a steady decline in the levels of capacity utilisation. This conclusion is borne out by exercises carried out in the Planning Commission which indicate that the capacity utilisation in a number of sectors did decline in the Ninth Plan period, especially in manufacturing in which the assessed level of excess capacity at the end of the Ninth Plan was about 21 per cent of the actual production.

The fourth feature of the change that has taken place in the Indian economy over the years and which needs to be factored into the growth strategy is the role of agriculture. In the past, when the share of agriculture in the Indian economy was high, the growth rate of GDP was strongly influenced by the growth of agriculture through its direct contribution to the GDP. Over the years, however, the share of agriculture in GDP has fallen significantly and, as a result, the aggregate GDP has become relatively less sensitive to fluctuations in agricultural performance. This factor is of course well recognised, but the role of agriculture, and particularly agricultural incomes, in influencing GDP growth indirectly through the demand side is less well understood. Table 2 presents the share of agriculture in

GDP and the share of nonfood consumption in rural expenditures over the last three decades.

While the share of agriculture in GDP has fallen from 44 per cent in 1973-74 to 27 per cent in 1999-2000, nonfood expenditure has risen from 25 per cent in 1973-74 to nearly 41 per cent in 1999-2000. In other words, a 1 per cent change in the growth rate of agriculture would have affected the GDP growth rate by 0.44 per cent in 1973-74 but only by 0.27 per cent in 1999-2000. On the other hand, the indirect effects of change in agricultural growth through the demand for non-agricultural goods and services has actually gone up from a little under 12 per cent of total aggregate demand in 1973-74 to nearly 14 per cent in 1999-2000. In the future, as average agricultural incomes increase, this indirect effect of agricultural incomes on nonagricultural growth will become progressively stronger as the bulk of the incremental income in rural areas will be spent on non-agricultural goods and services and not on food.

Table 2. Role of Agriculture in Growth

(per cent)

	Share of Agriculture in GDP	Share of Non-food in Rural Expenditures
1973-74	44.0	25.1
1983	38.7	34.4
1993-94	32.9	36.8
1999-2000	26.9	40.6

Keeping in mind these features of the Indian economy as they obtain at the end of the Ninth Plan, the growth strategy for the Tenth Plan period has to be decided. The most important feature that needs to be taken into account is the existence of large excess capacities, especially in the manufacturing sector. The existence of such unused capacity presents both an opportunity and a problem for accelerating the growth in the Tenth Plan.

On the one hand, if much of these capacities can be brought into productive use, it would be possible to accelerate the rate of growth significantly without a commensurate increase in the rate of capacity creation through fresh investment.

Thus, the aggregate investment rate can be significantly lower than would have been otherwise. On the other hand, the existence of large unutilised capacities is likely to curb the desire to invest by the private sector. Thus, the strategy will have to be developed in a manner in which these idle capacities are progressively brought into production during the early years of the Plan on the basis of demand generated from the non-private investment components of aggregate demand, with strong growth of private investment driving the growth process in the later years.

The other major components of aggregate demand are private consumption, public expenditure on goods and services, and exports. Of these three, the immediate prospects of export growth cannot be relied upon due to the conditions prevailing in the international economy. Although India is a small country in terms of total world trade, and therefore it is possible to increase exports through improvements in market share, the task will be a difficult one. Growth in private consumption demand has more or less kept pace with the growth rate of per capita disposable incomes, and it would not be desirable to try and push this up too aggressively since the relatively high level of savings of households will continue to be needed in the future in order to step up the rate of investment.

Thus, the principal responsibility for raising the level of aggregate demand, and thereby improving utilisation of existing capacities, will rest primarily on public expenditures at least in the initial years. In doing so, however, it further needs to be recognised that different components of public expenditure have very different multiplier effects on the rest of the economy. The strongest effect is through public investment, and the weakest through subsidies and transfers. It is, therefore, necessary to ensure that the growth in public expenditure comes about mainly through increases in public investment and not through a rise in current outlays, particularly on subsidies and other transfers.

It is estimated that the growth revival function of public investment will have to continue for at least the first two years of the Plan before private investment starts growing strongly enough to take up a major portion of the growth impetus. However, it should not be thought that public investment can be curtailed sharply thereafter. It must be remembered that private investment activity is extremely sensitive to the perceived trends in aggregate demand conditions. Since public investment is an important component of aggregate demand, abrupt reductions will inevitably lead to a loss of private investor confidence and a slow-down in the overall investment activity. Moreover, it should also be emphasised that public investment needs to be made in the infrastructure sectors in order to ensure that the availability of infrastructural facilities is commensurate with the demands of the economy.

In stepping up the pace of public investment, it is necessary to take into account two important facets of the role of public investment and public borrowings on the economy. On the one hand, efforts to increase the share of public expenditure in GDP through enhanced borrowings tend to reduce private investment by pre-empting investible funds and causing what is known as 'crowding out'. On the other hand, as has been argued above, private investment can be positively influenced by public investment, both through its demand-generating role and through creation of infrastructure. Thus, under certain circumstances, public investment can actually lead to 'crowding in' of private investment.

An objective appraisal of the Indian economy suggests that the danger of crowding out is practically non-existent at the present time. The excess of ex ante savings over investment demand implies that not only will public borrowing not lead to an effective reduction in resources available to the private sector, but that it may actually be necessary to absorb the excess savings and thereby prevent the emergence of deflationary pressure. Over the longer run, however, as private investment demand begins to grow strongly, the danger of "crowding out" can come into existence unless appropriate measures are taken. It is, therefore, extremely important that the increase in public investment that is being proposed during the latter half of the Plan be financed to the extent possible through corresponding increases in public savings.

The need to maintain a relatively high level of private consumption demand for non-agricultural goods and services demands that attention be paid to the growth and stability of rural incomes. Since 65 per cent of our population lives in rural areas, the potential and prospect of sustained growth in demand through enhancement of rural incomes are substantial. Mention has already been made of the growing share of non-food consumption in rural areas, and this process needs to be encouraged.

Growth Targets, Investment Needs and Resources

Taking into account the above factors, the macroeconomic requirements for achieving the target rate of growth have been projected on the basis of the planning model that is used for such purposes. The achievement of the Tenth Plan targets hinges critically upon an expected reduction in the incremental capital output ratio from 4.53 during the Ninth Plan to 3.58 in the Tenth Plan. Although the factors, which lead to this reduction, are discussed in more detail later, it may be mentioned at this stage that the measured ICOR was even lower during the Eighth Plan period at 3.43.

It can be seen that even with this reduction in the ICOR, the investment rate will have to be stepped up by more than 4 percentage points of GDP during the Tenth Plan period, and also conditions will have to be created for further increase of nearly 8 percentage points during the Eleventh Plan. In order to finance the increased investment requirement, the domestic savings rate is targeted to increase by 3.5 percentage points of GDP, and external savings, in the form of the current account deficit, to make up the rest. It is further expected that the rate of growth of imports will average more than 17 per cent per annum during the Tenth Plan, which arises partly out of the increased demand generated by the higher growth rate and partly from the planned reduction in the average level of tariffs.

Fortunately, it is expected that invisibles will continue to perform strongly and, therefore, the rate of growth of exports is determined more by supply side conditions than by the need to fulfill an exogenously set balance of payments target. Therefore, exports are expected to grow at the rate of 12.4 per cent on the basis of the projections made.

The size of national investment is required to rise substantially from Rs.2,507 thousand crore during the Ninth Plan to Rs. 4,082 thousand crore in the Tenth Plan at constant 2001-02 prices, i.e. by over 62 per cent. For this to be realised, investments in the economy will have to increase at an annual growth rate of slightly above 14 per cent. This is a fairly daunting task, since the long-run growth rate of investment in India has averaged around

6.5 per cent per annum. Nevertheless, there have been instances when investments have grown at over 20 per cent, and hence the task is not an impossible one.

Private consumption expenditure, which is a measure of the economic well being of the population, is expected to grow at a rate of 6.9 per cent per annum, which implies a per capita consumption growth of about 5.3 per cent per annum. At this rate, the per capita consumption level in the country will double in about 13 years. In order to appreciate the magnitude of the efforts that will be required to attain the Tenth Plan growth target, it may be more instructive to examine the macroeconomic aggregates as percentages of GDP.

As may be seen, the average investment requirement of 28.4 per cent of GDP involves a sharp acceleration in the investment rate from 24.4 per cent in the base year to 32.3 per cent in the terminal. Of this nearly 8 percentage points increase, more than five would be in the private sector and about 2.6 in the public. In order to finance an increase in the investment rate of this magnitude, domestic savings would have to rise by about 6 percentage points and the current account deficit by nearly 2 percentage points of GDP. Over the course of the Tenth Plan the size of the external sector is expected to expand substantially from under 27 per cent of GDP in 2001-02 to over 35 per cent by the end of 2006-07.

One of the most significant features of the Eighth Plan period was the sharp increase that occurred in domestic private savings. In the Seventh Plan, the private savings rate was 18 per cent, and it was expected to improve to 19.6 per cent. In actuality, however, it turned out to be around 22 per cent. This upward trend in the private savings rate continued in the Ninth Plan, albeit at a slower pace, with the average for the period being 24.1 per cent. Domestic private savings can be divided into two main components: (a) savings by household sector; and (b) savings by the private corporate sector.

It may be noted that in the classification used by the Indian statistical system, the household sector comprises not only of households in the common understanding of the term, but also of all unincorporated enterprises. Thus, the savings behaviour of the household sector is determined both by the level and growth of personal disposable income, and by the profitability and share in GDP of unregistered enterprises. Much of the increase in the savings rate of this sector during the Eighth and Ninth Plans has been the consequence of a higher growth in disposable incomes than of GDP arising out of the steady reduction in the tax/GDP ratio. In addition, during the Ninth Plan, the share in GDP of the unincorporated sector has gone up.

During the Tenth Plan period, however, fiscal imperatives demand that the tax/GDP ratio be stepped up significantly, which would tend to reduce household savings. On the other hand, the rapid increase in incomes arising from higher growth will tend to raise it. On the balance, therefore, it is expected that the household savings rate will tend to decline during the Tenth Plan period. The gross savings of the private corporate sector primarily comprises the depreciation reserve and retained earnings of corporate entities. The savings rate of this sector, therefore, depends upon its share in GDP, its profit rate and its capital intensity. This rate has registered a steady and sustained

As a result, the CAD will have to rise steadily in order to provide the necessary resources for the growth acceleration. By the end of the Tenth Plan, therefore, the CAD is likely to rise to 2.85 per cent of GDP. Balance of payments sustainability considerations demand that at the projected rates of growth of exports, the CAD should not exceed 3 per cent of GDP for any length of time.

Thus, by the end of the Plan period, the CAD will be approaching the sustainable maximum, and any further expansion of the CAD during the Plan period runs the risk of leading to a violation of prudential considerations.

The most critical, and perhaps the most contentious, element of the macroeconomic projections made for the Tenth Plan is the investment requirement that has been specified. After the experience of the Ninth Plan, there may be some scepticism about the possibility of raising the growth rate of the economy by nearly 2.6 percentage points with an increase in the investment rate of just above 4 percentage points. These figures taken in isolation would appear to indicate that the incremental capital-output ratio (ICOR) being used for the additional growth is only about 1.6. Such an interpretation would, however, be completely wrong. It may, therefore, be desirable to spell out with some clarity the nature of the relationship between growth and investment that is being contemplated for the Tenth Plan.

The incremental capital-output ratio (ICOR) is a summary expression for the existing technical conditions and structural configuration of the economy which captures the relationship between investment and additional productive capacity. The first point that needs to be made is that the ICOR relates investment to capacity and not to output. The difference between the two is the level of capacity utilisation. Although ICORs are usually estimated by using output data, it is implicitly assumed that the level of capacity utilisation remains unchanged or appropriate corrections are made. Second, the ICOR is an a-priori technical construct, and not a figure that arises in an ex-post sense.

It is therefore meaningless to refer to increases or decreases in the ICOR on the basis of short period changes in growth rates or investment rates. Third, the aggregate ICOR for the whole economy is a weighted average of sectoral ICORs, which can be very different from sector to sector. Indeed, for anything other than discursive purposes, it makes more sense to estimate ICORs at the sectoral level than for the GDP as a whole. Thus, the aggregate ICOR depends crucially upon the sectoral composition of growth and investment. The sectoral structure of growth, in turn, depends upon a number of factors such as pattern of demand, the nature of inter-sectoral linkages, and the possibilities offered by trade. These complexities are best handled by the use of planning models which are designed to capture the linkages and constraints.

Recent theoretical research suggests that the relationship between the investment rate and the growth rate of capacity is not constant. As a result, rates of growth that are significantly higher than experienced in the past require investment rates which are proportionately not as high. In addition, adjustment has to be made for the availability of excess capacities, which can be brought into use to raise the growth rate, which further reduces the required investment. As has already been mentioned, there is substantial excess capacity available in the Indian economy, particularly in manufacturing, in the base year of the Tenth Plan. These factors have been taken into account while working out the sectoral structure of growth during the Tenth Plan and the sectoral ICORs.

This information is presented in Table 3. As may be seen, the implicit sectoral ICORs, which have been computed as the ratio of actual sectoral investment rates to actual sectoral growth rates, have varied significantly between the Eighth and the Ninth Plans. Neither of the two sets of ICORs represents the true underlying technical relations because in the Eighth Plan capacity utilisation went up sharply, while in the Ninth it declined in most sectors. The ICORs for the Tenth Plan, by and large, lie between these two sets, and represent a possibly more justifiable estimate of the true ICORs, suitably corrected for the improved capacity utilisation that is expected during the Tenth Plan period.

It should perhaps be mentioned that the ICORs computed for the Tenth Plan period do not capture the significant improvement in efficiency that is sought to be brought about by policy and procedural reforms, and through better governance. It is expected, therefore, that if the policy and the governance imperatives that have been detailed in the Plan are carried out, there could be a further reduction in the ICORs. As far as the sectoral growth rates are concerned, specific mention needs to be made of four sectors that are critical for generating the desired growth in employment with relatively low capital investment requirements. These are agriculture, construction, other transport, and other services. The targeted growth rate in agriculture is significantly higher than in the Ninth Plan, but not as high as was recorded during the Eighth Plan.

The reason for this is that the public investment rate in agriculture has dropped steadily over the past two decades and, as a result, this sector continues to be sensitive to weather-related fluctuations. It is hoped that the strategy and measures detailed in the Plan will reduce the vulnerability of the sector during the course of the Tenth Plan and set the stage for higher growth in the future. The growth rate of the construction sector has improved significantly during the Ninth Plan, and this acceleration is expected to continue into the Tenth. Even faster growth can possibly be achieved if the various land-related suggestions made in the Plan are implemented expeditiously. It is realised, however, that these are sensitive issues, and progress may not be as rapid as desired.

The growth rate of other transport too is targeted to be significantly higher than in the Ninth Plan, although not as high as in the Eighth. In this case as well, even faster growth can be achieved if the requisite policy changes permitting greater involvement of the private sector are implemented. The potential of tourism has not been adequately harnessed by India, and it is expected that progress will be made in this direction during the Tenth Plan. This, coupled with expected high growth rates in the information, communication and entertainment (ICE) sectors, should lead to an acceleration in the growth of other services, of which these sectors are a part. Finally, there are segments within manufacturing which are also important as far as employment generation is concerned.

Encouragement to these segments is an integral component of the Plan, without which the target growth rate of the manufacturing sector is unlikely to be achieved.

Despite the higher growth rate targeted for agriculture, its share in GDP is expected to fall over this period. The sectoral target growth rates and the estimated ICORs yield the investment requirements of each sector for achieving the growth targets. The main challenge facing the planning and economic administration system of the country is to devise strategies by which the investment programme envisaged in the Plan are realised.

Even in the past, when there was considerable degree of governmental control over the pattern of investment through a high share of public investment, on the one hand, and industrial licensing, on the other, the sectoral pattern of investment tended to be somewhat different from the planned. With the substantial reduction in the share of public investment in recent years and the almost complete deregulation of private investment, the uncertainties involved in determining the likely pattern of investment have increased manifold.

In the Ninth Plan, a start was made in evolving a new method of investment planning, which explicitly recognised the uncertainties involved by determining the Central Government's sectoral investments residually from the desired investment programme. It involved estimation of the likely pattern of private investment, assessing the states' desired investment pattern, and then deriving the Central investment strategy as the difference between the desired sectoral investment programme and the sum of private and State investment estimates. The advantage of this method of planning is that it first of all explicitly recognises that the Central Government bears the residual responsibility for meeting the Plan objectives since both the private sector and the State Governments may have objectives and incentive structures which may not necessarily be coincident with the national Plan.

Second, it allows identification of sectors that may receive excessive or insufficient investment even after best efforts are made in suitably reorienting the Central investment structure. This information gives valuable pointers to the nature of policy changes that may be necessary to alter the investment pattern of the private sector through the market mechanism. This methodology of investment planning has been found to be very useful, and is continued in the Tenth Plan as well.

There are, however, a few areas of significant mismatch, which need to be noted and discussed. First and foremost, there are three sectors - Agriculture and Allied activities, Mining and Quarrying, and Construction - which apparently are likely to receive excess investments. Such an interpretation needs to be made with a great deal of caution, since they may reflect more the inherent limitations of the formal planning model than anything else. There are two main

Table 3: Sectoral Growth Rates and ICORs

	Sectors	Eighth Plan		Ninth Plan		Tenth Plan	
		Growth Rate (%)	ICOR	Growth Rate (%)	ICOR	Growth Rate (%)	ICOR
1	Agriculture & Allied activities	4.69	1.59	2.06	4.05	3.97	1.99
2	Mining & Quarrying	3.59	10.74	3.81	5.44	4.30	7.99
3	Manufacturing	9.77	6.67	3.68	18.37	9.82	7.77
4	Elect, Gas& Water Supply	5.50	18.00	6.46	15.43	7.99	14.97
5	Construction	3.56	1.74	6.82	1.00	8.34	0.99
6	Trade	9.06	0.54	5.86	1.09	9.44	0.91
7	Rail Transport	1.95	27.94	4.70	9.87	5.40	14.66
8	Other Transport	8.42	4.41	5.63	6.09	7.54	5.37
9	Communication	14.31	7.25	17.14	5.28	15.00	8.33
10	Financial Services	10.21	2.23	8.93	1.35	11.69	1.56
11	Public Administration	3.91	7.82	9.21	4.09	6.43	5.45
12	Other Services	6.22	4.19	8.19	3.70	9.26	3.53
	Total GDPfc	6.54	3.43	5.35	4.53	7.93	3.58

limitations. First, the inter-sectoral balancing is done mainly on the basis of past experience. As a result, sectors which have been under-emphasised in the past, tend also to receive less emphasis in the future projections.

Although some corrections are made in the light of the objectives of the Plan, these are based on heuristics and can seriously underestimate the true level of correction required. This is probably the case with both Mining and Quarrying and Other Transport. Second, the ICORs used to estimate the investment requirements are based on the investments made in the recent past, and may not fully reflect the needs of the future. This is probably true in the case of Agriculture, where the bulk of the investment in the recent past has been by the private sector in low capital intensive, short gestation investments, particularly in irrigation and mechanisation.

The irrigation technologies have been mainly extractive, such as tube-wells, and are not sustainable unless appropriate public investments are made in rain-water harvesting and recharging of ground-water sources. Moreover, the remaining potential of major and medium irrigation has been untapped due to inadequacy of public investment. On the whole, therefore, it is felt that the "excess" investment that these sectors may receive is probably desirable to meet the Plan objectives.

As far as major shortfalls are concerned, there are four sectors, which need to be considered the utilities sector of Electricity, Gas and Water Supply, Communications, Financial Services, and Public Administration and Community Services. In the first, although public investment, both by the Centre and the States, is proposed to be stepped up sharply as compared to the Ninth Plan, resource constraints place a limitation to what is possible. The gap will, therefore, have to be filled through greater private participation than has been estimated. In the Ninth Plan, there was high expectation that the private sector would come in to generation in a big way, which was belied. In the Tenth Plan, however, the focus has shifted to privatisation of distribution, which holds out better hope for higher private investment.

As far as communication is concerned, the estimates made for private investment is probably on the lower side due to the fact that private participation in this field is of relatively recent origin, and there have been a number of teething problems in the policy framework. Most of these have been ironed out, and there are expectations that private investment will accelerate sharply during the Tenth Plan and thereby bridge the differential. A similar situation obtains in the financial sector as well, and private participation in insurance should improve the investment level. It should, however, be mentioned that although the bulk of the financial sector is in the public sector, it does not fall under the purview of the public sector plan. There is some concern that unless the ability of the public sector banks to increase their capital base is enhanced, there could be a problem for them to enhance their lending ability due to capital adequacy constraints.

This can be done in two ways - either through the government increasing its equity contribution or by greater private participation in ownership. In principle, it has been decided to lower the government's shareholding to 33 per cent, but little progress has been seen in this regard in recent years. In view of the acceleration in the growth rate that is being proposed for the Tenth Plan, there is considerable urgency in taking the necessary steps.

The investment requirement for Public Administration and Community Services tends to be somewhat understated by the conventional planning methodology since the planning model does not adequately capture the non-economic benefits of public health and education expenditure and entirely misses both the economic and noneconomic contribution of law and order and justice. It is quite clear that the transition to a fully functioning market economy will be retarded unless adequate provision is made for these functions of the State. Unfortunately, fiscal constraints prevent further allocations in these areas, and every effort will need to be made by both the centre and the states to find additional resources for investment, since these are functions which cannot be taken up in the private sector.

Finally, mention must be made of Rail Transport, which too is likely to receive less than adequate investment during the Tenth Plan. The main problem here is the inability of the Indian Railways to raise sufficient internal resources to fund its investment needs, despite the existence of potential. Further subventions from the government will not be possible, given the competing claims, and every effort will need to be made by the railways to improve internal resource generation through the measures that have been proposed in the appropriate section of this Plan document.

Regional Balancing and Poverty

An important objective of the various Plans in the past has been balanced regional development. However, the Tenth Plan differs from the earlier Plans in one major respect and that is that it specifies targets for the growth rate for each State in consultation with the state governments. As has already been mentioned, such a break-down is necessary to ensure that there is non-trivial consistency between the national target and the State-wise growth rates.

During the Eighth and Ninth Plan periods the rate of growth in the better off States (i.e. States with higher per capita SDP), viz. Gujarat, Maharashtra, etc., have generally been higher than the States with lower level of per capita income like Bihar, Orissa and Uttar Pradesh. Such a phenomenon has resulted in higher income differences in the States. According to some studies, the regional disparities tended to increase gradually in the 1980s followed by a relatively steep increase in the early years after the reforms were launched, and a gradual increase through the 1990s. That different States have performed differently, despite the 'regionally unbiased' nature of economic reforms that have been pursued, can perhaps be attributed to the fact that some of the better off States have generally had better governance and followed growth-enhancing policies more effectively than others. The poorer States would have to raise their rates of growth to bridge this gap.

Table 4. Growth Rates in State Domestic Product in Different Plans

(percent per annum)

Sl. No.	State/UT	Eighth Plan	Ninth Plan	Tenth Plan
1.	Andhra Pradesh	5.4	4.6	6.8
2.	Arunachal Pradesh	5.1	4.4	8.0
3.	Assam	2.8	2.1	6.2
4.	Bihar	2.2	4.0	6.2
5.	Goa	8.9	5.5	9.2
6.	Gujarat	12.4	4.0	10.2
7.	Haryana	5.2	4.1	7.9
8.	Himachal Pradesh	6.5	5.9	8.9
9.	Jammu & Kashmir	5.0	5.2	6.3
10.	Karnataka	6.2	7.2	10.1
11.	Kerala	6.5	5.7	6.5
12.	Madhya Pradesh	6.3	4.0	7.0

13.	Maharashtra	8.9	4.7	7.4
14.	Manipur	4.6	6.4	6.5
15.	Meghalaya	3.8	6.2	6.3
16.	Mizoram			5.3
17.	Nagaland	8.9	2.6	5.6
18.	Orissa	2.1	5.1	6.2
19.	Punjab	4.7	4.4	6.4
20.	Rajasthan	7.5	3.5	8.3
21.	Sikkim	5.3	8.3	7.9
22.	Tamil Nadu	7.0	6.3	8.0
23.	Tripura	6.6	7.4	7.3
24.	Uttar Pradesh	4.9	4.0	7.6
25.	West Bengal	6.3	6.9	8.8
26.	A & N Islands	10.3	3.7	6.6
27.	Chandigarh		9.5	10.6
28	Delhi	4.3	9.4	10.6
29	Pondicherry	7.7	12.5	10.7
30	Chhattisgarh			6.1
31	Jharkhand			6.9
32	Uttaranchal			6.8

The achievement of rate of a growth of 8 per cent during the Tenth Five Year Plan will critically hinge on the achievement of higher rates of growth in the GSDP vis-à-vis the growth rates achieved during the Eighth and the Ninth Plans. It may, however, be mentioned that even if all the States perform as targeted, the inter-State income disparities are unlikely to decline. The Tenth Plan aims at reversing the pace of increase in inequality, and creating the necessary pre-conditions to help the worse-off States to catch up. The reduction in regional disparities could perhaps follow in the subsequent plans. Raising the growth rates is also important from the point of view of reducing the poverty levels prevailing in the country.

As against the overall growth rate of 6.7 and 5.4 per cent respectively in the Eighth and the Ninth Plans for the economy as a whole, the growth rates in the Gross State Domestic Product (GSDP) of different States are given in Table 4. The targets for the Tenth Plan are also placed alongside for ease of comparison, and for giving a feel for the magnitude of efforts that will be needed in the different States.

Given the vast variations that exist in the country, the incidence of poverty has to be treated as a region-specific issue. The overall growth of the economy cannot and should not be directly related to poverty, since it is entirely possible that the growth process may by pass those regions in which the poor are concentrated. Therefore, the methodology of poverty assessment in the country focuses on the State-level incidence, and builds up the national aggregates from these. The projections for poverty, therefore, also need to take into account the likely growth rates of the different States of the country.

Consistent with the target for the growth rate of GSDP during the Tenth Five Year Plan, the State-wise incidence of poverty by the end of the Plan, i.e. 2007, has been projected, keeping in view the trajectory that the following variables are likely to take.

— Per capita income of the State;

— Agriculture yield (output per hectare of foodgrains) in the State;

— Per capita plan expenditure incurred by the State; and

— Poverty line of the State.

The per capita income represents the amount of resources available for consumption and is expected to be inversely related to the poverty ratio. Poverty line is a summary statement of the level of prices in the State for a given basket of goods and services. Higher poverty line would be associated with a higher poverty ratio. Thus, a high per capita income may not necessarily translate to low poverty, if the poverty line is also high.

Agriculture productivity affects poverty in a number of ways. First, since poverty in India is predominantly a rural phenomenon, this variable captures rural incomes. Furthermore, since the rural areas are an important source of demand for urban products, an increase in rural incomes would have an impact both on rural and urban poverty. Second, it is not just the level of rural incomes, which is important for the incidence of poverty, but its potential distribution as well. Third, in the Indian context, consumer prices, both in rural and urban areas, are driven predominantly by the price of food, which is determined by agricultural performance. Of course, the poverty line would reflect to some extent this effect, but the latter is also sensitive to government actions in the field of food security and therefore captures an additional effect. It is expected that agricultural productivity will be inversely related to poverty.

One measure to capture the effect of government actions is the per capita State plan expenditure. It is expected that this variable will be inversely related to the incidence of poverty. It has been observed that the per capita GSDP growth is extremely important for poverty reduction and every Rs.1,000 increase in annual real per capita GSDP results in 1.6 percentage point reduction in the poverty ratio in the rural areas and 2 percentage points in the urban areas.

Based on econometric exercises, it is observed that every 5 percentage point increase in real GSDP, resulted in about 3 per cent increase in per capita terms, which would further reduce the poverty ratios by 0.33 and 0.42 percentage points in rural and urban areas respectively. However, if the inflation rate for the basket of goods and services consumed by the poor is 2.5 and 0.5 percentage points higher in the rural and urban areas respectively than the general inflation rate, then the income growth effect will be neutralised and there will be no decrease in the poverty ratio.

Another point to be noted is that the per capita State plan expenditure tends to affect poverty in both rural and urban areas and in almost equal measure. Reduction in such expenditures may seriously affect the process of poverty eradication. Agricultural productivity, as expected, does reduce poverty both in rural and urban areas, with an obviously larger effect in rural areas, and therefore, must form a central focus of our development strategy.

Based on these exercises and certain assumptions regarding the likely growth path for these variables during the Tenth Five Year Plan, the incidence of poverty for the year 2007 was projected.

— per capita gross State domestic product for the year 2007 is estimated applying Statespecific growth targets.

— the growth in the agriculture sector would be due only to the growth in yield.

— Per capita plan expenditure in the State for the year 2007 has been kept fixed at 1999- 2000 level.

— Poverty line is kept fixed in real terms.

The targeted macroeconomic and sectoral projections of the rate of growth during the Tenth Plan are achieved, the poverty ratio in India is expected to decline to about 19.2 per cent in 2006-07 as compared to 36 per cent in 1993- 94. However, most of the poor would be concentrated in only a few States - Bihar, Madhya Pradesh, Orissa, Uttar Pradesh, West Bengal and the North-Eastern States. Some pockets of poverty will also remain in Andhra Pradesh, Karnataka, Maharashtra and Rajasthan. With the overall growth target of around than 8 per cent accompanied by a high growth in agriculture in some of the States, the States of Haryana, Himachal Pradesh, Goa, Gujarat, Punjab, Chandigarh, Dadra and Nagar Haveli, Daman and Diu and Delhi, are likely to register negligible levels of poverty ratio. To take into account the migration factor from the relatively poorer States to these better-off states, the poverty level in some States has been kept at 2 per cent.

Issues in Aggregate Demand Management

One of the key differences between the Tenth Plan and earlier Plans is the attention that needs to be brought to bear on issues of demand management, which had earlier been neglected by the planning process. The Tenth Plan, however, requires a careful balancing between the demand and supply processes of the economy if the desired pace of acceleration of growth is to be achieved and the growth target met. There are a number of uncertainties regarding the generation of adequate aggregate demand, which need to be explicitly addressed if proper corrective measures are to be taken.

First, as far as private consumption demand is concerned, by and large there is little cause for concern since it has behaved fairly predictably in the past and there is reason to believe that any major change will occur in the future. There is, however, one aspect, which needs to be highlighted. As has been mentioned, the role of the agricultural incomes in supporting the growth and diversification of non-agricultural goods and services has been increasing and is expected to continue to do so in the future as the average income growth in this sector will be spent mainly on non-food consumption expenditure.

Nevertheless, it must be borne in mind that increased consumption of industrial products frequently involves life-style changes, and that such change may not be undertaken if there are large uncertainties regarding the possibility of maintaining the altered life-style in the future. It is, therefore, imperative that steps be taken to bring about greater stability to agricultural incomes. Indeed, in one sense, stability may be more important than the growth rate of agricultural incomes. In order to do so, emphasis must be placed on reducing the vulnerability of Indian agriculture to weather-related shocks through a much more intensive effort at droughtproofing, especially the rain-fed areas.

Strong and sustained growth of private investment is at the heart of the Tenth Plan strategy, and there are a number of issues that have to be addressed in this regard. The first point that needs to be recognised is that the Indian policy and procedural framework continues to be excessively investor-unfriendly. This is applicable as much to informal activities as to the corporate. There are too many hurdles that an entrepreneur has clear before undertaking any productive activity. Even after doing so, he is not immune to further harassment by various public functionaries. While there is good reason to enforce the laws of the land, this duality of control, which is exercised both at the point of entry and during operations, is completely unnecessary in most instances. Therefore, it is suggested that most rules, regulations and procedures which have to be complied with prior to investment or the entry point, should be scrapped, and greater emphasis placed on post-operation enforcement.

The corporate sector in India has not shown the kind of dynamism that had been expected of it at the start of the reform process. No doubt the policy and procedural rigidities mentioned above have contributed to this, but it is not a sufficient explanation. The growth dynamics of private corporate investment in India, as assessed by the Planning Commission, suggests that it is driven more by internal resource accruals than by any other factor.

Perhaps this is a reflection of the desire of Indian corporate promoters not to dilute ownership control, even if it involves loss of opportunities. This lack of entrepreneurial dynamism is most disturbing, especially at a time when the government is in the process of privatising most public sector enterprises.

It should be remembered that in many of the areas where the public sector dominated, non-corporate entities will simply not be able to shoulder the burden of creating new capacities, and the onus will have to be on the corporates. If the corporate sector does not fill the breach adequately, the economy runs the risk of serious imbalances emerging in certain key industries. Of course, with greater trade openness, this will not necessarily impede the growth of down-stream industries, since imports can bridge the difference between supply and demand, but valuable opportunities may be lost.

The projections made for the Tenth Plan on the basis of the past behaviour of the corporate sector suggest that unless steps are taken, private investment demand will fall significantly short of the target requirements. Removal of hurdles to the investment activity is clearly a crucial step, and this would have to be done within the first two years of the Tenth Plan, if it is to have the desired effect within the Plan period. Changes in labour laws too are likely to help in imparting more dynamism to this sector. It is equally important to realise that some of the lack of corporate dynamism, especially in recent years, can be traced to the huge excess capacities that exist in a number of industries. The principal responsibility for reducing this excess capacity through increased aggregate demand during the first two years of the Plan rests with the government, which will have to engage in an aggressive fiscal policy stance.

Another method of overcoming the weaknesses observed in corporate investment behaviour, primarily as a complementary measure, would be to encourage foreign direct investment (FDI), especially in those areas for which Indian corporates have shown little appetite. Indeed, it is suggested that, in the current context, the role of FDI in boosting corporate investment demand is probably far more important than its role as a support to balance of payments. This change should get reflected in the approach taken to FDI.

As far as the private unincorporated sector is concerned, there is fortunately no lack of entrepreneurial dynamism. This sector has played a key role in keeping the growth rate of the economy up when both public and corporate investments were stagnating. There are two important points that need to be made in the context of encouraging this sector to grow even faster, other than the general point made regarding policy and procedural barriers to entry.

First, the principal hurdle in expansion of the investment activity in this sector lies in its access to investible resources, especially from the formal financial sector institutions. The availability of long-term funds has always been a problem, and recourse has been taken to funds raised from the informal financial institutions. In recent years, even access to short-term bank finance has become problematic as commercial banks have turned excessively risk-sensitive and the brunt of this has fallen on the non-corporates.

The second issue relates to the nature of competition faced by this sector. There is a common perception that the main threat to the non-corporate sector comes from the corporates. While this may be true in some cases, it is equally true that a major vehicle for expanding the small-scale sector is ancillarisation by the corporates. There are policy hurdles in expanding the scope of ancillarisation, which have been mentioned before. These need to be corrected expeditiously. More importantly, it is suggested that the real barriers to entry for new small-scale entrepreneurs are the existing smallscale producers.

Since the small-scale units generally address a relatively small localised market, they are much more sensitive to the emergence of new competitors than the corporates. As a result, incumbent small firms tend to protect their turfs much more aggressively. The solution to this problem would be through an evolutionary process, whereby existing small firms grow into medium and eventually large firms, vacating space for new entrepreneurs. Unfortunately, in India this process is severely retarded because of the nature of policy protection given to small units, which prevents them from graduating without incurring heavy costs. This is one of the main reasons why it is proposed that the entire policy framework for small units should be thoroughly overhauled. The policy must recognise that dynamism involves both the growth of existing firms and emergence of new ones.

The importance of public investment, both as a component of aggregate demand and as a facilitator of private investment, has already been discussed. There are, however, serious concerns regarding the ability of the government to carry out public investment in the manner envisaged in the Tenth Plan. Insofar as the Centre is concerned, the principal vehicles for undertaking public investment were the central public sector enterprises. These not only generated their own resources through internal accruals and market borrowings, but were also conduits through which budgetary resources were transformed into investment.

With the commencement of the disinvestment and privatisation process, both the ability and the willingness of these enterprises to undertake investment activities has reduced considerably. The net result is a situation where not only are budgetary resources not utilised to create new capacity, even the internal accruals are being kept in liquid form and not put into productive use. This is an inevitable consequence of the disinvestment process, and should not be taken to imply that the process should be either stopped or retarded. On the contrary, the logic of the reform process demands that the pace of disinvestment be stepped up so that the currently idle resources can be used to create productive capacities, even if it is by the new private ownership.

The main problem, however, lies in the fact that the Central Government has not yet created sufficient alternative institutions through which public investment can be made, especially in the infrastructure sectors. The existing central public institutions, which are actively carrying out investment, have physical limitations on their ability to expand their investment programmes. It is apprehended that unless new institutional capacities are created in the appropriate areas, it may not be possible for the Centre to carry out the public investment programme even if the financial resources for doing so are available.

By and large, the institutional capacity of State Governments to undertake public investment today is better than that of the Centre. Although many of these institutions can improve their functioning quite significantly through better governance systems, most of them are limited in their activities by the availability of resources. As a result, the overall level of public investment in the country may be held back by a mismatch between the availability of resources and the availability of institutional capacity. The Central Government is likely to have a sufficiency of resources and a lack of institutions, whereas the position of the State Governments would be exactly the reverse. In recognition of this reality, the nature of the relationship between the Centre and States will have to undergo a change, with the Centre playing a progressively more important role in the funding of what are essentially State level public investments.

The modalities of this change would need to be worked out expeditiously so that unnecessary friction between these two arms of the Government does not take place. There is, however, one particular area of the institutional capacity of the State Governments which is a cause for worry. The Tenth Plan envisages not only the use of its financial resources but also its food stocks for augmenting investment in rural infrastructure. The Food for Work Programme is, therefore, being viewed not only as a device for bringing relief to disaster affected areas, but also as a major instrument of public investment. It is also central to the Plan for generating additional employment, especially for landless labour.

Unfortunately, the public work structure in many State Governments have more or less ceased to undertake public work programmes directly. Most of them are today no better than contract awarding organisations. The success of the Food for Work Programme and of the Rural Employment Generation Programmes hinge critically upon revitalising the public work systems at the State level so that its traditional functions of design and implementing rural public works directly is restored. Without this, it is feared that the desired level of public investment may not materialise since it would get confined only to financial resources available with the Government.

Finally, in view of the importance of public investment in attaining the Tenth Plan growth target, some mention needs to be made of the conduct of macroeconomic policy, particularly as it relates to the expenditure side. It must be realised that public expenditure on goods and services, especially public investment, is the only component of aggregate demand that is not behaviourally linked to the macroeconomic variables. These are policy decisions, and are therefore based on an appreciation of the role that such expenditures play in generating and maintaining the growth momentum of the economy. It therefore provides a degree of stability to the economic system and forms an important component of generating the required degree of confidence among private investors.

It is, thus, essential that the public investment programme, once determined, should be adhered to unless there are compelling reasons to do otherwise. The Five Year Plans were designed essentially to subserve this objective, but over the years the significant changes that are brought about through the Annual Plans has made the process much less effective. In view of the proposed acceleration in growth during the Tenth Plan, and the importance of public investment in the process, a greater degree of commitment in maintaining the required levels of public investment is essential.

4

Planning and Implementation Issues

The experience of planning at the State level over the last five decades seems to indicate that if we are to remove bottlenecks to progress, we have to step up growth rates and also ensure that the benefits of development are shared by all, in addition, qualitative aspects need to be paid at least as much, if not more, attention than the quantitative aspects of planning. The Approach Paper to the Tenth Plan had signalled that in order to achieve its Stated objectives, the Plan had to be a reform plan, and not a resources plan as before.

The Mid-term Appraisal has however drawn attention to a number of governance-related findings that have relevance at the State level as well. The beginning of planned development in India, both Central and State Governments have been implementing several programmes for eradication of poverty. However, it has been the experience of development planning since Independence that availability of funds by itself is not sufficient for tackling the problem of poverty. With liberalisation, there is an ongoing paradigm shift at the State level, with the Government increasingly playing the role of a facilitator rather than a direct provider. At the same time, more effective public intervention only can address the challenges of poverty alleviation. In this, the experience is essentially that better governance and implementation of programmes within a pro-poor policy framework is needed for effective results on the ground.

In the international context, good governance is often interpreted from a purely business point of view to mean policies that will attract foreign capital, such as effective rule of law, enforcement of contracts, protection of property rights, and reduction of uncertainties about decisionmaking by national Governments. In the context of development in a less developed country, good governance may be defined as the capacity of the Government to manage resources efficiently and formulate, implement, and enforce such policies and schemes that are in the interest of the poor and facilitate development.

However, good governance is not automatic. In the scarcity-ridden context of development in a poor society, the executive (both political and bureaucratic) may amass large monopolistic and discretionary powers for the apportioning of resources. This may result in a 'rent seeking' behaviour. With a view to preventing rent seeking, more rules and regulations may be prescribed, which may further result in delays, inefficiencies and corruption. Thus a vicious circle is set up, with noncompliance of rules leading to more rules and ending up in a situation where individuals in Government, whether from the legislature or executive, may, with the best of intentions find themselves helpless in changing the 'system', and ultimately find it more convenient to join the system rather than fight it.

Another tendency for any Government is to evolve a culture in which rules of decision-making or transaction are not easily amenable to scrutiny by the general public or the intended beneficiaries. Not only are the decisions difficult to be examined, they are also likely to be challenged or reversed, except by appeal to the munificence of the same executive which took them in the first place (thereby enlarging the ambit of power of the executive). Independent studies suggest that corruption and poor governance lead to lower growth and investment.

The South Asia Human Development Report also makes the point that low human development makes it easier for poor governance practices to survive, leading to a vicious circle. Thus, good governance and accelerated human development are inextricably linked and indeed, governance forms the bedrock on which gains in human development can be rapidly achieved.

Successful implementation of development programmes requires adequate funds, appropriate policy framework, and effective delivery machinery. Past experiences suggest that availability of funds alone may be a necessary but not a sufficient condition for tackling the problems of poverty and backwardness. The determining factor seems to be the capability of the funding Governments or Ministries to formulate viable schemes, and the delivery system to optimally utilise funds and achieve sustainable growth.

There is now substantial evidence, which corroborates experiential evidence, that even though there are variations, basic public services and programmes (such as those meant for the poor and the weaker sections) function relatively inefficiently in poorer and badly performing States. This is due to lack of motivation, accountability, absence of performance appraisal, absence of a system of incentives and penalties, understaffing and poor working conditions on the one hand, and large-scale leakages on the other.

This seems to be the case particularly for the numerous rural development programmes where studies suggest that the 'leakage' is estimated to be between 20 and 70 per cent! The weak track record of implementation of these programmes and failure to deliver intended benefits to the poor have been documented in various reports and studies including the reports of the Comptroller and Auditor General and surveys by international agencies and other independent bodies.

The implementation of development programmes by the State Governments must be more effective. Close monitoring can be organised in selected areas such as implementation of schemes relating to primary health, primary education, watershed development, empowerment of the local people to discharge their responsibilities effectively at the local level, as evidenced by the implementation of poverty alleviation programmes etc. The monitoring can be done on the basis of questionnaires designed by selected public institutions in consultation with the Planning Commission.

One way of doing so may be through a process of sampling, wherein randomly selected villages can be identified in every State for impact studies and obtaining progress reports in these sectors. These studies may be carried out either by academic institutes, consultants approved by the Planning Commission or by the Programme Evaluation Organisation of the Commission wherever possible. Incentives for improving implementation should be built into the criterion for the allocation of additional funds to the States in such a manner that the States which demonstrably perform better be entitled to more development assistance as compared to the States which do not implement these programmes effectively.

Governance reform thus needs to be at the center-stage of development planning, since without good governance and programme implementation, much of the vast quantum of resources being spent for development is wasted. It should be so designed as to bring about improved transparency, greater accountability, and streamlining of the structure of Government. Improved transparency should have the result of improving the flow of information to the general public on the modes of decision-making, and hence lead to less arbitrariness, as decisions come under closer public scrutiny. Greater accountability implies that the decision-making (and implementing) executive is answerable for the course of action that it pursues.

Since answerability is in any case implicit in the existing process, reforms should aim at improved accountability, which means that adverse results associated with wrong actions are quickly corrected and are not easily repeated. Similarly, changes in the structure and role of the Government are needed, involving a review of its role and functions, allowing it to concentrate on areas of key concern, and reducing its role in areas where it is not needed. In short, it means redesigning the structures of the Government so as to reduce distortions and allow it to optimally perform its key tasks.

Experience both within and outside the country has pointed to certain essential elements of any strategy for governance reform. This agenda of reform in governance, which is especially relevant at the State level, includes a multifaceted strategy based on decentralisation, civil services renewal, open and responsive Government, tackling corruption and strengthening the rule of law, and fiscal and environmental sustainability. Each of these elements of the strategy is outlined below.

Decentralisation

DeCentralisation of power from Centre to States, States to district, and areas within districts and villages can be one of the best ways of radically restructuring an over-

Centralised system of governance, which may be somewhat removed from people, and have limited direct accountability to them. Decentralisation results in empowering people, promoting public participation and increasing efficiency.

According to the Human Development Report 1993 of the United Nations Development Programme (UNDP), wherever decentralisation has taken place it has often been quite successful, encouraging local participation, increasing accountability of local officials, reducing costs and increasing efficiency. Decentralisation can help mobilise local resources, promote locally and regionally diverse solutions and promote equitable growth by bringing the poor into the mainstream of development. It may also increase the pressure on Governments to concentrate on those human priority concerns that are more likely to be chosen by the local community.

Decentralisation has been seen as desirable and necessary for public participation in the process of planned development. With the 73rd and 74th Constitutional Amendment of 1993, panchayat raj institutions (PRI) and urban local bodies have taken root all over the country. However, effective decentralisation has not taken place in most States, for various reasons, and efforts need to be made to strengthen and accelerate the process.

The 73rd Amendment envisages a polity where more and more powers are decentralised to the third stratum, but ironically, in many cf the States administrative and financial powers have been heavily concentrated in the secretariats and directorates. This process of centralisation of authority has particularly been going on in the last thirty years. The concentration of power, in addition to facilitating political corruption, results in making decisions the outcome of a long and tedious process that inconveniences the public. On the whole, the panchayat's role is still heavily influenced by the role of the development bureaucracy and the existing mechanisms and processes provide the space for considerable distortions and leakages. The present system is such that even honest panchayati raj institution (PRI) representatives find it difficult to carry out their functions.

In this connection, many lessons have been learnt from the experience of devolution in the wake of the 73/74Amendment. These point to the direction of desired reforms. Governments need to sustain the devolutionary process by transferring powers and functions specified in the 11and 12Schedule, to the local bodies at the appropriate level, and provide administrative control to local bodies over local functionaries. We must build commensurate capacity in the local bodies, its members and its committees through training and transfer of resources - physical and financial, encourage the local bodies to raise local resources for development, and put a system of incentivebased fiscal transfers in place.

At the same time, we have to inculcate attitudinal changes in the developmental bureaucracy, which should become a facilitator of the third level of government and help develop a healthy relationship between elected governments at all levels and the bureaucracy. The accountability of the local bodies, their standing committees and the representatives, need to be defined and strengthened. Panchayati raj institutions/urban local bodies (ULB) have to be helped to evolve a code of conduct for the newly elected members. Rules and procedures should be made simple and transparent. Financial management and audit procedures have to be strengthened with the objective of facilitating the tasks to be performed by the elected functionaries drawn from all walks of life.

Civil Services Reforms

In the area of civil services reform, State Governments face three critical challenges. They must enhance the productivity of the civil services and make certain that each employee is performing socially relevant tasks. They must ensure the longterm affordability of the civil services, and must enforce procedures for rewarding and promoting merit, and disciplining malfunction and misconduct, in order to strengthen accountability and enhance performance quality. Unfortunately, ever since higher education was introduced by the British, the State has been seen as the employer of first resort by the educated middle class in India.

This mindset has to change. Since the beginning of the 1960s, a rapid expansion of government employment has taken place, especially of the support staff. With the changing role of the government, the size and scale of the civil services no longer relate to the nature of functions that the government can or should undertake. Governments should identify the surplus staff, set up an effective redeployment plan, and a liberal system for exit. For the time being, recruitment should only take place for functional posts, and vacant posts of secretarial and clerical nature should not be allowed to be filled.

The Administrative Reforms Commission (ARC) Report, 1970 had recommended the abolition of clerical positions in the secretariat, by merging the field departments with the secretariat departments at appropriate levels, and by following the pattern prescribed in the army for decision making through the single file system. This can be done even now, as it will result in substantial reduction in the number of employees. Reducing the number of general holidays, as recommended by the Fifth Pay Commission can lead to better productivity of the existing staff. The Central

Government has already restricted the recruitment of fresh personnel to just one-third of the posts falling vacant each year, and some States have taken similar steps. These are moves in the right direction.

Open Government

Open Government is a key element of governance reform. The environment of secrecy that pervades government functioning encourages malpractices. There is no early check because decisions are taken behind closed doors. The sharing of information and making the entire system more transparent would certainly reduce the danger of the system being manipulated by a few in the name of many. Transparency builds external demand for reform and makes administration more responsive and performance oriented.

One way of sending a signal for reform is to encourage the enactment of legislation for Right to Information along the lines of the statutory scheme of the Government of India. If the right of the ordinary citizen to information is recognised, it will dramatically increase the strength of the citizen to understand and challenge corruption and the arbitrary exercise of State power. It should be the duty of the decision makers at all levels to proactively attempt to increase the power of the citizen in his or her relation with the State, through building in transparency in all official procedures and systems, and, suo-moto, making available all relevant information to the people.

There are many ways to bring about openness in government. The declared intention of the government should be in favour of transparency. All such information that is generally provided by the Assembly/Parliament to a Member should also be accessible to any member of the public. Departments such as the Police and Revenue, which have extensive public dealings, should be subjected to a social audit at periodic intervals. These audits, by eminent members of the public, should look at their policies and performance, and suggest constructive steps for their improvement.

The government also needs to make conscious efforts to increase its responsiveness to the ordinary people, whom it is meant to serve. At present the system of government is such that it is difficult for an average citizen to have access to information about schemes and programmes that affect him, and even about his rights and records. The complicated procedures not only distance Government from the very people that are sought to be provided with services but also create possible sources of corruption. Therefore, the stress needs to be on developing computer based information systems so that discretion and delay can be reduced.

Each department with a public interface should develop citizens' charters, establishing clearly enforceable norms. The citizens' charter should clearly define the standard for the services being rendered. It should also specify the remedial mechanisms available to the citizen. Merely notifying citizens' charters should not be an end in itself. After promulgating citizens' civil charters, departments should ensure that the necessary changes have also been introduced in every aspect of the functioning of the department and at every level to conform to the standards set in demand of these charters. Each department should organise largescale capacity building programmes to bring in attitudinal change in their employees.

The existence of widespread transaction costs in a governmental system corrodes the credibility of public institutions leading to widespread disenchantment with them, weakening the very fabric of governance, and making it virtually impossible to speed up development tasks. Accountability, transparency and the rule of law, are integral constituents of good governance. Transparency in government functioning will in itself reduce the possibilities of leakage and malpractice. The issue of accountability is crucial for effective financial management and a responsive civil service.

A responsive legal system is essential for the development of the private sector as well as for ensuring that all citizens, and particularly the poor, have access to justice. Streamlining of the civil and criminal justice systems with a view to reducing delays in disposal of cases is important. In addition, consideration of innovative mechanisms such as Lok Adalat (Peoples' Court for alternative dispute resolution) to reduce the burden on the courts may be necessary. The Nyaya Panchayat in the villages need also to be strengthened.

Procurements is an area especially prone to malpractices. Enactment of legislations/ regulations to mandate strictly competitive bidding of all contracts and procurement of works, goods and services by the government and its entities, with regular issuing of tender notices, bid closing dates and contract awards, should be effectively ensured to minimise opportunities for malpractices in procurement decisions.

Democratic Governments respond to pressures from below, and however well motivated and determined the reforms initiated by the government are, these can fructify only if government actions and decisions are subjected to continuous scrutiny and pressure by communities and the civil society. Yet, despite the enormous burden posed by weak governance, civil society action has been found wanting, on the whole. The pace of improvement in governance would accelerate only when countervailing forces in society develop sufficient confidence to oppose inefficiency and corruption in government. States should, therefore, not just tolerate, but actively encourage credible civil society organisations.

Sustainability

It is important for the fiscal policies of a government to be sound and sustainable. Unfortunately, as is well known, the fiscal situation of the Centre and the States has deteriorated continuously through the 1990s, especially after 1997. The combined balance of current revenues of the Centre and the States fell from minus 13,324 crore in 1996-97 to minus 92,969 crore rupees in 1999-00. Tax Revenue as per cent of GDP of the Centre has fallen from 11.3 per cent in 1989-90 to 8.8 per cent in 1999- 00.

Financially weak infrastructure sectors have placed a massive burden on the States; the problem has been accentuated by the deepening culture of non-payment by customers of public utilities. The share of plan expenditure of the Centre and the States in GDP has fallen from 13.4 per cent in 1986-87 to 8.6 per cent in 1998- 99, making plan outlay a residual item of Government expenditure. States' own contributions to plan financing is now totally nonexistent. The debt burden of governments is rising rapidly, and most governments are increasingly borrowing even to finance their current consumption.

A fiscal crisis has major developmental implications. First, declining capital investment leads to slower growth, which in turn renders it more difficult to increase the revenue yield. Slow growth also means that the incomes of the poor do not rise significantly. Second, a rising debt burden has the serious implication of sacrificing the welfare of future generations, who will sooner or later have to pay the price for the profligacy of today.

The key to overcoming the crises being faced is to curtail administrative expenditures, which are absorbing larger and larger shares of the public resources, leaving very little for spending on the developmental needs of the people. There is undoubtedly a historical legacy here that has to be overcome. The pressing need of the day is to put into place an action plan for rightsizing the government with a liberal system for exit of the surplus staff.

The Government of India has to take a lead in reducing its staff, especially in ministries dealing with State subjects. It is only then that the Centre will have the moral authority to seek similar action in the States. In the Ministries, there should be restraint on initial recruitment, and most vacancies caused by retirement should remain unfilled and the posts subsequently abolished. Steps have been initiated by the Centre and many States in this direction. As is the case in some countries, to reinforce the control on staff expansion, consideration may need to be given to a legislative ceiling on the total number of posts authorised for any particular department/ organisation. Other steps necessary to tackle the fiscal problems and improve resource mobilisation include:

External Aid: States should be encouraged to attract and improve disbursements of external assistance, which is a significant source of additionality to a State's resources. This is a source that does not presently have a ceiling, and the extent to which it can be tapped depends only on the willingness of a State to be pro-active, pursue sound policies and accord priority attention to timely implementation.

Single Economic Space: There is a need for the States to appreciate the mutual benefits of looking at the country as a single economic space, from which considerable economic advantages can be reaped by them. Greater integration and removal of barriers would encourage commerce and business and lead to a winwin situation for all concerned. Similarly, there is tax competition among States to attract private investments. Such policies are harmful, as States have lost tax revenue without influencing investment decisions. Better infrastructure, faster decision-making, and investor-friendly environment are more important in the decision matrix of the investor community, and State resources are better deployed in such areas.

State Guarantees: A practice that is pushing the States towards a fiscal crisis is the ready extension of guarantees to the borrowings of State-level public enterprises. These guarantees may devolve on State Governments, as the financial health of many such enterprises is not sound. This practice will hurt States' credibility and adversely influence their credit ratings and ability to raise resources in future. A legislative cap on guarantees, as has been done by some States, would improve the confidence of the investors in the States.

Similarly, there is a case for explicitly introducing Reform Linked Central Assistance: The medium-term fiscal strategy should include measures aimed at providing financial help to States to alleviate the fiscal stress facing them. However, the strategy would have to incorporate certain conditionalities. These would focus on critical issues facing the States on the fiscal and governance fronts. These conditionalities would be formulated with the agreement of the States concerned. The reform linked assistance would need to be phased over time with a view to accelerating the reform process at State level, and helping State finances to be put on a sound footing in the medium term.

In the last thirty years there has been enough empirical evidence to establish that environmental conservation must go hand in hand with economic development, because any economic development that destroys the environment will create more poverty, unemployment and diseases - as the poor depend on the nature much more for their day to day needs - and thus cannot even be called economic development. It may just be a transfer of resources from the poor to the rich.

Environmentally destructive economic development will impoverish the poor even further and destroy their livelihood resource base. In the absence of clean air and clean water not only is the productivity of the poor going down but their expenses on medical care is shooting up, resulting in their further misery. Denuded hills and barren pastures have resulted in falling groundwater levels, reduced availability of organic manure, and loss of soil and moisture for crops, thus affecting the productivity of rain fed agriculture and income through cattle. The environmental concern in India must go "beyond pretty trees and tigers" and must be linked it with peoples' lives and concerns.

Investment in better environment and forests however requires taking unpopular decisions like closing down of polluting industries, controlling vehicular pollution, reducing subsidy on forest raw material, etc. It also needs greater investments, the benefit from which is not easily discernible or immediate. When States are starved of funds, cuts are imposed on the budgets of these departments and activities, and money is diverted to paying salaries or civil works programmes. Therefore, improving governance must mean better policies and more funds for improving the quality of life through greater attention to environmental concerns.

Capital Investments

Capital investments are supposed to be the productive

and growth enhancing components of developmental expenditure. In the early years of the 1950's and '60s, plans consisted largely of capital investments. In those days, since we as a newly independent country were starting from a relatively low base, governments were concerned primarily with adding to the stock of public assets. Capital expenditures as a proportion of plan outlays have been steadily declining since, and have been estimated by the Eleventh Finance Commission to form now only about 42 per cent of the States Plan outlays.

In the case of some States like Kerala and Andhra Pradesh, this proportion is even less, at less than 25 per cent. States do realise the need for the plan outlays to consist of an adequately high proportion of capital investments. Nevertheless, they find it difficult to increase capital expenditures, because of fiscal constraints, and the immediacy of the pressure generated by the administrative machinery, most of which translate into revenue expenditure. At some point States would need to take a hard look at the situation, put aside short-term considerations, and see the big picture in this regard, even if it implies tough decisions. The capital content of the Plan needs to be protected, to enable plan funds to be utilised largely to create growth-inducing productive assets. This is in the long-term interest of the development of the State.

It may be argued that in the present day, with over five decades of planned development behind us, and a large stock of capital assets having been created, State Governments should be equally concerned about preservation of the existing public assets and schemes that have been built up over the years. The problem arises particularly since preservation and utilisation of these public assets imply recurring expenses on operation and maintenance (O&M), which are supposed to be the normal responsibility of a Government. These are therefore not seen as falling within the purview of "new" development expenditures, and are outside the Plan.

Fiscal constraints on non-plan expenditures are increasing due to rising establishment costs and interest burden. This leads to the tendency to under-provide for the maintenance of these capital assets, since establishment and interest payments have a compelling priority claim on resources, whereas the impact of under-funding of maintenance expenditures is not immediately visible. Over the medium term, however, the impact is felt through the productive assets that have been created over a long period of time having deteriorated due to lack of maintenance, and no longer serving the productive purpose they were intended to.

The expenses on maintenance, therefore, have to be provided for. A State cannot be said to be planning wisely if capital assets created at a great cost are allowed to run down for want of maintenance expenditures. Rational planning would mean fully budgeting these expenditures and recognising them as an essential component of developmental expenditure, since not providing for them would lead to running down of assets created over the years.

The immediate consequence of this approach is that O&M expenditures will gradually eat up larger and larger shares of development expenditures, crowding out new investments and giving rise to the question of sustainability. This need not happen. If this type of expenditure goes hand in hand with a policy of recovery of adequate user charges from the beneficiaries of the services provided, spending on O&M need not curtail plans for new projects and schemes.

If, on the other hand, governments make the policy choice to bear most or the entire O&M burden themselves, the implication for them is that in doing so they reduce their ability to sustainably create the much needed fresh capital assets. In an effort to improve the productivity of the existing capital assets, and efficiency of resource use during the Tenth Plan, however, selective use of plan funds has been permitted for the first time under the Plan for critical repair and maintenance activities, signaling thereby a positive development in this direction.

Today, there is a realisation borne out of the lessons of experience that investment in human capital is probably as much, if not more, important than "hard" capital investment. Human development is now seen not only as an end in itself, but also as a vital means to achieve the end of economic growth and prosperity for all. The Planning Commission has brought out in the first year of the Tenth Plan a National Human Development Report to signal the recognition of this.

This kind of investment creates another type of recurring expenditure dilemma, in that, the delivery of the services that create human capital is primarily through personnel and require a relatively heavy staff component e.g., teachers, health-care workers, etc. Further, unlike other capital projects, in which the bulk of the staff expenditures are linked to the construction phase of the project and such costs subsequently decline, in the case of human capital projects, staff expenditures are an essential and continuing part of the scheme or programme, since without them the desired development outcomes will not be realised.

Social services will continue to expand in the foreseeable future, until the desired levels of human development are attained. However, any planned expansion of facilities in the social sectors would need to factor in and provide for the long-term implications in terms of recurring costs. Innovative solutions have to be devised to reduce costs of delivery while retaining quality, in order that the expansion of services that must take place is sustainable.

In the context of the ongoing fiscal and administrative reforms, redeployment of personnel from other government or semi-government formations to social sectors, where possible, needs to be considered. The need is to move towards a dispensation wherein rather than recruitment for a specific project without flexibility of redeployment, there should be conscious attempt to redeploy personnel from project to project, once activity ceases in any one project and a new project commences. Further, options such as those adopted in Madhya Pradesh and Rajasthan of having contractual community appointed teachers with low infrastructure overheads, and in Uttar Pradesh of providing one time capital grants to encourage private educational institutions (rather than the policy of providing recurring grants-in-aid to such institutions) to help expand school education indicate that there are ways to move forward without compromising on the overall objective of expanding social services.

Yet another significant issue relates to the productive deployment of capital. "Projectisation" remains an imperfect art in Government. The problem is the delinking of project formulation and what in commercial world is called "financial closure". A common tendency is to underState the magnitude of the projects for Plan scrutiny, so as to squeeze them through a constrained resource envelope. Then, as the years go by, they emerge in their true colours. As a result, projects are not fully funded; implementation slips, and costs escalate markedly. Comprehensive project configuration, costing and full financial commitment is necessary for proper planning of capital outlays. It should be possible to consider the deployment of potentially productive capital as a business proposition, in which a sort of financial closure in the sense of a commitment of outlays required for the project is built into the plan, so that the requisite resources are arranged and a cap put on the costs including escalation.

Practically, this can be done with prospective effect, by loading subsequent plan outlays for concerned departments with an opening balance of committed outlays that are automatically set apart. While this will not immediately solve the problem of past overhang, which would be immense, this will at least ensure that what is henceforth committed, is realised. Decisions on the size of the plan have been traditionally driven by the tendency to present an optimistic picture to the media and the public of ever increasing development outlays. At the same time, State Governments tend to avoid hard decisions involving elimination or reduction in outlays for schemes/sectors, which have a reduced contemporary relevance. This leads to the overestimation of available investment resources by a substantial margin. This can also be termed as 'overloading' of the plan.

Overloading occurs when screening mechanisms are weak, and this implies that the top decision-makers are unable to set or enforce sectoral ceilings and priorities. When an overloaded plan comes up against the real constraints of State finances, the result is inevitable: ad-hoc adjustment of funds and allocations towards the close of the financial year. Making such ad-hoc adjustments usually means across the board cuts in plan allocations to different sectors. The State is thus forced to sacrifice or dilute the priorities that were initially set and reflected in the original plan allocations. Overloading thus tends to lead to surrender of priority setting, and is ultimately selfdefeating.

Overloading is to be distinguished from overprogramming. Used as a management tool, overprogramming means the deliberate inclusion of slightly detailed higher level of outlays in the Plan than can be realistically financed, to compensate for unanticipated project slippages. This would also go hand in hand with careful ex-ante prioritisation, so that the funds are made available for lower priority projects or schemes only if the higher priority projects fail to utilise funds to the extent programmed. And this is desirable only when full drawal of programmed funds is seen as a virtue; this may not be so if the funds are coming from high cost sources. In such cases, it may be better from a macro viewpoint to let the funds remain unutilised rather than over-programme.

Planning with a realistic resource framework, and the effective ex-ante prioritisation that results, remains the best bet for getting a developmental agenda implemented without loss of control. To assist the States in this task, the Planning Commission has taken the initiative of encouraging realism in State plans, for better planning and prioritisation. The concept of a "core plan", or the plan that would be protected in the event of resources not materialising as expected, has been recommended to States. Annual Plan outlays are now being finalised after discussion with the States, taking into consideration the visible resources at the time of plan finalisation, and adopting a realistic and conservative estimate of resources available for financing the plan. This initiative has been appreciated by the Chief Ministers of most States in their annual plan discussions with the Deputy Chairman. It has also led to reduction in the gap between agreed outlays and actual achievement of the annual plans.

A major share of available resources should go into the meeting of existing commitments i.e., incomplete works and ongoing schemes. Incomplete works that go on for a long time due to inadequate resource allocation breed cynicism, and a loss of faith in the ability of the

Government to deliver. In view of the large number of such works and schemes that may exist, it would be necessary to develop a simple transparent criterion for their prioritisation in order to enable the most productive use of resources. For example, the criterion could be to include works that are more than 80 per cent complete, and to review the possibility of termination of works on which not more than 10 per cent expense may have been incurred.

State Governments hesitate at laying down rational criteria for fear that their discretionary authority will be eliminated. The aim of transparent criteria is to reduce arbitrary discretion. But any criterion has the big advantage in so far as it helps ward off unreasonable pressures for misallocation of resources, and increases probability of productive outcomes within a visible time frame.

All existing commitments and incomplete works should ideally be fully funded as per their requirements, before taking up new investment for inclusion in the Plan. New investments may be considered in the event that ongoing works are fully taken care of, or that a conscious decision is taken to set apart a certain percentage of investible plan resources for new investments. The category of approved or sanctioned schemes, works or projects should constitute the bulk of any new investment. Limiting new proposals only to those duly sanctioned and approved by the competent authority increases the probability of timely implementation and productive use of the funds allocated.

Scheduling of Plan

Finally, the process and scheduling of plan preparation is almost as important as the content of the Plan. No matter how well the Plan may have been prepared, if it is not prepared in accordance with a strict annual schedule, the effort may be in vain. This is because a fundamental consideration for an effective investment plan is the use of the plan document in overall programming and management of public investments and as a regular tool of financial and economic management. Although most States have arrangements such that inclusion of schemes in the Plan is usually a precondition to a budgetary outlay for that scheme, the actual allocation for a particular scheme does not always bear a close relationship with the amount indicated in the plan document. This situation arises when there is a scheduling mismatch between planning and budgeting.

If plans are not prepared in time and in harmony with the budgetary cycle, they cannot be accurately reflected in the budget, and as such lose their relevance as a commitment of a Government's development priorities and as an instrument of economic management. To achieve integration with the legislative timetable for budgetary approval, internal procedural reforms for improving the scheduling, and some amount of rigidity in the deadlines for various steps in the planning process, with deadlines being laid down and enforced in the same manner as for the budgetary timetable, become quite necessary.

5

Plan Investments and Financing

The economic growth of a nation is dependent on the availability and quality of the economy's productive capacity, like literate, skilled and healthy human resources, effective transport and communication systems, adequate power and irrigation facilities, strong industrial base etc, which respond to demand pressures and create incomes for the nation. Governance of the economy facilitates the development of the productive capacities and delivers, inter-alia through Public sector investment.

Plan expenditure arises out of schemes freshly introduced in an ongoing Five-Year Plan (FYP) period. In the same period, non-plan expenditure arises out of schemes carried forward from previous FYP periods. Non- Plan expenditure, therefore, supports the old schemes of governments and plan expenditure, the new schemes. Since new schemes add to the economy's productive capacity as the old schemes did in the past, plan expenditure reflects government's investment in enhancing the economy's productive capacity. Thus non-plan expenditure maintains the existing capacities and plan expenditure adds to it.

A close observation of the States' budgets during the past decades reveals a blurring of plan and non-plan distinction of Government expenditure. Although inadvertent, this resulted in misrepresentation of non-plan as plan expenditure. Some of the new schemes, which States implemented during a new FYP period took longer than five years to get commissioned. Ideally, these schemes should have been considered as non-plan in the following FYP. However, this did not happen as States considered a larger Plan size as a positive reflection on their economic performance. For this very reason, even those plan schemes, which were completed and commissioned within the FYP period were not booked under non-plan budget in the following FYP.

Unfortunately, the misrepresentation of nonplan schemes as Plan schemes underestimated the genuine requirements for non-plan. Central Finance Commissions, which assess the genuine non-plan requirements of States and accordingly award necessary share of Central taxes and grants, ended up devolving a lower amount. As a result, the savings under non-plan, which States were banking upon, due to misrepresentation, did not materialise for augmenting plan resources.

As a result, the misrepresented non-plan schemes not only faced a tight plan budget but also found themselves in direct conflict with new schemes in matters of resource allocation. Consequently, provision for maintenance of existing capacities suffered both on account of lower devolution by Central Finance Commission and a limited availability of plan resources. The benefits gained from the creation of productive capacities enabled by new investments were therefore neutralised by the loss of existing capacities caused by curtailment of maintenance outlays.

States' budgets also bear testimony to the fact that plan expenditure at the onset of every FYP added new schemes in large numbers. While the intention of the states to rapidly and simultaneously develop all sectors of productive capacity cannot be disputed, the presence of large number of schemes in a limited plan budget led to a thin spread of resources. As a result, many new schemes virtually became non-starters due to inadequate funding, which highlights one more instance of plan expenditure not resulting in commensurate development of productive capacities.

The rapid growth in the number of schemes also entailed an undesirable build up of unproductive cost on administration and establishment. The need of the hour was to weed out low priority and irrelevant schemes as also transfer a few existing responsibilities to the private sector. This would have reduced the cost on administration and establishment and generated savings for both existing capacities and prospective ones. However, States chose to resort to borrowings in order to meet the resource crunch.

As a result the public sector draft on private savings increased - thereby reducing resources available for the private sector. High cost of borrowings impeded private sector investment. Thus, the contribution of the private sector in building the economy's productive capacity fell short of the available potential. In the beginning of the Tenth Five Year Plan, the interest burden arising out of past borrowings has added significantly to an already existing large overhang of administrative and establishment costs.

It appears unlikely that resources required for meeting existing capacities and developing new ones can continue to be sufficiently met by borrowings. The Centre, which directly as well as indirectly determines the borrowings of States has already indicated its resolve of reducing the fiscal deficit of the entire system. A favourable implication arising out of moderate growth of borrowings will be a restraint on the growth of interest burden. However, this alone will hardly be of any advantage in raising resources for existing and additional capacities as long as the large administrative and establishment cost is not reduced significantly.

Unless administrative and establishment costs are reduced, a meager additional capacities created would soon be outpaced by loss of existing capacities. A negative increase in productive capacities is thus a distinct possibility in the near future. The root cause behind the less than potential increments to the economy's productive capacity has been the large and growing presence of unproductive costs on administration and establishment. Its presence was permitted to become dominating due to the inability of the States to, first, curb the unbridled growth of new schemes, and second, to reduce, if not eliminate, the resulting growth of unproductive cost.

There are established norms, which need to be observed in deciding the number of new schemes affordable by States. One such norm is that new schemes at the onset of a FYP can be introduced only if the recurring expenditure arising out of maintenance of old schemes are accommodated within current revenues. Recurring expenditure arising out of old schemes is referred to as non-plan revenue expenditure (NPRE), which when deducted from current revenues determines the States' balance from current revenues (BCR). As per the above stated norm, BCR should be nonnegative. In other words, non-plan revenue account, which the BCR reflects, should never be in deficit.

Once the deficit on non-plan revenue account is ensured against, States are free to take up new schemes. The new schemes will also have a revenue expenditure component. This revenue expenditure stands to be financed by plan grants devolved by the Centre during the tenure of the said FYP. However, in the following FYP, this revenue expenditure cannot be financed by plan grants since the latter will be meant for new schemes specific to that FYP.

Therefore, the revenue expenditure in any FYP arising out of continuing schemes introduced in the preceding FYP should be met from revenue sources other than plan grants. This requires that at the start of a FYP, States must plan out additional resource mobilisation (ARM) and economy measures such that the non-plan revenue expenditure (NPRE) arising from continuing schemes at the end of the FYP is fully absorbed within a non-negative BCR.

It should be noted that even if introducing a fewer number of new schemes ensures the nonnegativity of BCR, it cannot address the problem of unproductive costs on administration and establishment. States will have to take direct steps to protect the provisions for maintenance outlays by curtailing unproductive costs. However, nonnegativity of BCR can enable States to plan a moderate growth in borrowings and prevent their interest burden from becoming insurmountable. A non-negative BCR enables a moderate growth of borrowings only because borrowings can be determined independently of the constraint of funding NPRE as would be the case under a negative BCR. It is precisely from this reason that the non-negativity requirement of BCR derives its rationale.

Apart from the States' own revenues, share in Central taxes and non-plan grants devolved by the Centre to States also contribute to the States' attempts at securing a non-negative BCR. The devolution of central taxes and non-plan grants is based on the recommendations of the Finance Commission, which is constituted every five years. The Finance Commission's recommendations are expected to strengthen the revenue resources of States to the extent the latter are able to achieve a non-negative BCR. Typically, Finance

Commissions set normative standards for NPRE levels, which therefore entail prescriptions for States to prioritise the expenditure on past commitments.

Finance Commissions also set normative standards for States' own revenue receipts comprising tax and non-tax revenue. Further, the share of Central taxes for each State is determined essentially on the basis of what is affordable to the Centre and, which fosters equity among States. If after all this BCR for any State is still negative, an equivalent resource gap grant is awarded. With a non-negative BCR in a new FYP, Central transfers for States' plans and States' borrowings are exclusively available for taking up new schemes.

Central transfers for State plan are devolved by the Planning Commission in the form of Central assistance and from Central Ministries as centrally sponsored/ central plan schemes. Some transfers are completely in the form of grants and others carry a debt component. The important point to note is that although all such transfers and borrowings are available in the on-going FYP for new schemes, the NPRE requirements these schemes generate in the following FYP cannot be met by central transfers and borrowings specific to the following FYP.

The institution, which can meet these if the States are unable to do so, is the Finance Commission. It is, therefore, essential that States in the following FYP transfer all recurring expenditure connected to new schemes introduced in the on-going FYP to the non-plan budget, so as to enable an accurate assessment of NPRE by the Central Finance Commission. Such transfers are referred to as transfer of 'committed liabilities'. In the absence of these transfers, Finance Commissions underestimate the NPRE requirements and thus devolve lower level of revenues, making it difficult to sustain a nonnegative BCR.

On the other hand, the continuation of 'committed liabilities' on the plan side, which is tantamount to misrepresenting non-plan outlays as plan investments, results in raising the revenue expenditure component of plan investments. A large revenue expenditure component of plan investments resulting from non transfer of the 'Committed liabilities cannot constitute the basis for demanding larger grants in lieu of borrowings from the Centre.

In fact a little reflection will bear out that if the transfer of committed liabilities takes place properly, the grant component of total central transfers will anyway increase. This is because non-plan central transfers, which is more grant-intensive than plan transfers will have to rise to accommodate transfers of committed liabilities. Although raising the grant component of Central assistance would achieve the same, it would also legitimise what States incorrectly represent as plan investments. Overstated public investment sends wrong signals in so far as macro-economic policies are made for promoting private investment.

On the basis of evidence available so far it can be observed that, due to unabated growth of new schemes, it had become increasingly difficult to ensure a non-negative BCR. When BCR finally became negative, it started shaping States' borrowing programmes in excess of sustainability levels. The consequent and rapid growth of interest burden further enlarged the negative size of BCR and thus resulted in unsustainable recourse to borrowings. Prescriptions of the Finance Commissions for raising own revenues and curbing NPRE were not heeded.

As a result even the share in Central taxes and non-plan grants recommended by the Finance Commissions fell woefully short of actual requirements. The Finance Commissions' devolution were also inadequate due to failure of states to transfer committed liabilities. The future course of action thus calls for setting time-bound targets for attaining a nonnegative BCR. In this regard, States are first required to correctly represent their NPRE, while disregarding a larger plan size as a benchmark for measuring economic performance.

A correctly estimated NPRE would enable Central Finance Commissions to bring into light the real targets of State-specific ARM and the economy in expenditure, the latter including the weeding out of irrelevant non-plan schemes and transfer of existing responsibilities to the private sector. A correctly estimated NPRE would also enable the Central Finance Commission to make appropriate devolution of central taxes and non-plan grants. Next, a cap on States' borrowings will have to be placed through a legislative process to ensure against any further increase in the public sector draft on private savings, although a lower draft compared to the present levels will be desirable.

The available borrowings will define the overall size of plan expenditure. However, for meeting the recurring requirements of plan expenditure in the following FYP, further Statespecific ARM and economy drive measures will have to be planned out in advance for maintaining a non-negative BCR. The number of new schemes introduced under the plan budget should be as few as possible for enabling a 'thick' spread of resources. Development of productive capacities, which are left unattended due to a realistic States' plan size should be canvassed for eliciting the private sector support.

Financing of States' Plan investments

An assessment of the financing of States' plan investments has been attempted in this section subject to the possible misrepresentation of nonplan outlays as plan expenditure. It is thus possible that the size of resources available for plan investments may not be exclusively for new schemes. The resources, available for Plan investments, referred to as aggregate plan resources, are taken to comprise the following :

— *States' own non-Debt contribution*: Includes non-plan revenue account (balance from current revenues) and non-debt Capital receipts net of non-plan capital expenditure (excluding repayment of debt).

— *Revenue plan transfers from the Centre*: Includes grant component of central assistance to State plan and centrally sponsored/central plan/NEC devolution.

— *Net debt receipts*: Includes net borrowings from various sources including those of the Centre for funding the gross fiscal deficit of State Governments.

The information on the above is taken from the Reserve Bank of India (RBI) documents on State finances, which report the States' budgets. The information covers the period from the Fifth to the Ninth Plan. There have been a few annual plans juxtaposed between two FYPs. However, these annual plans have been merged with the preceding FYP on the ground that government's policies of a FYP spill into the following annual plan before a new FYP mandates a change in the policy stance.

A notable exclusion from the measure of aggregate plan resources are the internal and extra-budgetary resources raised by State public sector undertakings. Data available in this regard were not found to be comparable among states. Therefore, the measure of aggregate plan resources only reflects the budgetary support to States' plan.

After an initial increase from the Fifth to the Sixth Plan, the aggregate plan resources of States has been decreasing in relation to GDP. This may be interpreted as signifying a diminishing presence of State governments in terms of incremental effort towards creating productive capacities. In fact, extra budgetary resources started contributing significantly during the Eighth and the Ninth plans, around the same time as the budgetary Plan resources were reducing.

In the Eighth Plan, total State guarantees issued amounted to 0.4 per cent of GDP, which jumped to 1.2 per cent in the first three years of the Ninth Plan. It is broadly indicated that, although in the last decade of the century, budgetary plan resources of State governments was on a diminishing trend, it was somewhat cushioned by the growth in extra budgetary resources. Indeed, at the turn of the century the task of building productive capacities have started getting entrusted more on Government backed agencies rather than on the Government perse.

States' own non-debt contribution has been showing a declining trend in its contribution to aggregate plan resources of State Governments since the Fifth Plan. However, the impact of this reduction was more than offset by increases in other sources of funding up to the Seventh Plan. In the Eighth Plan, the reduction in States' own non-debt contribution was accompanied by a falling contribution of other sources of funding. This led to a reduction in overall plan resources. Although in the Ninth Plan other sources of funding rose to an all time high, the achieved plan size stood at an all time low due to a severe fall in the States' own non-debt contribution.

It follows therefore that, in a medium term perspective, an increase in the Plan size cannot be sustained unless the share of States' own non-debt contribution takes on a rising trend. Plan. In the Seventh Plan, respective contribution of debt and non-debt receipts to Plan resources was maintained at the Sixth

Plan level. In the Eighth Plan however, net debt receipts fell along with the non-debt contribution, which resulted in a fall of Plan resources as well. In this period, hard measures of fiscal reforms necessitated at the Central level may have contributed to a fall in net debt receipts at the State level as well. Indeed, the debt component of Central Assistance, which had started falling in the Seventh Plan itself, fell significantly in the Eighth Plan, as well. States' own capital receipts also fell in the Eighth Plan reflecting a lower assignment of Statutory Liquidity Ratio (SLR) based borrowings and negotiated loans from financial institutions to State Governments.

During the Ninth Plan, net debt receipts climbed significantly and was entirely due to a rise in States' own capital receipts. This may have resulted from a slackening of control on the assignment of States' market borrowing programmes, negotiated loans from the financial institutions, and a significant growth in small savings collections. However, a more specific reason could be attributed to a rise in net States' provident funds due to impounding of arrears of revised pay scales. Despite the increase in net debt receipts, a sharp fall in plan resources could not, however, be averted.

The flexibility of the Government to roll over its outstanding debt also reduced from the Sixth Plan onwards only to rise again in the Ninth Plan. Other sources of funding include revenue plan transfers from the Centre, which rose from the Fifth to the Seventh Plan and fell thereafter almost to the Fifth Plan levels in the Ninth Plan. This trend was replicated in the share of Central taxes as well although the latter did not fall to the Fifth Plan levels. These two events together reflect the tightening of budgetary constraints at the Central level. In a situation where, due to a tight budgetary constraint at the Centre, central revenue transfers cannot augment a rapidly deteriorating States' own non-debt contribution,

States look up to debt receipts for protecting their plan sizes.

Net debt receipts of State Governments did more than compensate for a fall in the non-debt contribution in the Sixth Plan vis-à-vis the Fifth. This is borne out by the ratio of primary deficit to GDP, which fell from 2.1 per cent in the Sixth Plan to 1.6 per cent in the Seventh, 0.8 per cent in the Eighth but rose again to 1.9 per cent in the Ninth Plan. Again, but for the impact of the Pay Commission, the primary deficit could be expected to come down further in the future. Although a falling level of primary deficit may compromise on some development outlay as net debt receipts will have to be released for meeting the interest cost of debt, this policy may have to be given precedence if it helps in meeting a rising demand for domestic savings by the non-Government sector.

It is instructive to observe the behaviour of the primary component of the States' own non-debt contribution, that is balance from current revenues (BCR). BCR derived from subtracting non-plan revenue expenditure (NPRE) from States' non-plan revenue receipts (NPRR) is a major source of revenue support to States' Plan resources. Table 1 gives the break up of BCR into NPRR, NPRE and their respective components.

Table 1 confirms that it was basically the BCR, which steadily reduced States' own non-debt contribution, eventually driving it to a negative level in the Ninth Plan. The BCR itself became negative from the Eighth Plan onwards. In the Sixth Plan, where BCR contributed around 13 per cent of NPRE as revenue support to Plan resources, it withdrew the same percentage from other sources of funding in the Ninth Plan.

Table 1. Balance From Current Revenues

(As a percentage of GDP)

	V Plan	VI Plan	VII Plan	VIII Plan	IX Plan
I. *Non-Plan Revenue Receipts*	9.0	9.6	10.4	10.1	9.4
Share in Central Taxes	2.0 (22.2)	2.4 (25.0)	2.6 (25.0)	2.5 (24.8)	2.4 (25.5)
States' Own Tax	4.4 (48.9)	4.9 (51.0)	5.4 (51.9)	5.3 (52.5)	5.2 (55.3)
States' Own Non-Tax Revenue	2.0 (22.2)	2.0 (20.8)	1.9 (18.3)	1.9 (18.8)	1.5 (16.0)
Non-Plan Grants	0.6 (6.7)	0.3 (3.2)	0.5 (4.8)	0.4 (3.9)	0.3 (3.2)
II. *Non-Plan Revenue Expenditure*	7.6	8.5	10.0	10.3	10.8
Interest Payments	0.8 10.5)	0.9 (10.6)	1.5 (15.0)	1.9 (18.4)	2.1 (19.4)
Pension Payments	0.2 (2.6)	0.3 (3.5)	0.6 (6.0)	0.6 (5.8)	1.0 (9.3)
Other Non-Development	1.6 (21.1)	1.7 (20.0)	1.7 (17.0)	2.0 (19.4)	1.8 (16.7)
Development	4.9 (64.5)	5.5 (64.7)	6.1 (61.0)	5.7 (55.3)	5.7 (52.8)
Local Bodies	0.1 (1.3)	0.1 (1.2)	0.1 (1.0)	0.1 (1.1)	0.2 (1.8)
III. *Non-Plan (I - II) Revenue Account-BCR*	1.4 (118.4)	1.1 (112.9)	0.4 (104.0)	(-) 0.2 (98.1)	(-) 1.4 (87.0)

During the Fifth, Sixth and Seventh Plans, BCR deteriorated but remained positive. This was despite the fact that in relation to GDP, both NPRR and NPRE of the States increased by 1.4 percentage points from the Fifth to the Seventh Plan. However, as NPRE was at a lower level than the States' NPRR in the Fifth Plan, an identical increase in relation to GDP amounted to imparting a higher percentage growth to NPRE. Between the Seventh and the Ninth Plans, increase in NPRE was merely 0.8 percentage points. However, BCR continued to deteriorate due to a sharp fall of around 1.0 percentage points of the States' NPRR.

Ideally, NPRE should have also declined, having already achieved a significant increase of 1.4 percentage points in the past. A reduction of around 0.2 percentage points between the Seventh and the Ninth Plans did however take place in respect of items other than interest and pension payments, although a reduction of 1.3 percentage points was required in order to restore the levels of these items to that of the Fifth Plan. The increase in Pension and Interest payments, which was in the region of 1.0 percentage points between the Seventh and Ninth Plans more than offset whatever little percentage reduction that had taken place with respect to other items.

In fact, pensions and interest payments together increased from 1.0 percentage point in the Fifth Plan to 3.1 percent in the Ninth. Understandably, the share of pension and interest payments in NPRE increased from a little over 13 per cent in the Fifth Plan to around 29 per cent in the Ninth Plan. The increases in net debt receipts in the period under consideration, after all, did have a telling impact on debt servicing obligations of State Governments.

Consequent to the reforms in the financial sector, Government borrowings have been taken at market-based interest rates and this has also contributed to increased interest burden of State Governments. Further, the growing longevity of retired staff, compounded by the Pay Commission impact also increased the pension obligations significantly. To accommodate the rising burden of pension and interest payments, therefore, it was the development expenditure, which was compromised and its share in NPRE fell from 64.5 percent in the Fifth Plan to 52.8 per cent in the Ninth Plan.

The fall in the States' NPRR since the Seventh Plan was more or less uniformly spread across all its major components, although the impact was felt most in the case of states' own tax revenue and share in Central taxes, as these two together constituted more than 75 per cent of the States' NPRR. These two components reduced by 0.2 percentage points each between the Seventh and the Ninth Plans, reflecting the growing disparity between tax collection and tax potential. In fact, both at the Central and State level, tax potential has increased due to tremendous growth in the share of the services sector in GDP. The fact, that a comprehensive service tax is still not in place has implied a steady narrowing of the tax base. An expansion of the tax base will have to be necessarily carried out for tapping the full potential of both the Central and State taxes.

A deteriorating BCR or the non-plan revenue account may contribute to a fall in plan resources but not necessarily to a shortfall of recurring receipts in relation to recurring expenditure. A positive, albeit a deteriorating, non-plan revenue account still enables recurring expenditures to be funded only by recurring receipts and prevents the diversion of net debt receipts away from capital expenditure. It is only when the non-plan revenue account turns negative that concerns for appropriate application of debt receipts become as important as a shrinking Plan size. However, even with a deficit in the nonplan revenue account, recurring expenditure may still be fully financed by recurring receipts if an offsetting surplus exists on revenue plan account, the latter defined by central revenue plan transfers less revenue component of the State Plan.

Conversely, if a deficit exists on revenue plan account, it does not matter if an offsetting surplus exists on the non-plan revenue account. In any case, overall revenue account must be non-negative to enable full accommodation of recurring expenditure by recurring receipts and enable full application of Net Debt Receipts on Capital Expenditure. Table 2 indicates the revenue account position of States since the Fifth Plan, broken down into both nonplan and plan revenue account components. The overall revenue account of States deteriorated from the Fifth Plan onwards. However, it was positive in the Fifth and Sixth Plans, and turned negative only from the Seventh Plan. As Table 2 shows, this surplus was possible only due to surpluses on the non-plan revenue account as Plan revenue account remained in deficit throughout the period under consideration.

In fact, in the Seventh Plan, the deficit on the Plan revenue account was large enough to more than offset the surplus on the non-plan revenue account and obtain an overall revenue account deficit for the first time in the period under consideration. Thereafter, even the non-plan revenue account obtained a deficit. As a result, the overall revenue account position could not look up to either of its components for obtaining a balance.

Although the need for obtaining an overall revenue account balance is eventually emphasised, ideally, a balance on both the components should be targeted separately. A balance on the non-plan revenue account implies that States' own revenue receipts are adequate to meet the recurring expenditure obligations of the past. A balance on Plan revenue account implies that revenue expenditure burden arising from the creation of additional productive capacities is fully borne by the Centre in the concerned Plan period. It does seem that the Centre kept its part of the commitment, as revenue plan transfers increased from 1.1 percentage points of GDP in the Fifth Plan to 1.7 percentage points in the Seventh Plan, an increase of 0.6 percentage points.

However, the Revenue component of State Plan increased from 1.4 to 2.6 percentage points in the same period, an increase of 1.2 percentage points. There are two possible explanations for this. One States did not transfer their revenue plan commitments in appropriate amounts to non-plan at the end of the Plan period. If that had happened, the deficit on the revenue plan account would have reduced although surplus on the non-plan revenue account would have also reduced by the same amount.

The overall revenue account position would have remained unchanged but the responsibility of causing the revenue account deficit would have been more on the States. Two, revenue plan schemes for additional productive capacities could have grown in excess of what central revenue plan transfers permitted. If this were the case then it points towards the infringement, which States exercised in not confining their revenue plan outlay for incremental creation of productive capacities to the limit drawn by the central revenue plan transfers.

Table 2. Revenue Account Position of States

(As a percentage of GDP)

		V Plan	VI Plan	VII Plan	VIII Plan	IX Plan
I.	Non-Plan Revenue Account	1.4	1.1	0.4	(-) 0.2	(-) 1.4
II.	Central Revenue Plan transfers	1.1	1.5	1.7	1.6	1.2
III.	Revenue component of State Plan	1.4	2.2	2.6	2.2	2.0
IV.	Plan Revenue Account (II - III)	(-) 0.3	(-) 0.7	(-) 0.9	(-) 0.6	(-) 0.8

V.	Overall Revenue Account (I + IV)	1.1	0.4	(-) 0.5	(-) 0.8	(-) 2.2

Between the Seventh and the Ninth Plans, central revenue plan transfers fell by 0.5 percentage points of GDP. As against this, the revenue component of the State Plan fell by 0.6 percentage points. However, the revenue plan account in the Ninth Plan still remained negative due to inheritance of large deficits. The drop in revenue plan component could not have come about due to transfer of maintenance expenditure to the non-plan. The non-plan account enumerated in Table 1 does not indicate any evidence to this effect. It was in fact the shrinking size of the overall plan expenditure, which moderated the growth of new revenue plan schemes.

However, this moderation was more under capital expenditure, since the revenue plan component as a percentage of overall plan expenditure increased from 50.9 per cent in the Seventh Plan to 53.4 percent in the Ninth. If revenue plan outlay continues to get such a high priority, then revenue transfers from the Centre may require a significant step up in the future.

The growing deficit on States' revenue account was also on account of the growing support to State public sector undertakings. A case in point is that of State Electricity Boards (SEBs). SEBs were constituted by many States way back in the Indian planning history. However, their ability to perform was critically balanced on a sustained budgetary support provided by States for the purpose of meeting either their operating deficit or requirements of capital asset creation, or both.

With the passage of time it was felt that since SEBs are basically involved in commercial operations, there is no reason why they should not strive to become financially independent. This understanding therefore implied, that SEBs should not only wipe out their operational deficits but also earn a minimum return on their employed capital in order to display a financial strength adequate to raise borrowings for asset creation. There is ample evidence to suggest that SEBs have failed in their endeavour to attain the stated ends. The moot point however is to explore the way in which, States have reacted to it. The budgeted expenditure on the energy sector of the States provides a clue in this regard. In particular, the percentage share of energy expenditure in States' gross fiscal deficit reflects the extent to which the energy sector necessitated the borrowing programme of State Governments.

As indicated in Table 3, the share of energy expenditure in gross fiscal deficit shows a declining trend since the Fifth Plan. The share decreased from 49.4 per cent in the Fifth Plan to 20.2 per cent in the Ninth Plan. This clearly indicates that there were other reasons far more important than the energy sector, which dictated the borrowing programme of States. However, if one were to separately look at the plan and non-plan components of energy outlay, it is the plan component only which is showing a downward trend as against a rising trend of the nonplan component. This implies that States were increasingly unwilling to fund new schemes floated by SEBs, as against providing a higher priority to sustaining their current expenditure.

Revenuecapital break up of energy expenditure further substantiates this point. A rising share of revenue expenditure on energy in the gross fiscal deficit is indicative of widening operational deficits of SEBs, which were bridged by State Governments. However, States made up for it by more than reducing the capital expenditure on energy. Thus, since the Fifth Plan, although States did manage to relatively reduce their dependence on debt in providing for energy requirements, the quality of budgetary support went from bad to worse. State finances were dragged to unproductive ends of rising operational deficits, which in turn compromised capital expenditure on energy.

Although revenue expenditure on energy increased since the Fifth Plan in relation to gross fiscal deficit, its impact on overall BCR of States was felt as late as the Eighth Plan. Thus NPRE on energy was 4.8 per cent of fiscal deficit in the Fifth Plan as against a positive BCR of 68.9 per cent. In the Eighth Plan, NPRE on energy was 14.4 per cent of Fiscal deficit and could be taken as one of the important reasons for causing a negative BCR of 6.0 per cent. In the Ninth Plan, NPRE on energy fell to 8.5 percent as against a negative BCR of 35.0 percent. Although BCR turned significantly negative for other more important reasons, the contribution of SEBs to rapid increases in States' borrowings is fairly well established.

To sum up, at the end of the century the position on the revenue account and the size of the plan resources indicated a significant deterioration as compared to the late eighties. The falling revenue buoyancy at both the Central and State level started the downward trend, which was further aggravated by the implementation of the revised pay scales at the State level. Although the impetus to implement revision of pay scales at the State level emerged from the Centre, international practices do not support the policy of equating pay emoluments between the federal and provincial Governments in a federation.

If at all equalisation results, it is at best an incidental event arising out of the sound finances of the provincial Governments. That of course is ruled out in the Indian context if one goes by a secular deterioration of BCR. The end result has been a significant fall in capital expenditure despite a substantial increase in borrowings, which underscores the inappropriateness of the use borrowings were put to. Even to the extent capital expenditure did take place, financial returns were dismally inadequate as is indicated by the falling level of non-tax revenue in Table 1. Where returns are not commensurate with the debt servicing, debt burden is bound to become insurmountable.

State-wise Analysis of Financing of States, Plan Investment

The moblisation of plan resources of State Governments, particularly in the Ninth as compared to the Eighth Plan has been associated with three features of considerable fiscal concern. One, the falling share of plan resources / expenditure to GSDP, which is indicative of the diminishing role State investments are having on economic growth. Two, the rising level of net debt receipts (gross fiscal deficit) to Plan resources/ expenditure, which reflects the growing debt component of plan resources caused by rapid growth of non-plan expenditure. And three, the rising share of revenue expenditure in net debt receipts (gross fiscal deficit), which reflect the growing inappropriateness in the use of borrowings.

These features have been examined Statewise to isolate each States' relative performance. For this purpose, States have been grouped into four categories. The first three categories group the general category States into five States each, based on their per capita GSDP.

Group A comprises high income States, which include Goa, Punjab, Maharashtra, Haryana and Gujarat.

Group B includes middle income States of Tamil Nadu, Kerala, Karnataka, Andhra Pradesh and Rajasthan.

Group C comprises low income States of West Bengal, Madhya Pradesh, Orissa, Uttar Pradesh and Bihar.

Group D comprises all the special category States (excluding Uttaranchal).

Table 3. Energy Expenditure of States

(As a percentage of Gross Fiscal Deficit)

		V Plan	VI Plan	VII Plan	VIII Plan	IX Plan
1.	Total Expenditure	49.4	34.1	35.9	40.7	20.2
2.	Plan Expenditure	41.7	24.1	24.7	22.9	10.9
3.	Revenue Expenditure	5.4	6.0	10.1	15.8	8.8
4.	Non-Plan Revenue Expenditure	4.8	5.6	8.3	14.4	8.5
5.	Overall BCR	68.9	34.7	11.8	-6.0	-35.0

Table 4 confirms the diminishing role of plan expenditure on GSDP growth. All except the special category States registered a fall in plan expenditure in the Ninth Plan vis-à-vis the Eighth Plan. The low income category, Group C, however, registered a lower fall than the high and middle income categories. Within the high income category, Group A, Goa registered the sharpest fall, followed closely by Maharashtra. Along with Punjab, these States were lower than the group average. On the other hand, Gujarat recorded an appreciable increase easily reflecting the best mobilisation effort of Plan resources in its group.

Table 4. Plan Expenditure of individual States

(As a percentage of GSDP)

	Plan Expenditure /GSDP		
	Eighth Plan	Ninth Plan	Difference
Group A	4.0	3.7	-0.3
1. Goa	6.2	5.5	-0.8

2. Punjab	3.8	3.3	-0.5
3. Maharashtra	4.1	3.5	-0.7
4. Haryana	4.4	4.3	-0.2
5. Gujarat	3.6	4.0	+0.4
Group B	5.1	4.8	-0.3
6. Tamil Nadu	3.8	3.5	-0.3
7. Kerala	4.3	4.6	+0.3
8. Karnataka	5.9	5.3	-0.6
9. Andhra Pradesh	5.0	5.3	0.2
10. Rajasthan	6.7	5.8	-0.9
Group C	4.6	4.4	-0.2
11. West Bengal	3.5	3.5	0.0
12. Madhya Pradesh	5.1	4.8	-0.3
13. Orissa	7.5	7.4	-0.1
14. Uttar Pradesh	4.5	4.2	-0.2
15. Bihar	4.0	4.0	0.0
Group D	12.7	12.8	+0.1
16. Arunachal Pradesh	38.3	37.0	-1.4
17. Assam	6.5	6.3	-0.2
18. Himachal Pradesh	14.1	15.9	+1.8
19. Jammu & Kashmir	14.4	14.2	-0.2
20. Manipur	20.4	20.2	-0.2
21. Meghalaya	14.8	13.7	-1.1
22. Mizoram	31.5	31.6	+0.1
23. Nagaland	19.8	18.8	-1.1
24. Sikkim	36.5	33.8	-2.7
25. Tripura	18.1	16.4	-1.7

In the middle income category, Group B, Rajasthan recorded the maximum fall, followed by Karnataka, which was significantly higher than the group's average. Kerala came out to be the best in the group as it recorded an increase in the plan expenditure. In Group C, Madhya Pradesh and Uttar Pradesh recorded a decline whereas other States retained their Eighth Plan expenditure efforts in the Ninth Plan as well.

In the special category, Group D, Arunachal Pradesh, Meghalaya, Nagaland, Sikkim and Tripura recorded significant decreases. However, more significant was the improvement of Himachal Pradesh, which in fact marginally raised the group's efforts in the Ninth Plan.

Midway through the Ninth Plan, the share of plan expenditure in GSDP is recorded to be highest for special category States, followed distantly by Group B. Group C is the next, followed by Group A. These relative positions were the same in the Eighth Plan as well, which underscores the crucial importance of State Government investments on economic growth for the special category States, but not so for other categories. The fact that plan expenditure to GSDP ratio is the lowest for Group A is consistent with the view that high income States must take the lead in promoting non-governmental investment for the purpose of building productive capacities. This will enable the Central Government to focus on the deficiencies of Public investments in low income and infrastructurally poor States.

Table 5 indicates that while growth in the debt component of plan resources was common to all the States, the highest growth was recorded in the case of high income category, Group A, marginally lower for the low income category, Group C, but much lower for the middle income category, Group B. Special category States, Group D recorded the smallest decline.

Table 5. Gross Fiscal Deficit (GFD) of Individual States

(As a percentage of Plan expenditure)

	Gross Fiscal Deficit/ Plan Expenditure		
	Eighth Plan	Ninth Plan	Difference
Group A	66.9	95.2	28.3
1. Goa	43.5	70.3	26.8

2. Punjab	113.1	153.1	40.0
3. Maharashtra	60.4	89.8	29.3
4. Haryana	61.5	82.3	20.9
5. Gujarat	61.1	87.5	26.4
Group B	62.5	77.4	14.9
6. Tamil Nadu	63.9	84.8	20.9
7. Kerala	77.6	96.4	18.8
8. Karnataka	49.4	59.6	10.3
9. Andhra Pradesh	62.9	68.1	5.1
10. Rajasthan	67.2	90.8	23.6
Group C	77.8	105.2	27.5
11. West Bengal	96.6	148.1	51.6
12. Madhya Pradesh	45.1	61.2	16.1
13. Orissa	69.1	86.2	17.1
14. Uttar Pradesh	94.0	121.6	27.6
15. Bihar	75.0	95.5	20.5
Group D	28.3	39.0	10.7
16. Arunachal Pradesh	10.0	12.1	2.2
17. Assam	28.7	36.3	7.6
18. Himachal Pradesh	54.8	59.2	4.4
19. Jammu & Kashmir	10.5	35.1	24.5
20. Manipur	22.3	42.4	20.1
21. Meghalaya	23.0	33.5	10.4
22. Mizoram	23.6	29.5	5.9
23. Nagaland	61.9	55.6	-6.3
24. Sikkim	25.7	33.8	8.1
25. Tripura	21.5	28.7	7.2

In Group A, Punjab utilised the largest proportion of borrowings for non-plan expenditure and Haryana the lowest. All other States within the category were at equal distance from these two extremes. Non-plan expenditure was a significant impediment in raising the plan resources of highincome states. For Group B, growth in non-plan expenditure was a relatively less significant impediment. Rajasthan topped this group, with Andhra

Pradesh recording the lowest growth. In fact, Andhra Pradesh recorded the lowest growth among all non-special category States. Perhaps in this middle income category, growth in nonplan expenditure was significantly outpaced by growth in borrowings.

For Group C, the impediment of non-plan expenditure growth was almost as significant as that of Group A. However, West Bengal caused a significant distortion as its growth was not only distantly highest in its respective group but also among all non-special category States. Madhya Pradesh recorded the lowest growth in this lowincome category. For Group D, special category States, the growth in GFD/plan expenditure was by far the lowest. However, the burden of non-plan expenditure growth must have been taken up by large central plan grants, which constitute 90 per cent of central assistance unlike that of nonspecial category States, where it is only 30 per cent. Nagaland in fact recorded a negative growth, implying large grant-intensive central plan transfers to the State. Jammu & Kashmir and Manipur recorded non-plan expenditure growth comparable to non-special category States.

In the Ninth Plan, the burden of carrying the liability of non-plan expenditure on its borrowings is largest for the low income States. This is despite the fact that central debt transfers to this category is largest vis-à-vis all other categories as is indicated by the relative sizes of central assistance. The requirement of pruning and consolidating the non-plan expenditure is felt most in this category.

Finally, the inappropriate use of borrowings as reflected in the growing share of revenue deficit in net debt receipts or gross fiscal deficit is examined. Among Non-Special category States, the high income category, Group A recorded the largest increase, followed by the low income, Group C, and least by the middle income,

Group B. This suggests that the high income category was the most imprudent as far as appropriate use of borrowings is concerned.

Within Group A, as also among all general category States, Goa recorded the highest growth in inappropriate use. In fact for Goa, the contribution of revenue account changed significantly from a large surplus in the Eighth Plan to a deficit in the Ninth Plan. Gujarat recorded the second highest growth, which was half that of Goa. Punjab recorded the lowest growth.

Within Group B, all States except Andhra Pradesh recorded by and large similar growth rates. Andhra Pradesh in fact recorded a negative growth, which was against the trend of events and indicative of an improved application of borrowings. Andhra Pradesh was isolated in this effort among States from all other categories. Kerala recorded the highest growth in Group B. Among the low-income category, Group C States, Bihar's performance was most exemplary as it recorded a nil growth and stood second next to Andhra Pradesh. In this Group, Madhya Pradesh recorded the highest growth.

The special category States, recorded the highest growth which was at least three and a half times that of any other category. This was despite the fact that large plan grants were available to this category for sustaining the surplus on the revenue account. The only reason which can explain this phenomenon is a significant growth in revenue plan expenditure, which easily outpaced the growth in their borrowings. Although the overall revenue account contribution still showed a surplus, it is possible that the revenue plan component may have been significantly blown up due to inadequate transfer of committed liability from plan to non-plan during preceding Plan periods. Inadequate transfers blur the distinction between plan and non-plan expenditure.

Table 6. Revenue Deficit of Individual States
(As a percentage of Gross Fiscal Deficit)

	Revenue Deficit/ Gross Fiscal Deficit		
	Eighth Plan	Ninth Plan	Difference
Group A	24.7	40.9	16.1
Goa	-38.5	18.7	57.2
Punjab	53.7	64.2	10.5
Maharashtra	16.5	31.9	15.4
Haryana	38.9	53.3	14.5
Gujarat	10.6	36.4	25.7
Group B	33.5	46.0	12.5
Tamil Nadu	48.8	64.4	15.6
Kerala	38.3	57.3	19.0
Karnataka	11.5	28.3	16.8
Andhra Pradesh	41.5	38.1	-3.4
Rajasthan	25.4	42.7	17.3
Group C	45.5	58.6	13.1
West Bengal	51.9	65.7	13.8
Madhya Pradesh	33.3	51.2	17.9
Orissa	43.2	57.8	14.6
Uttar Pradesh	44.1	57.9	13.8
Bihar	54.4	54.5	0.1
Group D	-72.8	-17.9	54.9
Arunachal Pradesh	-490.0	-347.5	142.5
Assam	-21.7	7.4	29.1
Himachal Pradesh	27.2	43.0	15.8
Jammu & Kashmir	-558.0	-84.0	474.0
Manipur	-144.4	-28.6	115.9
Meghalaya	-112.2	-48.0	64.2
Mizoram	-104.5	-64.9	39.6
Nagaland	21.4	16.1	-5.3
Sikkim	-89.1	-33.6	55.5
Tripura	-90.5	-45.2	45.3

In the Ninth Plan, the largest share of revenue deficit to gross fiscal deficit is still being reflected by the low income category, Group C. However Group D and Group A are fast catching up, with only Group B, the middle income category showing some signs of restraint. To sum up, the role of public investment in effecting GSDP growth is negligible for the high-income category States. This could be the result of a spurt in economic activites, which is independent of public intervention.

In deference to this trend, high income States must promote private investment for building additional productive capacities while using their resources for consolidating their existing capacities. Given that in relative terms these States have their non-plan as well as revenue expenditure consuming the largest proportion of borrowings, consolidation of existing capacities would again be consistent with the present trend. Middle income States must also follow in the footsteps of high-income States. Although this is desirable for low-income States as well, their infrastructural deficiencies are too significant for diluting the role of public investment.

A significant increase in non-plan revenue transfers to the lowincome States may be required for meeting their social sector needs, which are spilling into larger revenue account deficits. For the special category states, the continued significance of public investment and therefore Central transfers cannot be over emphasised. Given the inevitability of such transfers resources of these States need to be permanently strengthened by raising their share of Central taxes.

Sectoral Distribution of Plan Investments

Allocation of aggregate Plan resources among the various economic and social sectors is the next important consideration after the determination of its size. In this section, allocation of plan resources has been assessed by broadly classifying plan expenditure into the following five broad categories.

— *Education and Health*: This comprises education, sports, art and culture, medical, family planning, public health and water supply & sanitation.

— *Agriculture and Industry*: This comprises agriculture, rural development, special area programmes, industry & minerals.

— *Infrastructure*: This comprises irrigation & flood control, energy and roads & bridges.

— *Other Social and Economic Services*: This mainly comprises housing and urban development, welfare, social security and nutritional programmes and economic services apart from Infrastructure sectors.

— *General Services*: This includes debt servicing and assignment to local bodies.

For a given sector, incremental expenditure like Plan expenditure eventually augments its recurring expenditure. As already stated, the genesis of recurring expenditure lies in the cumulative impact of past policies, which were designed to create productive capacities existing as on date. It is the maintenance requirement of currently existing facilities under the given sector, which finds shape in recurring expenditure. The recurring expenditure of such type is referred to as non-plan expenditure under plan-non-plan classification.

At the end of the Fifth Plan, the non-plan expenditure, which now carried the Plan efforts of the Fifth Plan period included the maintenance expenditure on facilities created in the Fifth Plan. Thus, if total expenditure on Agriculture & Industry accounted for 2 per cent of GDP at the beginning of the Fifth Plan and 3 per cent at the end, then the increase in 1 percentage points is ideally made up of 1 per cent of GDP as plan expenditure.

However, more often than not, the increase in 1 percentage point is made up of any combination of plan expenditure and increases/ reduction in non-plan expenditure. Where nonplan expenditure increases, it reflects a deepening of the thrust of existing facilities instead of creating newer facilities. And where it reduces, it reflects a weeding out of outdated existing facilities in favour of newer ones. The important point to note is that for a given sector, a variation in plan expenditure between two successive plan periods does not necessarily imply a shift in sectoral emphasis between two time periods. A change in sectoral emphasis can be unequivocally stated only on the basis of the variation in total expenditure.

Table 7 on total plan disbursements indicates that across the period under consideration, plan expenditure on education and health increased by 0.2 percentage points between the Fifth and the Sixth Plan. Whereas, Table 8 indicates an increase of 0.5 percentage points in total expenditure, this may be interpreted as an increase in sectoral emphasis carried out more on the non-plan than on the plan side. This tendency is observed to be further reinforced in the entire period under consideration as total expenditure on education & health increased by 0.8 percentage points and Plan expenditure by 0.2 percentage points.

The deepening of the thrust of existing facilities is clearly more in evidence than adoption of newer facilities. This is not entirely unexpected as reasonable facilities under this sector were significantly created in the past, thereby requiring only an increase in their capacities in order to cater to a rising level of population. Education & health in the Ninth Plan comprised around one-fifth of plan and one-fourth of total expenditure.

Agriculture and Industry on the other hand indicates a fall in both plan and total expenditure indicating a reduction in sectoral emphasis. The fall in total expenditure is more on total than on plan expenditure. This indicates a greater emphasis on newer plan schemes than on deepening the impact on existing ones. This again is on expected lines as these sectors mainly comprise subsidy and welfare schemes that require reconstitution with changing times. In the Ninth Plan, Agriculture & Industry comprised one-fourth of plan and one-tenth of total expenditure.

Table 7. Total Plan Disbursements (Revenue & Capital) of States

(As a percentage of GDP)

Major Sectors	V Plan	VI Plan	VII Plan	VIII Plan	IX Plan
1. Education & Health	0.6 (13.7)	0.8 (16.4)	0.9 (17.3)	0.8 (19.0)	0.8 (22.4)
2. Agriculture & Industry	1.1 (25.4)	1.6 (30.7)	1.5 (29.8)	1.2 (27.8)	0.9 (23.8)
3. Infrastructure	2.0 (46.0)	1.9 (36.8)	1.8 (35.8)	1.5 (34.8)	1.2 (33.2)
4. Other Social & Economic Services	0.5 (13.4)	0.7 (14.6)	0.8 (14.3)	0.6 (16.2)	0.7 (18.0)
5. General Services	0.1 (1.5)	0.1 (1.5)	0.1 (2.8)	0.1 (2.2)	0.1 (2.6)
Total	4.3 (100.0)	5.1 (100.0)	5.1 (100.0)	4.2 (100.0)	3.7 (100.0)

The infrastructure sector was characterised by a declining trend in plan but a firming up of total expenditure except in the Ninth Plan, when total expenditure also fell under the influence of a sharp fall in plan expenditure. Although this may suggest that more emphasis were laid on maintaining existing facilities, it also implied a diversion of funds away from creation of additional infrastructure facilities, which throughout the period under consideration, has continuously been felt as the most pressing requirement.

Since the maintenance expenditure could not have been compromised upon, additional plan funds for infrastructure stood requisitioned by withdrawing the same from other sectors. That did not happen as is evidenced from Table 7, where the share of expenditure on Infrastructure in total plan fell from around one - half in the Fifth to one-third in the Ninth Plan. In total expenditure, the share fell from one -fifth to around one-sixth.

Table 8. Total Disbursements (Plan & Non-Plan) of States

(As a percentage of GDP)

Major Sectors	V Plan	VI Plan	VII Plan	VIII Plan	IX Plan
1. Education & Health	3.0 (22.5)	3.5 (22.7)	3.9 (24.2)	3.6 (23.6)	3.8 (24.7)
2. Agriculture & Industry	2.3 (17.0)	2.8 (18.0)	2.6 (15.7)	2.1 (13.5)	1.8 (11.5)
3. Infrastructure	2.8 (20.9)	2.9 (18.7)	3.0 (18.7)	2.8 (17.9)	2.3 (15.2)
4. Other Social & Economic Services	1.4 (10.8)	1.8 (11.6)	1.8 (11.3)	1.6 (10.6)	1.6 (10.1)
5. General Services	3.8 (28.8)	4.5 (29.0)	4.9 (30.1)	5.3 (34.5)	5.9 (38.5)
Total	13.3 (100.0)	15.5 (100.0)	16.2 (100.0)	15.4 (100.0)	15.4 (100.0)

Other social and economic services followed a similar pattern as that of agriculture and industry, where the emphasis was more on plan expenditure in quest of locating newer schemes while restricting the coverage of existing schemes. In the Ninth Plan, the share in plan expenditure was around one-fifth and in total expenditure, one-tenth.

Although general services in total plan expenditure constituted a miniscule proportion, its share in total expenditure was not only the highest but increased from 29 per cent in the Fifth to 39 per cent in the Ninth Plan. This was clearly due to a large and growing chunk of debt repayment obligations, which could be taken to be the primary impediment in enabling a reasonable application of total receipts to important infrastructure and social sectors.

In the section under Plan investments funding, a deficit on the revenue plan account was noted throughout the period under consideration. It was suggested that this was due to a large revenue plan component arising out of two possibilities. One, appropriate and thus adequate transfers from plan to non-plan budget did not take place as should have been the case at the conclusion of each Plan period. And two, new revenue plan schemes at the State level were introduced in excess of what Central revenue plan transfers permitted.

Table 9 indicates that it was Agriculture and Industry, which accounted for the largest share of the revenue plan in the period under consideration and can therefore be attributed with causing a large revenue plan. Although its share diminished steadily it still remained the largest education and health accounted for the second largest share. It also declined from the Fifth Plan onwards but only till the Seventh Plan.

Thereafter, its share increased in the next two Plans, at the time overall plan expenditure of States was diminishing in relation to GDP. This emphasises that in recent years, it is education and health, which have shown an increasing tendency of blowing up the revenue plan outlay of States. Education and health along with agriculture and industry has constituted more than 70 per cent of revenue plan outlay of State Governments throughout the period under consideration.

Table 9 also indicates that the share of infrastructure in the revenue plan outlay remained constant at 5 to 6 per cent. When observed in relation to Table 7, which indicates a declining plan outlay for infrastructure, it follows that it was the capital component of the plan outlay on infrastructure, which was compromised upon. Table 8 on the other hand indicates a steady growth in the overall expenditure on infrastructure. This implies that when the plan outlay on infrastructure, together with its capital component was declining, non-plan expenditure was steadily increasing.

Table 9. Revenue Plan Outlay of States

(As a percentage of GDP)

Major Sectors	V Plan	VI Plan	VII Plan	VIII Plan	IX Plan
1. Education & Health	0.47 (33.2)	0.66 (29.9)	0.71 (27.4)	0.65 (29.4)	0.68 (34.2)
2. Agriculture & Industry	0.59 (41.9)	1.06 (48.1)	1.19 (45.8)	0.94 (42.3)	0.71 (35.7)
3. Infrastructure	2.8 (5.4)	2.9 (3.0)	3.0 (8.8)	2.8 (6.8)	2.3 (5.5)
4. Other Social & Economic Services	0.24 (17.2)	0.38 (17.5)	0.43 (16.3)	0.43 (19.6)	0.43 (22.3)
5. General Services	0.03 (2.3)	0.03 (1.5)	0.04 (1.7)	0.04 (1.9)	0.05 (2.3)
Total	1.41 (100.0)	2.20 (100.0)	2.60 (100.0)	2.21 (100.0)	1.98 (100.0)

The rising non-plan expenditure could be taken as indicative of a rising non-plan revenue expenditure as the capital component of Infrastructure Non-Plan is negligible. The rising non-plan revenue expenditure is explained by the substantial growth in subsidies and grants to State electricity boards and road transport corporations. It also suggests, particularly in view of the revenue plan component being very small, that staff recruitment for both irrigation and roads and bridges sector was done way back in the past and continued at net rising levels ostensibly for enabling better maintenance of created assets.

Sectoral emphasis on agriculture and industry was more on building additional capacities, which is expected for a rapidly modernising sector. Policies aimed at developing the entrepreneurial abilities in this sector and that too on a sustainable basis however will only reduce the burden of subsidies under both nonplan outlays and plan investments. The sectoral emphasis for the infrastructure, like education and health was again on consolidating non-plan outlays at the expense of large plan outlays enriched with capital component. It is in this sector that the capital content of plan outlays needs to be enhanced by reducing the unproductive component of the nonplan outlays. Private investment may be a viable option for supplementing public investment, particularly in States where cost of availing these services are affordable by the general population.

During the pre-1974 period, the real growth of GDP fell from 3.9 per cent in the First Plan to 2.8 per cent in the Fourth Plan. In the post-1974 period, the real growth of GDP rose from 4.1 per cent in the Fifth Plan to around 6 per cent mid-way through the Ninth Plan. A rise in the real growth of GDP in the post-1974 period is indicative of the effective utilisation of productive capacities created by States' plan investment in the pre-1974 period. Similarly, a realisation of the growth rate of 8 per cent and above in the Tenth Plan is critical on the augmentation of productive capacities expected out of plan investments in the post-1974 period.

It has been indicated that augmentation of productive capacities by States' plan investments in the post-1974 period fell below potential. This was because the maintenance requirements for sustaining productive capacities created in the pre-1974 period proved to be too large for the revenues available with the States. When, despite this handicap, States attempted to build additional capacities and for this purpose, diverted resources from maintenance outlays towards plan investments, it led to the loss of existing capacities. Plan investments also could not effectively add to productive capacities since a large number of new schemes, which States introduced at the onset of every Five-Year Plan secured only a thin spread of resources not conducive to creating capacities fit for deployment.

Along with the growth in the number of schemes, the requirement for maintenance outlays as well as unproductive expenditure on establishment and administration also grew. In fact, the presence of unproductive expenditure was more significant since, as compared to maintenance outlays, it was inflexible downwards. As a result, sometime in the latter half of the post-1974 period, unproductive expenditure became a serious deterrent in securing adequate resources for plan investments, since unlike maintenance outlays, unproductive expenditure could not be easily reduced. Augmentation of productive capacities continued to fall below potential.

In the nineteen nineties, States resorted to large-scale borrowings for securing adequate resources for plan investments. This may have contributed to some growth in productive capacities. However, recourse to large-scale borrowings for funding plan investments can continue only till such time as the consideration for avoiding the crowding out of private investment applies brakes to the growth of public sector borrowings.

At the turn of the decade the restraint on public sector borrowings is being seriously considered since it has already been felt that the public sector draft on private savings has become large enough to crowd out private investment. Unfortunately, this consideration has come after the growth of States' borrowings in the nineties significantly added interest payments to other unproductive expenditure. In the Tenth Plan a restraint on further growth of States' borrowings, coupled with a large overhang of unproductive expenditure can only obtain a very small amount of resources for Plan investments and therefore capacity building.

The path ahead therefore is to focus on ways to protect existing productive capacities and building additional ones by not repeating the pitfalls of the bygone era. The following action-points are emphasised.

— States must protect the productive capacities already acquired under their jurisdiction by adequately providing for their maintenance outlays.

— Maintenance outlays should be accommodated within the constraints of a non-negative BCR.

— The inclusion of all maintenance outlays under a non-negative BCR would require a political will to curtail administrative and establishment costs.

— For seeking adequate assistance from the Finance Commission for maintenance outlays, States must cease to misrepresent these as plan investments.

— Growth in borrowings should be planned such as to sustain or even reduce the public sector draft on private savings from current levels.

— Following from lower levels of borrowings and consequently the States' plan size, private investment must be promoted to build additional productive capacities.

— States can eventually compliment private investment by raising their resources for plan investments through mobilising own revenues.

— For mobilising own revenues, priority areas include expansion of tax base, plugging tax leakages and levying cost recovery commercial user charges.

— For making plan investments effective in creating productive capacities fit for deployment, States must restrict new schemes to a manageable few.

— The number of new schemes must entail a future maintenance burden not more than what is reasonable to be accommodated within a non-negative BCR.

— In order to be able to put restrictions on the number of new schemes, States must divide the responsibilities of building productive capacities with the private sector.

— The division of responsibilities could be one where private investment focuses on infrastructure requirements and States' plan investment on social sector needs.

The aforementioned action points basically seek a stance from State Governments, which protects the existing capacities and build additional ones in partnership with the private sector in order to achieve potential increments to the economy's productive capacity. However, such action points could be implemented only if the 'resource illusion' of the States is broken. Hitherto,the liberal access the States had to borrowings cultivated such 'resource illusion'. Given the control, which the Central Government exercises on States' borrowing programmes, the onus is largely on the Centre to break this 'resource illusion'- all for, enabling the potential increments to the economy's productive capacity.

6

Employment Perspective

The Approach Paper to the Tenth Plan, approved by the NDC in September 2001, prescribed provision of gainful high-quality employment to the addition to the labour force over the Tenth Plan period. A subsequent assessment of unemployment situation in the base year of the Tenth Plan 2002 showed that to clear the backlog of unemployment, 35 million employment opportunities are required to be created. The Tenth Five Year Plan, however, aims at provision of gainful employment in excess of the addition to the labour force.

New Trends in Employment and Unemployment

There was a slight decline in population growth between the periods 1983-1993/94 and 1993/94-1999/2000 from 2.0 per cent per annum to 1.9 per cent. Though growth of output in the economy accelerated between these two periods - from 5.2 per cent gross domestic product (GDP) growth to 6.7 per cent, the pace of employment growth slowed down from 2.7 per cent to 1.07 per cent as per National Sample Survey Organisation (NSSO) employment surveys. Slow-down in pace of employment growth, in the nineteen nineties, is also borne out by demographic census data - growth of main workers decreased from 2.34 per cent to 0.81.

Similar trends in deceleration of employment growth are revealed for specific segments of employment-growth of workers in establishment covered by economic census came down from 2.84 per cent annum in 1980-1990 to 1.71 in 1990-1998; employment in establishments covered by Employment Market Information System of Ministry of Labour grew at 1.20 per cent per annum during 1983-1994 but decelerated to 0.53 per cent during the next five years 1994-1999. However, the latter decline was mainly due to a decrease in employment in public sector establishments, whereas the private sector showed acceleration in the pace of growth from 0.45 per cent to 1.87 per cent. Thus, the employment intensity of the growth process of the Indian economy is coming down.

The decrease in employment intensity of output growth can be explained by either an increase in capital intensity or increase in labour productivity, releasing labour. Both happened partly in this period. Incremental capital output ratio (ICOR) increased greatly and also capital substituted labour. Both suggest strategies to look for labour intensive areas and technologies.

At micro level, the increase in productivity of labour should be reflected in higher growth of real wages. Some indicator of this trend is seen when the growth of real wages of rural casual male workers is seen during 1994-2000 compared to in the preceding period 1983-1994. However, the rise in the real wages of casual labour only cannot be a conclusive evidence either of an increase in the real income or of tightening of labour market when the incidence of unemployment has not reduced, and has rather gone up. For example, unemployment rate reduced from 8.3 per cent of labour force, measured on current daily status (CDS) basis, in 1983 to 5.99 per cent in 1993-94; however it rose to 7.32 per cent in 1999-2000.

Further, youth unemployment has increased between 1993-94 and 1999-2000: among rural males in 15-

29 years age group from 9.0 per cent to 11.1 per cent, and from 7.6 per cent to 10.6 per cent among rural females. In addition, there are sharp variations in the unemployment rate across States. Against the all India average of 14.7 per cent unemployment among the urban male youth (15-29 years) in the year 1999-2000, while Gujarat, Haryana, Rajasthan and Punjab have 8 to 9 per cent unemployment, it is much higher in Assam (22.4 per cent), West Bengal (23.4), Bihar (24.0) and Kerala (26.6). Moreover, the incidence of unemployment is much higher among the poor. In the lowest consumption expenditure class the unemployment rate is more than twice the level compared to the highest expenditure class.

The growth of labour force decelerated from 2.43 per cent to 1.31 per cent per annum between the periods 1983-1993/94 and 1993/94-1999/2000. However, the growth of population in the working age group (15+) has continued to accelerate despite the fall in growth of population, as the younger cohort grows older. The decline in the growth of labour force, inspite of a higher growth of population in the working age group is because a substantial part of those in the working age group have withdrawn from the labour force. While a part of the decline in labour force can be explained by an increase in the attendance at educational institutions, it cannot be ruled out that some of those in the working age group have withdrawn from labour force due to non-availability of work.

The changes in the age structure of population, given the present demographic transition of the Nation, are such as to lead to a much faster growth of population in the working age group than the entire population, and this, given the different participation rates in different age groups will lead to a faster growth of labour force as compared to the working age population (Tables 1 and 2).

Table 1. Age Structure of Population
(age distribution in per cent; population in millions)

Age group	2001	2006	2011	2016
0 - 14	35.6	32.5	29.7	27.1
15 - 59	58.2	60.4	62.5	64.0
60 +	6.3	7.0	7.9	8.9
All age groups	100.0	100.0	100.0	100.0
Population	1,027.0	1,113.7	1,194.4	1,267.5

There was a substantial gap in the growth rates of working age population and labour force in the period 1993/1994 - 1999/ 2000, leading to a sharp fall in the growth of labour force to 1.31 per cent per annum from 2.43 per cent during the preceding period 1983 - 1993/94. The Planning Commission Special Group on Creation of 10 million Employment Opportunities a Year in Tenth Plan noted that the causes underlying this sharp fall need to be investigated further. One view is that withdrawal from labour force is to invest one's time in acquiring education for better returns in future, while the Special Group observes that this factor can only partially explain withdrawal from labour force, and suggests that lack of work opportunities can also lead to complete withdrawal from labour force.

The decline in the rate of growth of labour force, however, is not expected to continue unabated in future. Hence the special Group adopted the higher of the two alternative labour force growth scenarios suggested by the Task Force on Employment Opportunities. Accordingly, the Group has adopted a 1.8 per cent growth rate of labour force in the Tenth Plan period, i.e. a much slower decline in the age-specific participation rates in the period beyond (2007-12). Therefore, the projections of labour force are made here on 1.8 per cent growth.

Table 2. Growth in Population and Labour Force (per cent per annum)

	2002 - 2007	2007 - 2012	2012 - 2017
Population (All age groups)	1.63	1.41	1.20
Population (15 - 59 years)	2.41	2.08	1.70
Labour Force (15 - 59 years)	2.42	2.15	1.78
Population (15 +)	2.57	2.26	1.93
Labour Force (15 +)	2.51	2.25	1.92

In the Ninth Plan, the calculations of employment and unemployment were based on Usual Principal and Subsidiary Status basis (UPSS). The Report of the Special Group has viewed that current daily status (CDS) is a better measure to capture unemployment and underemployment, than the usual status, and therefore recommended the use of CDS basis for estimation purpose. The rationale for using CDS as measuring employment and unemployment is the following.

The Approach Paper to the Tenth Plan recommends creation of gainful employment opportunities for the entire additions to labour force in the Tenth Plan and beyond. Therefore, policies and programmes to fill the gap between requirement and availability of gainful employment opportunities are to be worked out. At any point of time, there is a large unemployed and under-employed workforce i.e., not having any gainful employment, although by using the measurement on UPSS basis, several of them are declared employed. This results in overestimation of the level of employment. To avoid this, largely, the Special Group suggested estimation of the extent of employment and unemployment on CDS basis.

According to the NSSO employment and unemployment survey report of 1999-2000 'The usual status approach adopted for classification of the population is unable to capture the changes in the activity pattern caused by seasonal fluctuations. But the estimate obtained by adopting the current weekly or current daily status approaches are expected to reflect the overall effect caused by the intermittent changes in the activity pattern during the year. The latter (CDS) reflects also the changes, which take place even during the week. The estimate of the employed based on current daily status gives average daily picture of employment.' Therefore the Special Group regarded the CDS measurement as the most appropriate measure to have an estimate of the gap i.e., jobs to be created on gainful basis, in order to bring out recommenda-tions as to how they can be filled up by changes in policies and programme.

The NSSO Report also provides estimates of the likely under-employment that is hidden in the number of the employed category, calculated by the UPSS approach when they are compared with CDS. The activity pattern of the usual employment during the days within the reference week is indicated by the distribution of their activity by current daily status. The relevant results for rural and urban India are presented in Table 3. It is observed that the proportion of person days of the usually employed, utilised for work, is lower for females as compared to the males throughout the period 1987-88 to 1999-2000.

During 1999-2000, this proportion was estimated at about 68 per cent and 79 per cent for females in the rural and urban India respectively, as against 90 per cent and 94 per cent for males in rural and urban India respectively. If the work is not available, large portion of the females withdraw from the labour force rather than report themselves as unemployed. The distribution obtained from the 1999-2000 survey is presented in Table 3.

The employment generating capacity of output growth has been seen to be reduced in recent years. The baseline scenario of growth of GDP is 6.5 per cent, as indicated in the Tenth Plan Approach Paper.

Business as usual basis the percentage of unemployed will grow up to 11.0 at the end of the Tenth Plan, giving a total unemployed labour force of 45.56 million person years. This picture is not acceptable on any socio-economic or political ground. Therefore, a much higher growth rate (8 per cent) is needed for the future along with positive policies and programmes for changing the sectoral pattern and technology in favour of labourintensive production, if unemployment is to be tackled.

The estimates of unemployed for the year 2001-02 have been given around 34.85 million person years (defined on CDS basis) when the unemployment rate went up around 9.21 per cent. It also provides the estimates of addition to labour force over the Tenth Plan period as 35.29 million person years. Thus, over the Tenth Plan, we have to deal with the problem of creating job opportunities against a potential job demand of more than 70.14 million person years (i.e., 34.85 million base period unemployment and 35.29 million new labour entry net of exits).

Against this perspective, the employment objective of the Approach Paper to the Tenth Plan has to be addressed. The Approach Paper recommends providing gainful employment opportunities to all the additions in the labour force over the five year period, and reducing significantly the rate of unemployment over the Tenth Plan, so that by the end of the Eleventh Plan, the unemployment rate will be near zero.

Table 3. Per 1000 Distribution of Person-days of Usually Employed by their Broad Current Daily Status

Current daily status	Rural						Urban					
	Male			Female			Male			Female		
	1999-00	1993-94	1987-88	1999-00	1993-94	1987-88	1999-00	1993-94	1987-88	1999-00	1993-94	1987-88
(1)	(2)	(3)	(4)	(5)	(6)	(7)	(8)	(9)	(10)	(11)	(12)	(13)
Employed	897	909	926	676	.663	638	942	949	938	791	766	716
Unemployed	53	40	27	41	30	26	27	27	37	22	24	37
Not in Labour Force	51	51	47	283	306	336	·31	25	25	187	210	247
All	1000	1000	1000	1000	1000	1000	1000	1000	1000	1000	1000	1000

Increased employment opportunities of around 29.67 million person years will be created with the help of a 8 per cent per annum growth over the next five-year period. This 'business as usual' scenario means, an employment growth of 1.7 per cent per annum as against a labour force growth of 1.8 per cent per annum. The result: even with as high a growth as 8 per cent, the objective of providing employment opportunities to all additions to labour force will not be achieved; an additional 5.62 million employment opportunities will have to be created. This, added to the base period stock unemployment of 34.85 million, will give an unemployment rate of 9.79 per cent at the end of the Tenth Plan, an increase from 9.21 per cent at the base.

This arises largely due to the near jobless growth character in many sectors of the economy especially in the organised sector, and a growing capital intensity in many of the organised sectors and even in some of the unorganised sectors including some small scale industries. The unemployment rate at the end of the Tenth Plan can even go up by a minimum onepercentage point (adding four million more unemployment) if the labour force growth increases to 2.0 per cent per annum. The answer is, therefore, to look for a development strategy, which will revamp the activities in those sectors where the comparative advantage lies in a labour-intensive nature of production. But as the economy is now operating under the impact of globalisation, all care should be taken in the reallocation of activities between sectors and sub-sectors, so that every sector can meet the open market competition.

To give a simple example, without the changes in the overall growth rate of agriculture, the sub-sector compositions can be changed by changing the cropping patterns and resources allocated between food and non-food, from less to more labour intensive sectors. Even this strategy may not always need additional investment resources. In fact, it is often said that a change in favour of labour intensive activities is accompanied by saving of capital by substitution of capital by labour and knowledge/ technology. Specific programmes and projects are to be identified and launched, keeping this goal in view. In this effort, extensive discussions with Ministries and sector specialists have been undergone.

At present, the awareness of the need for employment generation is generally very poor while formulating the plan programmes/policies. This applies to most of the concerned Ministries and authorities. As per the findings of the Special Group on Employment Generation, agriculture and allied sector activities have a very large employment generating poten-tiality. This is to be achieved not necessarily by heavy additional investment, but by reallocation of funds and choice of appropriate technologies. But to be sustainable under the present globalised system, this should be supported by appropriate policies to increase their productivity and competitiveness, which would make them viable.

The Tenth Plan aims at provision of gainful employment opportunities to the entire additions to labour force during the Tenth Plan and beyond. This is an essential condition for improving the quality of employment of an average worker. For, if labour markets do not clear, no strategy for improving the quality of employment is likely to succeed. In a large labour surplus situation, there may be employment of a high quality but only for a select group. Hence, the first strategy to improve the quality of employment is to increase the aggregate demand for labour.

While a higher rate of economic growth is a necessary condition for increasing the demand for labour, the pursuit of growth objective in isolation may not be sufficient, at least in an immediate foreseeable future, to gainfully absorb the annual additions to labour force. Therefore, in the shortterm perspective of a Five Year Plan, growth will have to be supplemented by increasing the employment content of growth in order to fulfill the employment objectives of Plan.

Labour Intensive Sectors

There are many labour intensive sectors, where employment-generating growth can be rejuvenated if right kind of sectoral policies can be put in place

Agriculture

The food security perspective guided the sectoral policies and related programmes in agriculture during the past three decades. This ensured rich dividends in terms of agricultural output and food prices. Employment was an incidental objective. Certain agricultural crops, mainly wheat and paddy, and the parts of the country where these are produced, benefited immensely. Wages of labour improved at such locations.

However, growth of employment in agriculture decelerated to a very low level in the nineties. Considering the consumption needs of our large population, agricultural production and the linked processing, distribution, trade, financial and commercial activities still have a very large potential for (i) sustaining the demand for labour and (ii) improving the quality of employment. At the sub-sector level, however, many structural changes in the pattern of growth of agriculture and its forward linked activities are required.

Having more or less achieved the objectives of food security, the development perspective towards agriculture needs to undergo a change. This is necessary for improving the growth performance of the sector as also for improving the pace of labour absorption. The two important issues from the point of view of employment creation in this sector are diversification of agriculture and removal of control on storage, movement and marketing of agricultural produce. Some of the initiatives that can have substantial benefits towards opening up more employment opportunities in new areas linked with the agriculture sector are mentioned as follows.

— Public investment in irrigation, power and roads should be sufficiently stepped up by reducing subsidies on fertilizers, water and power.

— The control and regulatory measure introduced earlier in an era of food deficit on marketing, storage and movement of agricultural produce (such as Essential Commodities Act, Milk and Milk Products Control Order, canalised export etc.) need to be reviewed.

— Private and co-operative sector participation in the marketing of agricultural produces should be allowed in order to break the monopolistic/ oligopolistic supply structure. Also, forward trading in agricultural commodities should be permitted.

The Minimum Support Price for foodgrains and other commodities needs to be so adjusted as to promote diversification of agriculture. This should be done both in terms of geographical coverage and crop diversification. New areas like pulses and oilseeds are more labourintensive; shifting of cropping pattern in their favour will boost employment generation per unit of output. A higher output of these crops is also necessary to increase the weight of these items in the average food consumption basket, necessary for meeting the nutritional requirements Agricultural Land Use and Liberalization of Land Laws

To increase growth in agriculture, all policies for better utilisation of land and water should be pursued.

For example, policies on utilisation of all types of hitherto unutilized lands, especially the cultivable and afforestable lands owned by the governments need to be given priority. A back-ended, beneficiary-oriented subsidy scheme for reclamation of degraded lands like ravines, un-levelled lands, saline, sodic, alkaline and water-logged lands, has been contemplated by the Ministry of Agriculture at the Centre. Some incentive for computerising land records and lowering the stamp duties substantially can avoid pseudo legal and illegal conveyance systems as well as litigation in rural areas.

Legalising the land leasing-in and leasingout systems and promotion of contract farming through standardised contract formats enforceable on both parties will help in increasing the size of holdings and improving the viability of agri-units. Minor irrigation and watershed development will increase the employment-generating capacity of agriculture. The semi-arid and rain fed areas of the Central regions, which have higher potential for increasing productivity, would be the focus of attention in the Tenth Plan. These measures selected for the Tenth Plan can accelerate agricultural growth as well as trigger growth in other sectors, besides reducing poverty.

There are better social returns in promoting agro-forestry models in the rain fed or semiarid regions, which contain most of India's marginal lands. The NSSO survey results show that there is high female unemployment in the rural sector. Therefore, the Tenth Plan must also focus on programmes for increasing the work opportunities and productivity of female farmers. Increasing women's access to productive land by regularising leasing and share cropping of uncultivated agricultural land by women's groups, encouraging collective efforts in bringing wastelands under cultivation, and providing policy incentives to women in low input subsistence agriculture will have immediate benefits in terms of the household's food security and women's empowerment along with additional employment generation.

Agricultural Reforms

Reforms initiated in 1991 had largely bypassed the agriculture sector. The purpose of reforms was removal of poverty, and employmentgenerating growth was taken to be the principal strategy for removal of poverty. In this process, the role of the agriculture sector is crucial. A few initial steps have been taken now, but this process will require close involvement of State Governments, Local Governments, Panchayats and other local authorities. Planning will need to play a proactive role through appropriate programmes. Agricultural exports should contribute to employment generation because they are labour using, and a more rapid growth of agriculture would increase the demand for labour in the agriculture sector.

If the reforms are implemented successfully, employment in non-cereal crops, and within cereals, in the labour intensive pulses and oilseed crops, should increase. Animal husbandry, fisheries, floriculture and horticulture, and extended areas of agriculture, have very high employment potentials but their growth has comparatively gone down in the 1990s. Agricultural reforms should give a boost to such activities, and benefits of such employment growth are expected to be more equitably distributed across regions.

Food Processing

Food processing is an important employment generating activity. While India is the second largest producer of fruits and vegetables in the world, its food processing industry remains underdeveloped. The purpose of reforms in agriculture is to increase the income of farmers, and of those who are employed in agriculture. Given the very large proportion of our farm produces that perishes, any expansion of food processing activity should improve the off take on commercial terms of agricultural output.

The absence of an assured electricity supply and poor road connectivity are two of the major constraints in the development of the food processing industry. In addition to addressing the basic infrastructural needs of power supply and road connectivity, certain promotional measures, fiscal as well as creation of facilities specific to the sector, need to be taken simultaneously to impart dynamism to the sector. The success of food processing industry is crucially linked to a continuous food chain starting from farming to food processing to marketing. Corporations or modern cooperative organisations are needed to develop the chain. Some of the specific issues requiring attention in order to develop a culture of food processing are :

While the agriculture sector has been exempted from all taxes (like excise and income tax), the agricultural produces attract a number of levies like infrastructure cess, market cess, sales tax, mandi tax, turnover tax, inter-state transfer regulations, etc. At the point of conversion, i.e., value addition, excise, income tax and other taxes are levied. The packaging material used is also subject to heavy taxation. All these taxes increase the cost of food products and it becomes a food/commodity for the rich, thereby reducing its demand.

It is necessary to facilitate contract farming with its backward and forward linkages, especially in the hinterland of proposed food parks, to be set up in the Tenth Plan period. This would enable greater value addition and consolidation of operations. Equally important is to provide post-harvest infrastructural facilities in the hinterland of the food parks, such as harvesting equipment, sorting, grading, packing, pre-cooling, washing operation, etc. Setting up of these facilities would improve the level of food processing, reduce post-harvest losses, contribute to value addition and generate new jobs in rural areas.

For reducing the post-harvest losses, which are estimated at Rs.50,000 crore annually, it is necessary to take urgent steps to set up irradiation plants, cold storages based on vapour absorption technologies, pre-cooling, etc. To bring our food products at par with and conforming to international safety and quality standards, it would be necessary to set up a network of quality testing/certification laboratories across the country. There is an urgent need to set up a retail chain for distribution of standard and hygienic quality food products. This would help in creating sustained demand for quality food products from customers. Synergies between the food parks and the agriculture export zones is necessary so that facilities/provisions set up for one zone may be considered for the others.

Within the Government the responsibility for development and promotion of the sector is scattered among different Ministries and Departments. An illustrative list of such Ministries and Departments, along with their areas of responsibility is given in Box 5.2. Similarly, there is a multiplicity of laws and regulations governing this sector. There is an urgent need to harmonise the working of different Ministries, as also among the provisions of various laws and regulations for the sector.

This group of activities is the main provider of employment outside the agriculture sector. Its importance increases with reduction of employment opportunities in traditional agriculture. In the immediate future, the strength and weakness of policies here will determine the employment scenario of the country, and its influence on social situation. In each of these activities there are government supported institutions, which have a long experience of implementing the programmes and policies.

The focus of the programmes for weaker social sections, women, unemployed youth, migrant workers, construction workers, bonded labour, child workers and other over-exploited workers, is also at such economic activities. Almost all the support through plans for development of economic and commercial infrastructure - microcredit, cess driven worker welfare funds, social security/insurance for low income groups, vocational training, apprenticeships, rural infrastructure for electricity, transport, and industry, in the final analysis, concerns these activities. A coherent approach to this group of activities can yield very large benefits in terms of employment and income of a majority of households.

There are many administrative structures that reach these activities, but for want of a better term, all of them put together within the sweeping term 'unorganised sector', whereas what the term really implies is all the non-incorporated establishments. This sector or group is very large in terms of workforce, it responds to competition, and is therefore vibrant. These decentralised economic activities, which are self-adjusting, contribute in no small measure to harmony and social stability in the Indian polity.

In the following section further development of these economic activities is explored. Rural Non-farm activities/industries, including Khadi & Village Industries (KVI) Principal planning initiatives on rural nonfarm activities are taken through the Khadi and Village Industries Commission (KVIC). The efforts needed to further improve the effectiveness of KVIC programme are:

— KVIC should focus at traditional artisan based activities because the present coverage is very small. Special initiatives by the KVIC for north eastern region, hilly and border areas.

— Involvement of Self Help Groups (SHGs) under KVI sector in order to widen the programme at the grass root level.

— Planning process in KVIC should involve the beneficiaries - State Khadi & Village Industries Boards, cooperative societies, etc.

— Cluster development approach should be adopted by KVIC so as to strengthen backward and forward linkages.

— R&D ties should be established between the KVIC and the National Institute of Design, National Institute of Fashion Technology, Indian Institutes of Technology etc.

— An IT-based data bank of KVIC assisted units should be created to facilitate research and information flow across KVIC establishments spread across the country.

— Policy support to village industries should be ensured.

— A Ministry of Agro and Rural Industries as separate from SSI has already been set up.

— The KVIC should play the role of a nodal agency for the whole village industry sector in the country.

— The Khadi programme has social objectives, and the subsidies/concession should be considered from this angle.

— Registration with the KVIC should enable a unit to avail of the same benefits as with the State Directorate of Industry.

— The KVIC should be given the status of an export promotion council.

Small and Medium Enterprises

A number of high-level committees have suggested that there should be uniform policy for all small and medium enterprises; it should not remain confined to the manufacturing sector alone, but should include all activities - trade, transport, and financial services. Fiscal support is given to small industry because it is labour intensive and hence employment generating. Therefore, the fiscal incentives (excise and income tax), preference in State Government levies, sales taxes, excise and credit support, technology development and marketing support, should be linked with a criterion of employment generated.

A new 'cluster development approach' should be adopted to focus at locations, which have high employment intensity. There exists a number of programmes for the benefit of small and micro enterprises. These include:

— Credit for modernisation

— Credit guarantee for tiny units without collateral

— Market development assistance through industry associations

— Local infrastructure development through industry associations

— Testing laboratories for product quality

Besides these enterprise-specific programmes, the general programmes aimed at the households are:

— Housing for low-income groups

— Micro-finance

— Skill Development

— Health care

If all these programmes could be focused at a particular cluster, the returns in terms of better productivity, higher income of workers and a better quality of job will be immense. In other words, rather than having multiple programmes, each having a spread over a large area, the Tenth Plan may emphasize these micro development programmes at specific clusters.

Credit for Informal Sector

A major problem in all developing countries is that the formal banking system is ill suited to meeting the credit needs of the informal sector. And yet this sector accounts for the bulk of the total employment generated. The banking system must be encouraged to reach out to the enterprises in the informal sector through innovative means. This is effectively what is intended by the various targets specified for priority sector lending by commercial banks. However, priority sector lending has created a culture of mechanical lending in public sector banks in which there is little effort at credit appraisal of lendings made to priority sectors. The Narasimham Committee suggestion of limiting priority sector lending to a more precisely defined target group was not accepted.

Banking practices and procedures need to be reviewed to enable banks to adopt a more proactive approach to lending for economically viable activities in the informal sector. The cooperative credit structure can play a major role in extending credit to the informal sector but it has become very weak in most States. A great deal of informal sector activities can be more effectively serviced by non-bank financing intermediaries, which are perhaps better able to handle such intermediations, charging interest rates, which cover the high cost of managing an inherently more risky informal sector loan. They are also able to enforce claims on collateral. It is necessary to review the regulatory constraints on commercial banks, which may prevent them from lending to such non-bank financial intermediaries for on lending to finance informal sector activity.

Another important mechanism through which banks can meet the credit needs of the informal sector is the self help groups (SHGs), which provide micro credit for informal sector activities. A pilot project linking SHGs to banks was launched in 1992. It was envisaged that NGOs could help build up capacity among the poor to organize themselves into SHGs and approach the banks for financing. In 1992-93, a total of 255 SHGs were linked with banks under this project. The number had expanded to 1,21,744 as on September 30, 2000. The programme has provided credit to 1.9 million poor families. More than 85 per cent of the SHGs are exclusively women's groups.

The experience thus far has been very encouraging. Recovery rates of SHGs are very high (over 90 per cent) reflecting the impact of peer pressure in ensuring loan recovery. Impact studies of micro credit extended by SHGs show very positive outcomes in terms of the effectiveness of the loans reaching the poor and in improving their income levels. An important aspect of the programme is that it envisages a process of graduation whereby families can begin informal sector activities through micro credit extended by SHGs but can, in due course, access larger amount of loans directly from the banks.

The Reserve Bank of India has taken a number of steps to encourage bank lending to SHGs as a part of mainstream banking activity. Credit extended by commercial banks to SHGs is treated as part of priority sector lending in order to encourage banks to engage in this type of activity. Banks have also been given considerable flexibility to determine procedures and design loan products for SHGs responding to local conditions. A micro finance development fund has also been established in NABARD to give training to SHGs members, partner NGOs, banks and government agencies, provide start up funds to micro finance institutions and meet their initial operating deficits, and meet the cost of formation and nurturing of SHGs. The programme of providing credit to SHGs, which has made a good start, is a potentially important mechanism for expanding credit to the informal sector and should be greatly expanded in future.

Health and Nutrition Services

Access to quality health services of the population at large is one of the main indicators of social development. The existing facilities in the areas of health and nutrition services are highly inadequate, especially in rural areas. The implications of poor health services or non-availability of these services at a reasonable cost can be economic as well. Data from NSSO indicate that escalating cost of health services is one of the reasons for indebtedness not only among poor but also among the middle-income group.

There are sharp inter-state/inter-district variations in availability and utilisation of health care services. Considerable expansion is needed to provide minimum level of access to every citizen. Thus, in terms of the need for services, this sector affords promise of immense employment opportunities. There is also a very large scope for more efficient use of the available infrastructure, which will enable increased use of health services, and associated demand for health and related workers.

During the Tenth Plan the effort would be to universalise access at least to primary health care facility, not only in terms of creating physical infrastructure but also in terms of equipping each health care centre with adequate medical and para medical staff. The State will be required to play an important role in providing these services at affordable cost. However, within the Government sector there have been persistent gaps in manpower and infrastructure especially at the primary health care level in remote, rural, tribal and urban slum areas where health care needs are greatest. Also, as it is today, there exists a mismatch between personnel and health infrastructure. Expansion of health facility and its adequate manning as per the existing norms will create demand for educated and skilled manpower for this sector.

The critical constraint of course is availability of resources with the State Governments and local authorities. The initiatives at collection of user charges in public services, and risk pooling through insurance should supplement the resources of the Government. New initiatives to improve the efficiency of the public health delivery system will also augment the resource base. Still, a large part of the health care is procured from private establishments. However, outside the government, the capability to manage hospitals has remained confined to a few corporate groups.

On the other hand, the medical insurance industry has not evolved to a reasonable level of professionalism, which can inspire confidence among the buyers of insurance. Insurance mechanisms, designed especially for the low-income groups, need to be developed. Introduction of health care support as a part of the social security insurance of workers in the unorganised sector will help in reducing risk to the individual and also make available resources for investment.

Education Services

Out of approximately 200 million children in the age group 6-14 years, only 120 million are in schools and net attendance in the primary level is only 66 per cent of enrolment. To achieve education for all, the Sarva Shiksha Abhiyan has been launched. The process of integrating our educational system with the economic needs of the people and of the nation must begin at the primary school stage itself. Assertion of the dignity of labour and vocationalisation of curricula are essential to ensure that a disjunction does not take place between the educational system and the work place.

Universalising access to primary education and improvement of basic school infrastructure in the Tenth Plan would mean targeting the provision of one teacher for every group of 40 children for primary and upper primary schools, opening of a primary/alternative schooling facility within one km of every habitation, provision of free textbooks to all SC/ST children and girls at the primary and upper primary school, management and repair of school buildings through school management committees, provision of opportunities for non-formal and alternative education for out of school children in the most backward areas and from un-reached segments of the population in response to local needs and demands articulated at the grass root level.

Mere establishment of schools without hiring teachers happens in many parts of the country, especially in rural areas. It is therefore essential that control over schools and teachers be transferred to local bodies which have a direct interest in teacher performance. States should be encouraged to implement the 73rd and 74th Amendments of the Constitution, which facilitate the transfer of management of primary and upper primary schools to panchayats/local bodies. Planning, supervision and management of education would have to be through local bodies at district, block and village levels. Efforts should also be made for social mobilisation of local communities for adult literacy campaigns and for promotion of primary education.

Laws, rules and procedures regarding facilitation of educational institutions must be modernised and simplified so that honest and sincere individuals and organisations can set up universities, colleges and schools. Controls on fees, teacher salaries, infrastructure, and staff strength must be replaced by a strong regulatory frame work. The regulatory system must also put the greatest emphasis on fraud detection and punishment while letting normal individuals function more freely.

Vocational Training Services

There is a very large unmet need for imparting vocational training to the new entrants to labour force as only about 5 per cent or so enter the world of work with any kind of formal vocational training. If the employers, the educational infrastructure and labour administration can join, this gap can be filled. Outturn from schools at 10+ stage has so far been a small fraction of those in the 15 to17 years age group. However, after the introduction of compulsory education in 6-14 years age group, which is the target in the Tenth Plan, the utilisation of youth in occupations appropriate for educated persons has to be considered.

The educated youth can take up better occupations than manual work or petty business. To bring them to the mainstream of economic activities, imparting of some production and professional skills is essential. The present approach is to put most of the youth through a higher technical, medical or management education system. Simultaneous with the incidence of rising unemployment among those with higher education, is also shortage of trained technicians, paramedics, accounts, insurance, legal and other commercial assistants. These requirements are met at present by employing those who acquire the requisite skills through 'hands-on' experience. And such opportunities are restricted to those youth who somehow find an entry point in a good establishment.

As part of education, vocationalisation schemes have been tried. But, these have not succeeded because requisite equipments, and teachers, who have requisite work experience, are not available. Moreover, as a part of school education, the vocational stream carries a lower priority among the students. The other approach has been the apprenticeship scheme, whereby educated or trained youth can be placed in establishments. Establishments are required to pay a stipend to trainees. However, the number of seats in this has remained rather small. Further promotion of vocational training as a part of entrepreneurial activity can provide employment opportunities

Information Technology

The potential contribution of information technology to employment generation is both direct and indirect. The indirect impact of IT is far greater than the direct impact. In the USA, it is estimated that for every direct job created in the IT industry, three to four jobs are created by indirect ones. This does not include the non-IT jobs created by the growth of other sectors of the economy under the stimulus of information technology. It is assessed that IT will contribute to approximately 0.2 million jobs per year and around one million at the end of the Tenth Plan as additional direct employment.

The real employment potential of Information and Communication Technology (ICT) will be realised when such services support the community, social and personal services required by the Indian masses. This is the issue of digital divide, on which adequate policy attention has not so far been focussed in India. Many efforts have been made at at the use of ICT in education, health, nutrition, housing, real estate, banking, insurance and other personal services, However, not all of them have been designed with the perspective of a low budget consumer. The cost of research on technology keeps the cost high. The real purpose of planning for ICT, which is to narrow and eliminate the digital divide, will be defeated if the issue is not considered in its proper perspective.

Development of Tourism

Development of tourism needs to be taken up on priority basis as India has large untapped tourism potential, which can be successfully harnessed for the benefit of development of areas, that have remained underdeveloped despite being potential destinations of tourist attractions. The employment impact of development of tourist destinations can be substantial as the activity in itself is labour intensive and also has extensive forward and backward economic linkages. The focus during the Tenth plan would be to encourage public-private partnership in development of tourist centres in which the government would be the active facilitator and catalyst, with the ultimate goal of creating world-class infrastructure and innovative products.

Real Estate Development

The real estate development and construction are linked activities and are employment intensive too. Unfortunately, development and growth of housing and the real estate sector has been severely constrained by outdated laws and polices governing land development and rent control which have pushed the market underground and spawned a host of undesirable practices. The construction activities are very much influenced by the real estate developments. The recent repeal of the Land Ceiling Act, likely to be followed by the States, to free land market will largely boost the real estate activities. The proposed repeal of the Rent Control Act will further encourage the growth of this sector.

In a package proposed in the Tenth Plan to give incentives to the cities and States for urban sector development, there has been a proposal for recommending selective freedom to convert rural land for urban use, reduction of stamp duty on transfer of property and laws facilitating private development of township - all of which will increase the real estate growth, and thereby generate increased demand for construction.

It is noticed that in the organised and mechanised segment, there has been a very low employment elasticity and, at this point of time, very little contribution to the employment generation in this sector, whereas in the unorganised segment employment elasticity is very high. But unfortunately, their wage rates are very low because of low productivity in this segment along with, heavy exploitation of labour by the employers in the absence of proper legislative safeguards.

Both the large mechanised activities and the small and medium ones have their own respective roles and will survive alongside. In the area of bridges, major irrigation and dam construction, highrise buildings etc., the large mechanised construction activities will be unavoidable. But at the same time, in the areas like rural road building, low cost housing, minor irrigation etc., the small construction units with minimum improvement in mechanisation can serve the purpose and fulfill the need for generating more jobs.

Road and Transport

Transport and allied activities provide employment to around 15 million persons. The largest share in this is of those engaged in transport of freight and passengers by road. It has potential for three to four million additional employment opportunities during the Tenth Plan period. With the completion of various stretches of the National Highways Development Project, the traffic flows, and thereby the employment opportunities, can expand much more than this projection.

The activity is highly decentralised and work conditions are strenuous; it carries a high risk. Since the administration of this activity is with the State transport authorities, the conditions of employment do not get any significant attention. There are however sufficient resources generated in transport activity. Just like construction workers, the welfare measures for transport workers need attention.

Distributive and Retail Trade

The Group of activities 'trade, hotels, and restaurants' is estimated to provide employment opportunities to around 41 million persons. The importance of trade in providing an outlet to newly emerging industries - processed food products, milk and milk products, khadi and village industries products, etc., has been noted earlier. The large firms producing consumer products and consumer durables have established their own retail chains - as for example KVIC, National Dairy Development Board (NDDB), shoe industry etc. But productspecific stores have a large share of overhead expenditure. Other large corporate firms, which deal in group of personal toiletry, edible oil, food products, and automobiles etc., have evolved direct arrangements with retail trade, bypassing the wholesale trade.

Given the large employment potential, there has been a keen discussion on policies concerning distributive and retail trade. A betterorganised retail trade can open up a large number of gainful employment opportunities to youth, either as self-employed or as shop managers, supervisors, and assistants. So far the organised retail trade establishments have remai-ned confined to public sector-government owned societies, bazaars, and emporia. But many of these failed as direct financial support or purchase price preference from Government reduced. The private corporate sector should be encouraged to set up retail chains in small and medium towns and metros.

Requisite changes in laws concerning rents, land use, property acquisition, and bank finance policies may be made so that the prime retailing activity does not remain confined to the property owners (also the local governments), which keeps the entry cost at exorbitant levels. In the process, the gainful and productive employment to those who work in shops suffers since the fixed cost uses up the bulk of the resources of the new ventures.

7

Special area Programmes

Planning and development of an area within the State is primarily the responsibility of the concerned State Governments. Within an overall State oriented approach, certain regions across and within States have for historical and special reasons called for a focused area development approach. Developmental problems are faced by certain areas arising out of their distinct geo-physical structure and location and concomitant socio-economic development.

To deal with the specific problems of these areas, region-specific plan strategies are formulated keeping in view the basic needs of the people and priorities of the State Governments concerned. A core element of the Planning Commission's strategy in this regard has been to supplement the efforts of the State Governments by targeting such disadvantaged areas with funds for capital investments. The Commission would continue in the Tenth Plan to advocate the area approach and aim to strengthen decentralisation of planning. Focused developmental programmes for backward areas are expected to help reduce imbalances and speed up the economic development of these regions.

North Eastern Region

The north eastern region comprises the seven contiguous

States of Arunachal Pradesh, Assam, Manipur, Meghalaya, Mizoram, Nagaland and Tripura. It covers an area of 255,000 Sq. Kms, representing around 7.7 per cent of total geographic area of the country. It is a distinct geographical unit connected with the rest of the country through a narrow land corridor. Ninety-eight per cent of its borders are with other countries: Bhutan and China in the north, Myanmar in the east and Bangladesh in the south and west. The region has wide variations in physical features ranging from the plains of the Brahmaputra in Assam to the dissected mountains of eastern Himalaya in Arunachal Pradesh.

It can be broadly classified into the north eastern hills and basins which accounts for 65 per cent of the total area, the Brahmaputra valley which covers 22 per cent of the region and the Meghalaya plateau covering 13 per cent of the total area. The North-East supports a population of 38.4 million, around 4 per cent of the country's total population, with Assam accounting for 70 per cent (26.6 million) of the region's population. The decadal growth rate during the period 1991-2001 has been at 21.9 per cent which is slightly higher than the national average of 21.34. The population growth in individual States (1991-2001) has been above the national average of 21.34 per cent, except in Tripura and Assam.

The decadal growth of population in Nagaland; 64.41 per cent; is the highest in the country. Excluding Assam, tribals represent around 60 per cent of the total population in each State. Assam has only 13 per cent tribal population. The region has great ethnic diversity with people of Aryan, Dravidian, Indo-Burmese, Indo-Tibetan and other races inhibiting its hills and valleys.

The trauma of partition, political evolution and insurgency combined with the geographical location, transport bottlenecks, natural calamities, etc., have hindered the progress of the North East, and the region has experienced relatively slower economic growth compared to the rest of the country. Most of the north eastern States joined the planned development process later than many other States. For development purposes, Sikkim too is treated at par with the other States of the north east region. Special focus had as such been given on the economic development of the north eastern region and Sikkim during the Eighth and Ninth Plan periods, and strategies adopted for removal of infrastructural bottlenecks, provisioning of basic minimum services and creating an overall environment for private investment.

Despite these efforts, the recent growth performance of these States has not been encouraging. During the period 1993-94 to 1999-2000, only the economy of Tripura grew at a rate higher than the national average. All the other States had lower growth rates.

The continued efforts of the Government towards removing the impediments to lasting peace in the North East, and the improved security scenario during the recent past has raised hopes for faster economic development of the region. The Government of India's commitment to accelerating the pace of socio-economic development of the region is reflected in the creation in 2001, for the first time, of a dedicated Department of Development of North Eastern Region to coordinate and give impetus to the Centre's development efforts.

The Approach Paper to the Tenth Five Year Plan, adopted by the National Development Council, spelt out the objectives of economic growth with enhancement of human well being by way of provisioning for adequate level of consumption of food and other consumer goods; access to basic social services, especially education, health, drinking water and basic sanitation, expansion of economic and social opportunities for all, reduction in disparities, greater participation in decision making etc. State Governments of the north eastern region have identified the priority areas in their Tenth Plan in the light of the objectives laid down in the Approach Paper, and the various departments of the Central Government have drawn up their sectoral strategies for implementation.

Recognising the special problems of the region, significant levels of Central assistance to State Plans have been a feature of planning in the north eastern States. Even among the special category States, the per capita levels of Central assistance are among the highest in the country, as indeed they are intended to be. For example, for the year 2001-02, average per capita Central assistance for State Plans for all the States in the region taken together was Rs.1,546, compared to Rs.356 for the country as a whole. Further, a number of special arrangements and initiatives have been taken and will be followed up in the Tenth Plan which will help accord priority to the development of the region.

The North Eastern Council (NEC) was set up in August 1972 under the NEC Act, 1971 (with its Secretariat at Shillong) for regional planning and development. As per provisions of the statute under which it was constituted, the Council is envisaged as an advisory body empowered to discuss matters of common interest to the Union and the north eastern States, and recommend to the Central/State Governments any matter of common interest, interalia, in the fields of economic and social planning, inter-State transport and communications, power and flood control, etc. For securing a balanced development, the NEC may formulate, for the member States, a regional plan in regard to matters of common importance to more than one State of the region, and indicate priorities of the projects/schemes included in the plan and their location.

The projects financed by the NEC are implemented either by the State agencies or by the Central public sector undertakings/organisations. The functions of the NEC can be grouped into three categories:

a) Regional Planning

b) Zonal Council

c) Security

NEC has been focusing largely on its role as a regional planning body and a zonal council. The approved outlay for the Ninth Five Year Plan (1997-2002) of the NEC was Rs. 2,450 crore which represents an increase of about 31 per cent over the Eight Plan outlay of Rs. 1,867.50 crore. The year- wise details of the expenditure during the Ninth Plan period are given in Table 1.

Table 1. Year-wise details of the Budget Estimates, Revised Estimate and Expenditure of NEC during Ninth Plan

Year	Budget Estimates	Revised Estimates	Expenditure	Utilisation over BE
1997-98	324.00	324.00	319.16	98.50
1998-99	440.00	370.00	368.55	83.76
1999-2000	450.00	425.00	413.53	91.89
2000-01	450.00	410.90	409.48	90.99
2001-02	450.00	450.00	414.82	92.18
Total	2114.00	1979.90	1925.54	91.08

It may be seen from Table 1 that against the agreed outlay of Rs. 2,450 crore the budgeted outlay for the five years of the Ninth Plan period was Rs. 2,114 crore, which represented a shortfall to the extent of 13.7 per cent in the budgeting of the agreed outlay. Further, it can be seen from the figures given in the Table that the utilisation of the budgeted outlay has also fallen short of the amount provided for during the Ninth Plan period.

The outlay for the Tenth Plan of the NEC has been fixed at Rs. 3,500 crore. The strategy to be adopted by the

North Eastern Council for the Tenth Plan is to put more thrust on completion of on-going priority works, initiation of a few major projects to have better impact on areas of intervention instead of taking up large number of smaller projects, consolidation of schemes, better monitoring, and improvement in project implementation. The Council is responsible for taking up projects for balanced development of the region and would continue to emphasise financing of projects with a regional approach.

Pursuant to the announcements made by the Prime Minister in October 1996 at Guwahati, all development Ministries/ Departments in the Union Government have been directed to earmark and spend at least 10 per cent of their annual gross budgetary support for the Plan for specific programmes in the north eastern region. Under this initiative, a total of more than Rs. 5,000 crore is expected to be budgeted annually by various ministries for the region.

In case any Ministry fails to achieve this target, the unutilised portion with respect to the 10 per cent norm is pooled in a Non-Lapsable Central Pool of Resources which is re-utilised to finance infrastructure development projects in the north eastern region including Sikkim. This approach has succeeded in increasing the Plan expenditure of the Central Ministries in the North East from 6.25 per cent in 1999-2000 to 7.28 per cent in 2001-02. The percentage flow of Central funds is expected to improve further in the Tenth Plan.

During the last four financial years, a large number of development projects have been directly supported from the pool for which an amount of Rs.1346.72 crore has been released. Detailed break up of the funds released are given in Table 2

Table 2. State-wise Release of Funds from the Non-Lapsable Central Pool of Resources, 1998-99 to 2001-02

State	Funds released (Rs. crore)			
	1998-99	1999-2000	2000-2001	2001-2002
Arunachal Pradesh	15.00	19.65	43.96	74.24
Assam	28.81	105.86	69.31	89.18
Manipur	20.34	121.67	23.85	18.56
Meghalaya	8.79	3.00	32.63	22.39
Mizoram	9.00	62.15	27.06	69.86
Nagaland	20.01	44.08	15.91	52.16
Sikkim	10.00	32.01	23.78	49.71
Tripura	10.00	22.50	67.08	115.71
Common to NE and Sikkim	—	9.00	9.46	—
Total	121.95	419.92	313.04	491.81

The role of the newly created Department of Development of North Eastern Region (DONER) would be to create synergy and ensure convergence of programmes by coordinating the efforts of both Central agencies and the State Governments and by meeting the last mile resource needs for completion of projects. The department would act as a catalyst in stimulating the development process and focus on increasing opportunities for productive employment, strengthening infrastructure, particularly connectivity and communication, together with ensuring accountability in the implementation of projects.

An important initiative that is being closely followed up is the PM's Package. Reflecting the special attention needed for the region, announcements have been made by the Prime Ministers during the last five to six years for giving an impulse to the speedy economic development of the north eastern region. These announcements, inter-alia, included specific schemes/ programmes to be implemented on priority basis. Most recently, on 22January 2000, at Shillong, the Prime Minister announced an Agenda for Socio-Economic Development of North Eastern States and Sikkim. This Agenda covers 28 programmes/schemes.

The financial requirements for implementation of these programmes/schemes, as per the present estimates, aggregate to Rs. 13,388.90 crore. The entire financial requirement is to be met through the plan/non-plan budgets of the Central Ministries/agencies and through the financial support from the financial institutions such as the National Bank for Agriculture and Rural Development (NABARD) and North East Development Financial Institution (NEDFI). The execution of these programmes during the Tenth Five Year Plan period is expected to help bridge infrastructural gaps particularly in the sectors of power, rural infrastructure, roads, air-links, horticulture, medical and health services, information technology and vocational training, and provide a conducive atmosphere for expansion of border trade and strengthening of security.

DONER is now the lead department in the Government of India for coordinating all Central initiatives and programmes in the North East. The following would be the strategic focus of the Government of India in the Tenth Plan for the north eastern region.

(A) Improving Implementation and Ensuring Better Delivery of Results

(i) Timely implementation of the Agenda for Socio-economic Development;

(ii) Completion of ongoing, centrally assisted projects, and proper prioritisation of projects for effective use of resources;

(iii) Ensuring better implementation of projects with transparency and accountability, through close monitoring and reviews, in coordination with the sectoral departments/State Governments;

(iv) Strengthening infrastructure, particularly connectivity and communications.

(B) Providing Upstream Assistance and Policy Support

(i) Reviewing the policies of both the Centre and the States from time to time with a view to focusing greater attention on the region;

(ii) Providing assistance in resolving policy bottlenecks to development efforts and in expediting the clearance of projects;

(iii) Facilitating the efforts of the States in the mobilisation of financial resources;

(iv) Ensuring adequate availability of funds for essential public capital investments, especially where "last mile" gaps need to be filled to bring benefits to the people;

(v) Encouraging credit flow in the priority areas through banks and financial institutions.

(vi) Facilitating better utilisation of economic infrastructure for enhancing income generation, keeping in mind the ethnic and social setup of each State of the region;

(C) Strengthening Capacity and Public Involvement

(i) Capacity building through training programmes for educated youths in high growth sectors having large employment opportunities, and encouraging private sector participation in these programmes;

(ii) Capacity building of State Government personnel in project formulation, appraisal, evaluation and monitoring;

(iii) Ensuring greater participation and involvement of the people in project formulation and implementation;

(iv) Building awareness through seminars, workshops for prospective private sector investors.

Planning and development of an area within the State is primarily the responsibility of the concerned State Governments. However, the Central Government is supplementing the efforts of the State Governments in this direction through special Central assistance for special area programmes such as Hill Area Development Programme (HADP) and Western Ghats Development Programme (WGDP), Border Area Development Programme (BADP), etc.

Special area programmes have been formulated to deal with the special problems faced by certain areas arising out of their distinct geophysical structure and location and concomitant socio-economic development. Funds under special area programmes are meant to deal with the specific problems of these areas. Hence special plan strategies are formulated and schemes drawn up by the State Governments keeping in view the basic needs of the people and existing environmental and socio-economic considerations.

Areas under HADP were identified in 1965 by a committee of the National Development Council (NDC) and areas to be covered by WGDP were recommended in 1972 by the High Level Committee set up for the purpose. After the formation of Uttaranchal in 2001, the designated areas covered under HADP / WGDP include:

a) Two hill districts of Assam - North Cachar and Karbi Anglong.

b) Major part of Darjeeling District of West Bengal.

c) Nilgiris District of Tamil Nadu.

d) One hundred and fifty nine talukas of WGDP comprising Western Ghats in Maharashtra (62 talukas), Karnataka (40 talukas) Tamil Nadu (25 talukas), Kerala (29 talukas) and Goa (3 talukas).

The HADP will continue to be funded through Special Central Assistance (SCA) on 90:10 (Centre:State) basis. The SCA will be apportioned between the Hill Areas Development Programme / Western Ghats Development Programme in the ratio of 60:40. As in the earlier plan periods, the SCA will be divided among the designated hill areas on the basis of area and population, giving equal weightage to both. In the case of the Western Ghats Development Programme, the criteria will be the same but the weightage for area will be 75 per cent and population 25 per cent.

The main objectives will continue to be ecopreservation and eco- restoration with a focus on sustainable use of bio-diversity, recognising the needs and aspirations of local communities. The planning approach would aim to facilitate community participation in the design and implementation of strategies for conservation of bio-diversity and sustainable livelihoods. During the Ninth Five Year Plan, the two programmes (HADP and WGDP) were being operated differently.

While under HADP, a subplan approach was used and almost all the sectors were funded from Special Central Assistance, in the case of WGDP, the Watershed Approach was used and only a few additional sectors/ schemes were funded. While the WGDP approach has been more in line with ecological development, the HADP States have been requested to include schemes for ecological preservation and restoration in the sub-plan.

In the hill areas of Assam and West Bengal, the use of special Central assistance for payment of salaries/ other expenses of non-plan nature should be phased out slowly and schemes for environmental preservation and restoration introduced such that by the year 2003-04, the salary/ establishment would be reduced to 20-25 per cent and schemes for preserving the ecology and restoring the fragile eco system of these areas would be increased by a similar proportion.

The thrust areas of HADP/WGDP during the Tenth Plan will be :

(a) Watershed Development

(b) Participatory Approach

(c) Innovative Schemes for Technologies suited to Hill Areas

(d) Schemes for Bio-Diversity Conservation

(e) Schemes for Income Generation

(f) Gap-filling Infrastructure

(g) Maintenance

In the Tenth Plan, the State Governments can use up to 15 per cent of the annual allocation for maintenance of assets in HADP areas.

Developmental Programmes in the Tenth Plan

The programme will continue in the Tenth Plan as a separate programme and will be operational in the border blocks of all the States which have international land borders. The main emphasis of the programme will continue to be on meeting the special needs of the people living in remote, inaccessible areas situated near international borders.

Special Central Assistance under the programme will be provided as 100 per cent grant. The existing criteria of the length of international border, area of the border blocks and population of the border blocks (with equal weightage to each) will be the basis for the division of funds amongst the BADP States. Schemes under the programme are to be designed such as to take care of the special problems faced by people living in the border areas.

A long-term Perspective Plan for each border block is to be prepared by the State Governments keeping in view the objectives of overall balanced development of the region. The State Governments may undertake a study of remote villages in the border blocks in order to assess the needs of the people and the critical gaps in physical and social infrastructure. Schemes for employment generation, production oriented activities and schemes which provide for critical inputs in the social sector would also need to be identified.

Security related schemes and construction of houses for crucial functionaries such as teachers, doctors, nurses etc., may also be taken up in border blocks under the programme along with construction of small culverts, bridges, bridle paths and feeder roads. Up to 15 per cent of the total allocation could be used for maintenance of the assets already created under the programme. The BADP is expected to help address the special developmental needs of the people living in the border areas during the Tenth Plan.

Development of Kalahandi, Bolangir and Koraput (KBK) Region of Orissa

The KBK region comprises the original Kalahandi, Bolangir and Koraput districts situated in the southern and western parts of Orissa. These three districts have been reorganised since 1992-93 into eight districts, namely, Kalahandi, Nuapada, Bolangir, Sonepur, Koraput, Nabarangpur, Malkangiri and Rayagada comprising 80 blocks, 1,171 gram panchayats and 12,104 villages. This area has become the Centre of attention owing to the high levels of poverty and consequent adverse effects on the quality of life of the people of the region.

The State Government had drawn up a revised Long Term Action Plan (LTAP) (1998-99 to 2006-07) with a total outlay of Rs. 6,061.83 crore, consisting of a Central Plan and Centrally Sponsored Schemes in various sectors, namely Agriculture, horticulture, watershed development, afforestation, irrigation, health, drinking water, emergency feeding, welfare of SC/ST and rural connectivity. In order to fill critical gaps, an additional central assistance of Rs. 243.95 crore was allocated by the Planning Commission from 1998-99 to 2001-02 to the KBK districts. However, apart from this additionality, most of the other fund flow to these districts comprised only normal flows under various Centrally Sponsored Schemes.

Hence, it was decided that a more concerted effort was required if the living conditions of the people of these districts were to be ameliorated. In order to adopt a more holistic approach to the development of the KBK districts and to tackle the basic problems of drought proofing and essential support to disadvantaged groups and economically weaker sections, the State Government was requested to prepare a projectised plan for critical sectors. The Annual Action Plan for the year 2002-03, prepared by the Government of Orissa provided for Rs. 200.00 crore as Special Central Assistance and Rs. 164.69 crore as central loan assistance under the Accelerated Irrigation Benefits Programme with emphasis on the following sectors:

(i) drought proofing (soil & water conservation, afforestation, irrigation, and drinking water;

(ii) livelihood support (agriculture, horticulture, animal husbandry, fisheries, agri-business, agri-market, handloom and sericulture);

(iii) support for disadvantaged groups (special nutrition programme,. emergency feeding, tribal development and women's self-help groups);

(iv) Health;

(v) Rural Connectivity; and

(vi) Administrative Support.

It is proposed to provide Special Central Assistance to the special plan for the KBK Districts during the Tenth Plan period, subject to satisfactory physical and financial progress of the schemes. The main aim is to use a project based approach and local participation along with transparent and responsive administration to ensure that field level results are visible in a time- bound manner.

8

Micro Credit for Women's Empowerment

A Case Study of Dhan Foundation

The concept of empowerment is being used increasingly in many context as a tool for understanding what is needed to change the situation of poor and marginalized people. Availability of micro finance services do widen the range of options open to marginalized and poor women but still do not enable them to exercise their choices due to constraints like lack of confidence, skill and information and also the social, cultural and political influence. As Shrilata Batliwala puts it "there is often an assumption that power comes automatically through economic strength - it may, but often does not, depending upon local gender relations and class/caste relations."

Micro Finance at the outset attempts to achieve specific aspect of poverty and also aims to fulfill the gap between the poor and formal financial system. The proponents of micro finance consider economic empowerment as an entry point and a road map towards the overall empowerment. It is believed that certain benefits seem to be flowing automatically as a consequence of this approach. Whether extending micro finance and micro credit is sufficient to bring the empowerment is questionable? There are issues of human development related with the empowering processes. Is it not that the vulnerable socio-cultural position of women inhibits the benefits accruing due to availability of micro finance services? There are thus, multi dimensional issues, which are non-economic in nature, reinforcing the disempowering status of women.

It is increasingly realized that an empowerment approach to development centered on economic entry needs to pay attention to the processes and structures. These processes and structures need to be designed to create opportunities for empowerment processes to happen. These could be slow, however, will have perpetual impact. United Nations Development Programme (UNDP), Delhi commissioned the study with an objective to understand the role of micro credit on social mobilization for women's empowerment.

For this purpose UNDP has identified different micro finance organizations to assess and analyze the impact of micro credit on processes of empowerment and outcome of processes on individual women as well as on collectives. In addition to this the task was also to look into design and management of the micro credit programme and perspective and approach of implementing organisation to understand the role of the organisation in contributing to processes and structures that leads to empowerment.

Against the backdrop of broad TORs of UNDP, the objectives of the study are defined as follows:

— The role of Dhan foundation as an institution, its perspective and approach in contributing to empowering processes.

— The design and management of micro finance programme of Dhan foundation, its out reach and the process through which the women's position is strengthened.

— The changes in the life of individual women as well as collectives of women are also examined. The changes may be fall out of direct intervention or consequential impact (on account of changing socio economic situation) of micro finance interventions of DHAN Foundation.

Intensive field visits and investigations and direct observation formed the basis of examining and assessing the empowerment processes happening at individual level and collective level at grassroots. It needs to be mentioned that it was not possible to use structured sample survey due to lack of time and coverage of different strata. The attempt is to identify the qualitative changes taking place among the women through their own voices. Following methodology was adopted to analyze the empowerment impact at individual level as well as group level. Interviewing the non members, male members as well as other institutions was also done to triangulate the information collected from the women.

— Informal and Focus group discussions with group members, leaders at group, Cluster leaders and federation level on group formation, decision making processes, savings and lending operations and different products offered and issues of financial and social sustainability,

— Individual discussion at family level for discerning the impact on household level,

— A participatory analysis of division of labour, work load, mobility and intra-household decision making before and after the DHAN Foundation intervention to see whether the work load has increased or decreased after being members of the group, expanded women's mobility, may be due to only being part of group activities or initiatives taken by the self and also the enhanced women's role in household decision making,

— Informal discussions with primary School teachers, Aanganwadi workers, local administration, bankers, local law protection officers, village leaders, male community who are related to women members or otherwise,

— Formal and informal discussions were held with the senior functionaries of DHAN Foundation, Programme Leaders, Managing Directors of federations and staff of clusters to triangulate the information collected and also to understand the long term perspective of the organization,

— Review of secondary material like annual reports, newsletters and case studies.

Dhan Foundation operates its micro finance programme in viz. Tamil Nadu, Andhra Pradesh and Karnataka and in Pondicherry. Dhan's micro finance programme is named as Kalanjiam Community Banking Programme. The basic philosophy of Dhan Foundation is building institutions, which has led to evolving of people's organisation thus forming 20 registered federations of SHGs, federated at block level. Out of 20 registered federations three are urban, one is semi urban, 16 are rural. Out of these 20 federations, 3 federations are identified for the study in consultation with Dhan functionaries. The relative context of each federation is different and also care was taken to select young and older federations in order to assess the impact at different time intervals of implementing the programme.

Within each federation, though the sample group visited was identified randomly, yet the care was taken that the selection of oldest group, new group and relatively older group is covered. Different groups in three federations have been studied namely

— Pothigai Vattara Kalanjiam (PVK) federation located at Madurai West block in Madurai Region is a relatively new and semi-urban federation. In PVK federation discussion took place with 6 groups and 81 women participated in the discussion. A Focus group discussion was arranged with 8 cluster leaders. Daily routine of the two members' individual families was mapped.

— Kadamalai Kalanjia Vattara Sangam (KKVS) federation in Mayiladumparai Block in Theni Region is chosen as one of the oldest federation in rural areas. In KKVS federation interaction was done with 60 women of four groups. Also participated in all cluster meeting of KKVS federation and had a dialogue with 60 cluster leaders. Close interaction was undertaken with 18 cluster presidents. Also got an opportunity to deliberate with the 10 Board of Directors members of federation. Daily routine mapping was undertaken with three families. Intensive discussion and probing was done with 6 women belonging to different age groups and different status.

— Mugavai Kalanjiam Mahalir Vattara Sangam (MKMVS) federation in Mandapam Block in Ramnad Region is selected as one of the most backward areas and on coastal line of Tamilnadu. In MKMVS federation 9 groups were visited and discussion took place with 97 women members. Two groups of fisher women were visited and interacted with. Individual discussion took place with 3 women members for mapping daily routine. Two Executive Committee meetings were attended and deliberations took place with 15 members. A meeting of 6 federation leaders was arranged for deliberations on policy issues.

Overall, 378 women members of the programme were interacted. Besides this, discussions were held with functionaries of DHAN Foundation, government departments and banks that helped to triangulate the information collected from the women.

Limitation of the Study

This study is the outcome of two weeks field visit to Dhan Foundation. It was the attempt of the researcher to look at the programme with an outsiders view throughout the visit. Looking at the vast expansion and structure of the programme it is possible that some aspects of the programme are missed out or have not captured the impact as perceived by the organisation itself. As it was difficult to cover the programme in its entirety. Such a large programme must have undergone different processes, actions and phases over a period of ten years which have now stabilised among the women members and Dhan functionaries.

It is possible that the study and fieldwork conducted in such a short time may be missing certain important processes and aspects of the programme and therefore may have captured certain views on the basis of first observation, which may be different in reality. It is to be stated that, in all the discussions and field visits, an open and friendly attitude and transparent exchanges took place. A special word of thanks and gratitude to all the women needs to be expressed for untiring response to all the queries enthusiastically.

It was also felt that opportunity given to share the experiences and ideas with the top functionaries of Dhan Foundation was well received and appreciated. This is also to acknowledge and express thanks to UNDP, Delhi for commissioning the study on such an important and relevant topic. It is expected that findings and observation will make meaningful contributions to the purpose of the study commissioned by UNDP, Delhi for ICICI.

Perspective of DHAN Foundation

DHAN foundation (Development of Humane action) was initiated in October 1997 incorporated under Indian Trust Act in January 1998 with an objective of bringing highly motivated and educated young women and men to the development sector in order that rural innovations are brought. Dhan Foundation has its operations in viz. Tamil Nadu, Andhra Pradesh, Karnataka and Pondicherry in 17 districts. Dhan Foundation was created as a spin off organization from erstwhile Pradan organization to expand and deepen its base in Southern India.

The aim of Dhan Foundation is to address poverty alleviation directly. Dhan Foundation's mission is building Institution for development innovation and upscaling for impacting livelihood to enable poor communities. This mission emanated from the basic organizational values like Grass Root Action, Enabling, Innovation, Excellence, and Collaboration. Thus the three broad purposes are defined as follows:

— Mothering of development innovations: The institution aims to promote and nurture new ideas on different development themes in the region.

— Promoting institutions to reach scale: Exclusive thematic organizations will be promoted with an objective to ensure that benefits reach a large number of poor.

— Human Resource Development: The institute will attract young professionals in to development sector with a focus to built up their skill and competence to undertake development work.

From the purpose it is very clear that Dhan has clear agenda of working as a support and facilitative body for institutional development and capacity building of the people for the transfer of new technology at different levels. Dhan believes in making institutions and taking them to the masses to produce a significant and sustainable change in the household of the poor and marginalized. In its processes it tries to build the capacity of the people in planning, organizing, conflict resolution and organizing them into a collective body at different levels to achieve a significant upscaling of programme.

People are then enabled to adopt and enact a generic skill of developing viable alternatives to their situation by working on single activity focus. Dhan therefore does not deliver services but facilitates and supports to get access to the choices and demand made by the people. The successful economic initiatives are expected to lead towards grass root democracy by occupying the legitimate political space without getting into party politics.

Most of the efforts are directed towards localized institution building for the poor. In order to achieve above purposes, Dhan has introduced community banking programme for women, Tank Fed Agricultural Development Program for farmers. The Kalanjiams (name given to the programme, literally meaning a storage bin made of mud used to store grains) and Vayalagams (Tank Farmers Associations) at the village level are federated at block level or district level.

The strategy of Dhan is to introduce the theme, support it and move to the next theme. After successful demonstration of specific activity Dhan moves to next theme and moving into civic programme like health and education which is a larger agenda is taken up by the peoples organisations promoted. Collaboration with other agencies is seen as an instrument to enable the poor people to mainstream with overall system. Upscaling the activities and collaborating with the agencies on policy issues, funds, training and networking are part of the empowering processes. This enables the poor women to develop leadership quality and linkages with the mainstream system which has been unheard of by the poor women.

After achieving the above two themes, Dhan has moved to new themes - Dhan Academy - a development management institute for nurturing and developing young professionals for development work and a pilot project on Information technology for the poor.

A strong bias in Dhan is towards the fact that economic strength is considered the basis of social, political and psychological power in society. Executive Director Shri Vasi Malai in his discussion said with anguish that he had experienced poor women (even men) in villages working as bonded labour and suffering drudgery but never coming out of debt. The compensation will go for interest payment and principle amount inherited by the next generation. Dhan thus focused an intervention based on the needs of poor people, with their participation, ownership and control.

The poor people's need for money emanate for consumption, sudden events like deaths or sickness and lifetime events like marriages. Sometimes these are also attributed to factors beyond their control. Therefore primary focus of Dhan is to create access and control over financial services like savings and credit by poor women by promoting localized self managed institutions. Thus micro finance services are considered as an essential tool of addressing poverty alleviation.

The effort towards integrating with macro economic processes is of course built in the structure of community banking programme linking the poor with mainstream system through people's participation and building up their capacities. Dhan has also made the substantial contribution at the macro level for the cause of micro finance for the poor by impacting on policy issues through various national level committees on micro finance. However, Dhan also responds to the changing internal and external environment and this has led to new initiatives like housing, insurance and also possible of opening of women's bank for urban poor.

Women's Empowerment

The recognition of women's powerlessness and addressing it with the base of low economic status of women is internalized at all levels in the organization. During different deliberation with Dhan functionaries and even during discussion with women members clear message of understanding on women's issues was observed. Basic issues to be addressed are internalized in the system that women are restricted to low paid work, lack of access to education, training and credit, lot of invisible and unpaid work, restricted mobility of women, lack of any opportunities to express women's abilities, gender discrimination intermixed with cultural issues. With this understanding, community-banking programme for women has moved with clear reflection of fundamental core values and purpose of Dhan.

These core values and objectives are reflected in each of Dhan's initiatives and actions. Discussion and the review of the documents indicate that Dhan has actually not used the word 'empowerment' though it does realize that these are empowering processes happening. The outcome of its processes is seen more in Access and Control and decision-making through democratic processes. The strong belief is to allow the women to learn in their own way and not short-circuiting the processes.

The ultimate goal is selfreliance and empowerment through interdependence with community. For this purpose, Dhan has adopted four generation strategy achieving one after the other. The first generation process is social intermediation followed by financial intermediation process in second generation with livelihood and business promotion during third generation and finally the fourth generation process will address civic programme interventions. Dhan itself has perceived the time frame of 10 to 12 years for four generation but to the researcher's mind certain process were evolving due to women being together and women are demanding to address the civic issues like health intervention. The generation gap is thus reducing over the years.

Therefore in this sense, empowerment may be interpreted for Dhan as the process by which the women and community gain control over social and economic conditions; over democratic participation in their communities and over their own stories. Dhan thus believes that social change will evolve over a period of time with economic strengthening and thus views economic empowerment as the beginning of the social change. Dhan hence has adopted the economic entry approach.

Competence and Skill of Staff

Dhan foundation is a spin off institution of PRADAN, one of the foremost development agencies in India. Asserting a clear mission, working on value based principles and fundamental and associating professional staff with high values and commitment. An organization promoting 'participation of poor women' of course has in-built system of including participation of its programme staff. Dhan recruits professionals who are willing to work for the development. Various consultative processes existing indicate that all the staff are also allowed to reflect their voices and concerns through structured and unstructured interactions.

These interactions are further developed, refined and also validated through their experiences of working with the poor people. Programme staff is considered a critical link to work with the women. The strong qualities of perhaps each programme staff is a scientific method of social analysis, continuous learning, two way communication skills and the ability to cope with tension and conflict resolution skill mixed with strong sense of ownership and fundamental values of Dhan. However, the researcher felt that the long hours the team puts in on a day to day basis should be having pressures and stresses of varied kinds. The noteworthy point is that Dhan has a policy of gender balanced recruitment unlike other organizations who appoint only women for women's programme. The thrust is on recruiting and grooming the professional suitable for the development sector.

Community Banking Programme

The focus of community banking programme is to create sound local financial institutions managed by women at each hamlet, cluster, & block level to link with main stream financial institutions.

Programme Components

— Organizing poor women into groups of 15-20 and giving them an opportunity to experience and share their economic position and the nature and causes of exploitation - Social Mobilization;

— Mobilizing of own resources and managing them for their own benefit through regular savings and management of credit;

— Regular interactions, exchanges and exposures;

— Linking the women groups with formal financial institutions; The credit management is by women groups and the transaction with bank as clients and not as beneficiaries;

— Training and building leadership qualities through transferring the roles and responsibilities to manage their own groups and activities;

— Skill building and training in specialized business activities (Dairy, Poultry, Charcoal, etc,) and financial management;

— Formation of women managed financial institutions at village, cluster and block level for gaining collective strength and Power.

Structure of People Institutions promoted by Kalanjiam Programme

Community banking operates at group level, at cluster level and at federation level. Each group has three leaders decided by the consensus of all the members. The executive committee thus manages the group, which consists of the president, secretary and treasurer, a vice president and joint secretary. The secretary will be responsible for looking after operational and administrative matter and the treasurer would take care of cash and accounts. The executive committee would divide the following operational responsibilities among themselves viz. Banking, community issue, monitoring and evolution, expansion and training.

Once a set of 5-6 groups in a contiguous area has attained stability in their operations, they are encouraged to meet periodically and share their experiences. Over time these meetings are formalized and a cluster association is formed. The task of cluster association is to

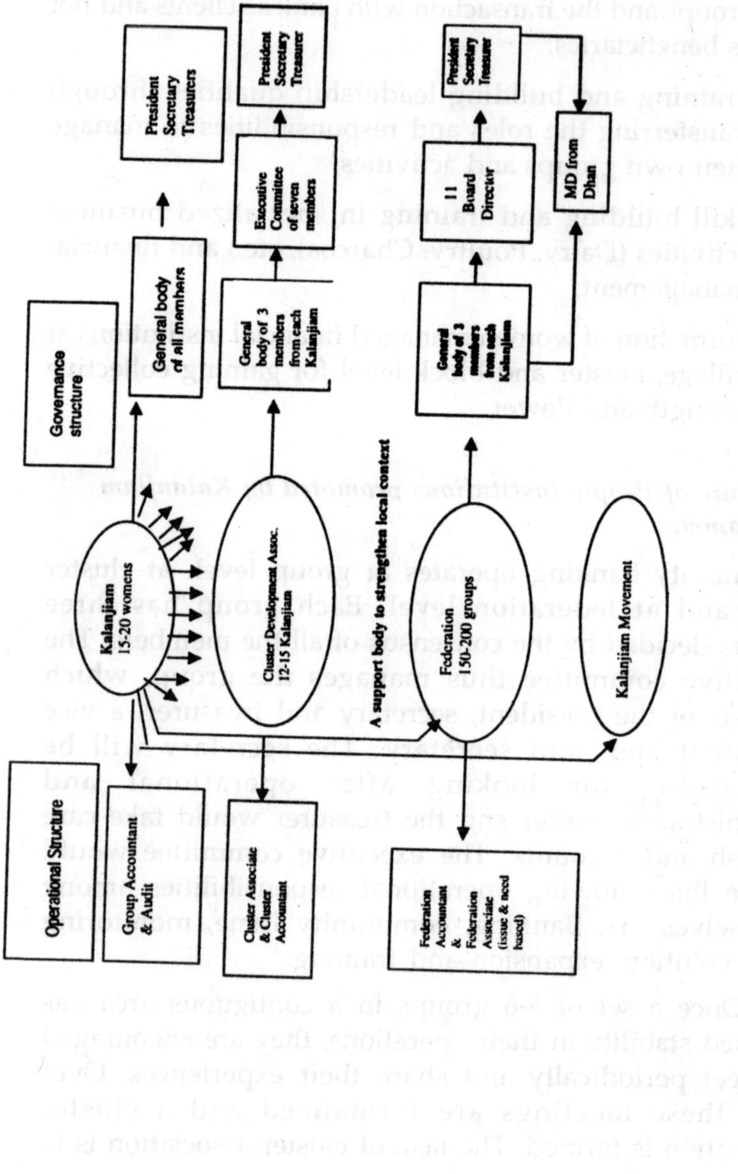

Community Banking Structure of Dhan Foundation

monitor the progress of the groups, conflict resolution promoting new groups and also training group members. This has further evolved towards helping groups in creating bank linkages and also a forum for addressing the civic issues. Each group has three representatives in cluster of which seven members executive committee is elected at cluster level. Cluster constitute of 15-20 groups.

The federation is made of 150 - 200 Kalanjiams. Federations get support for three years from Dhan. All the groups will promote in to federation at the block level. These federations are registered as society or trusts. The general body of the federation consists of all the leaders of the member groups. From which 11 members are selected for the constituting executing committee of federation board.

The primary objective of the federation is to strengthen and sustain the primary groups and mobilize external funds from banks, and apex financial bodies. Federation acts as a support body for training and managing specialized services such as insurance, health, and education. Federations provide economies of scale, better bargaining and negotiating power with banks, government, outside agencies, while facilitating local initiatives and promoting leadership development.

Within the overall structure each level operates as an autonomous body. Each level has to cover the cost by itself. The autonomy is to ensure the responsibility of the group and group leader, strong ownership, awareness of cost coverage, developing community & financial management skill and also to ensure transparent system. These are empowering processes, leading to devolution of qualities essential for development of the women. For e.g. leadership- quality asking questions, negotiations, analyzing and consciousness to monitor the groups money.

The present structure of groups also allows for the participation of women at all level. A norm of one person - one post is followed to avoid burden on one person. Normally SHG leaders graduate to cluster leader and cluster leaders graduate to federation leaders. This process brings in the experience of the local context and also ability to share more responsibility by the leaders. Once this graduation happens the earlier role is taken over by the new member. This process assists in rotation of the leadership and gives opportunity to all the members to participate and share higher level responsibilities.

While women members take governance roles, local staff are appointed for maintenance and management functions. The costs of the local staff are paid by the people out of their own sources. There are around 1500 local staff working at group, cluster and federation level. At present a total of Rs.30 lakh per month towards the salaries of these staff are paid by people. In essence these groups are also creating employment opportunity at local level. One group accountant keeps the record for 5-6 Kalanjiams. One of the important things is to be noted here is that the money transaction does not take place through the hands of accountants. They are merely facilitators for writing the accounts and record keeping. Similarly the cluster appoints cluster accountants and cluster associates.

The women members primarily are landless agriculture labors, masonry workers, and construction workers or undertaking small activities of fruit and vegetable vending or running a petty shop. The classification of families is categorized in survival, subsistence and self-employment. Almost 80% of the women belong to survival and subsistence category having wage income with deficit household budget leading to greater indebtedness. Village mapping and wealth ranking in the village under take identification of the women members.

The Kalanjiam is a basic hamlet group with 15-20 members residing in the same hamlet. The programme is implemented by mobilizing the target women in homogeneous group. Homogeneous group here means organizing group of target women with more or less similar economic status. The first generation group formation took longer time sometimes 5-6 months to formalize the group. Dhan staff made the initial facilitation efforts through addressing the social issues. In KKVS federation issues like girl infanticide or suicide were addressed to build confidence and rapport among the women. The second generation Kalanjiam formation was motivated on the experiences and example setting of older groups.

Over the years, this process has shifted to the group members and the group leaders. Many Kalanjiam have emerged as a ripple effect of the groups functioning in that area. This has now transformed into institution building through Kalanjiam movement exclusively constituting of poor women. Kalanjiam movement of group expansion has emerged in to creation of women led managed kalanjiam Foundation.

The process of initial grounding goes on for 3-4 months and follows process of "quality check" followed by the registration process (not legal body) at programme level for allotment of group code. Books of accounts are introduced after six-month period with opening the bank account. The norms for group functioning such as saving rate, loan amount, interest rate, meeting schedule, agenda setting and group leadership are decided by the group.

The members as convenient to them decide the timings of group meetings. In semi urban areas the women prefer to meet generally at 10.00 am in the morning as they are free of household work. Most rural groups prefer to meet in the afternoon after becoming free from the work. Frequency of the meeting is monthly or fortnightly, usually monthly in rural areas. Fisher women's group in Ramnad district meets four times a month.

Meeting place is usually outside the village under the big tree. In semiurban area women meet in a common garden or common open space of the hamlet. One of the groups is meeting at the temple place, which also happens to be the house of village panchayat leader (Man). Due to the temple place, women during "periods" are not attending the meeting. In one more group few women do not attend the meeting for the same reason as this is held at one of the better of members' house.

At this juncture women should negotiate to obtain space for "Mahila Kutir" to have common place of meeting which may also serve the purpose of shelter for the women. The attendance in the meeting appears regular and member not attending the meeting will take permission or inform. Some groups have the practice of imposing penalty for not attending the meeting. It was observed that the participation by the women in the semi-urban area or town areas was higher. The participation also depended on the literacy level.

Normally, the younger women in the age group of 25-32 years are more participative, initiating the issues and also playing the facilitator's role. The older women are matured and able to understand the issues. Extremely poor category, sickly or very many elderly and totally illiterate women are seen excluding themselves from the discussion. The women in semi-urban areas are seen more articulated and organised in conducting meetings and sitting in a round sitting arrangement. In the rural areas even now, articulation is less and does not tend to sit in a way that allows eye to eye contact.

Evolution of the Community Banking Programme

Erstwhile Pradan project initiated 1989 made a modest beginning and started with forming 20 self help groups in 11 villages with a total membership of 286 women. This has under gone various phases of expansion with different strategies like initial promotion and strengthening, older group mobilizing new groups, replication in new location and saturation in a particular village and also in the block, revival of defunct groups and collaborating with other NGO. In the year 1998 a revolutionary movement started with a decade of community banking experience resulting in the beginning of people led movement.

The year witnessed the celebration of Kalanjiam movement and women taking oath to spread the concept of the Kalanjiam to all poor women and also to reach one Lakh women within three years. During the year 1999-2000 itself the Kalanjiam covered additional 33,000 families. The VVK Federation has made 100% coverage of all the poor in 39 out of 80 villages saturating the coverage of poor in the region. The effort is targeting all the poor in the panchayat and in a block so that 100% coverage of poor is ensured.

The expansion strategy is further strengthened by the initiative of cultural team, by movement workers and collaborating with local government and banks. This approach has enabled to transform from a mobilization and service delivery approach to people led movement and also cost efficient approach. The next strategy is to have a Kalanjiam Foundation a separate thematic institution to upscale the Community Banking Programme and reach a million poor over next decade. The major approach of the programme in meeting its objectives is through the promotion of people's organization at different levels.

The programme has been successful in promotion of more than 6100 SHGs in almost 2000 villages with 400 cluster development associations and 20 federations. As on December 2001 there are more than one-lakh Kalanjiam members. As a support body facilitating the development of local institutions and enabling the women to manage and become self reliant for own development, Dhan appears to be the only institution to achieve such a large scale.

The growth in terms of savings and lending activity is equally impressive. Most distinguishing is the fact that this is all poor people's money. Average saving is Rs 1300 to Rs.1500 while average loans arrive at Rs 2500 to Rs 2800 at their doorstep. Though the average saving and average loan will not the capture the strength of some of the older members but gives an indication of large scale outreach of the benefit of the services.

Kadamalai Kalanjia Vattara Sangam (KKVS) Federation

Kadamalai Kalanjia Vattara Sangam (KKVS) is located in Mayiladumparai, a remote block in Theni district of Tamil Nadu, 100 k.m to the North West of Madurai, in the foothills of Western Ghats. The block has 18 panchayats that have 115 villages among them. The main reason for selection for operating community banking programme was the remoteness of the block and its constituent village and low development status both social and economic. This development status is greatly influenced by migrant nature of population and the area being pre-dominantly dry agriculture.

The villages were selected on 4 major criteria remoteness of villages, small villages with less than 100 households, villages with more women issues and finally the prospectus of forming clusters due to contiguity of the villages. The federation was registered in August

1995 under the Society Registration Act 1860 after a period of 2 years of association with Kalanjiams.In terms of resources land and forest are the major resources of the block but with the degrading quality. There are 924 females per 1000 males as of 1991 census indicating poor female male ratio. Scheduled Cast Scheduled Tribe constitutes nearly 24% of the overall population in the block.

Of the total work force 46% are female workers while female agricultural labourers are 49% of total agriculture labourers. The literacy rate is very low at 35% with female literacy at 24%.The major development issues of the block are as female infanticide, the marriageable age of girls between 12-16 years, desertion of women by men, large number of widows, high incidence of money lending. Some of the infrastructure issues of the blocks are high deforestation and high erosion, land alienation, migration of men in search of employment and extensive cultivation of cannabis. Similarly, lack of approach roads to villages, poor health and educational facility are other features of the block.

Mugavai Kalanjiam Mahalir Vattara Sangam (MKMVS) Federation

MKMVS is operating in the entire Mandapam block having 28 panchayat and two-town panchayat and in 7 panchayat of Tirupulani block of Ramnad District. The community-banking programme was initiated in 1992 in Mandapam Block and in 1995 the Kalanjiams got promoted into Federation. This block was selected for development intervention, as it is one of the most backward blocks in Ramnad. Livelihood of most people is dependent on coastal and marine resources. Fishing and palm mat weaving are major source of income to meet their basic and social needs.

Agriculture is not suited for this block due to sandy soil. Special feature of this block is that the male population is less than female population. The population of Mandapam has religion based diversity as equal number of Hindus and Muslims are residing in this block. Many poor Muslim males are migrating to Arabian countries for earning but most of the time they are cheated by the middleman. The socio-economic situation of the block is very poor. Different occupations have different wage rates in the same range of Rs.20 for women and Rs.35-70 for men. This block is also characterized by large number of women headed families.

Alcoholism is wide-spread and men are spending their money only on alcohol and give meager amount for family expenditure at home. There is a large scale desertion of women and prevalent bigamy. The villages covered under the block are remote villages not connected by pucca roads; inadequate drinking water and electric facility, exploited money lending. The general profile of the members covered are landless labourers, widows, prevalent child labour, female headed families, people living in huts and earning less than Rs.1200/- per family per month.

Pothigai Vattara Kalanjiam (PVK) Federation

PVK federation is located in Madurai west block having urban influence as it is situated around 8 kilometers away from heart of Madurai City, with community banking programme initiated in the year 1999. Nearly 60% of the total geographical area is used for agriculture purpose while rest is wasteland and used for non agriculture purpose like institutions and industries. The female population is 974 per 1000 of male population. Female agriculture labour force constitutes 45% of the total agriculture labour. The total female workers are 34%

of the total labour force. The female literacy is 44%. The main employment opportunity for the block is agricultural work. This block is one of the paddy belts in Madurai district.

The wage rates vary from Rs.25-30 for women and Rs.50-60 for men. Main reasons for selecting this block for community banking programme is that 60% of people are agriculture labour, money lenders operations at exorbitant rate, high percentage of scheduled caste population and no infrastructure facilities. Most of the people are employed as agriculture labourers, road and building construction workers, fruit and vegetable venders, mill worker or undertaking activities like coir making, dairy, and miscellaneous small business activities. The targeting of the villages was done on the basis of remoteness and population less than 1500 in a village of which majority villages targeted are with population of less than 500.

Only two villages have population above 1500. This federation has attempted classification of poor into three categories of survival (who find it difficult to fulfill their daily needs), subsistence (wage employment available more or less regularly) and self-employed. The major development issues in this block are alcoholism, child labour, high dropout rates of children from the school and infanticide.

Growth of Financial Services

Providing diversified financial services is considered a vehicle to address poverty. Widening of financial services is addressed by penetrating the market by geographical saturation through replacing the informal sources of credit. Dhan strongly believes that deepening of financial services is possible through providing options and choices for the poor. Once poor are utilizing the services it will help them to link and influence the mainstream system. Alternate financial services thus are provided in an organized manner with an understanding of varied dimensions varying in each local context and situation. Savings, credit and insurance services are provided to suit the convenience of the poor women.

Saving is considered a powerful tool to build the stakes of local community in the financial system. Started with level of Rs.5/- for each member, women are saving up to Rs.100/-. There was no concept of saving earlier and whatever was earned, was spent. The saving collection in the group is weekly, fortnightly or monthly. In Mandapam block in Ramnad District groups have achieved the saving level of Rs.10 million. The total savings of all the Kalanjiams are Rs.1067 lakhs as of March 2001 as compared to Rs.627 lakhs in March 2000.

The average savings by member per year increased from Rs.55 in 1991 to Rs.337 in 1995-96 and has risen to Rs.1329 as of March 2000 and to more than Rs 1500 by December 2001. In older groups the average savings range from Rs.3000/- to Rs.5000/-. The saving lending ratio for all the Kalanjiams comes to 51%indicating the extent of people's own contribution for rotating the funds.

Two types of saving products are available primary saving and diversified savings. Primary saving is the regular contribution and internal lending is used for rotation within the group with out any lock-in period. Primary savings are non-withdrawable until the death of the member or on discontinuation of the membership from the group. The withdrawble diversified savings are contributed for specific needs like education, marriage, festivals, social obligations etc. There is a special deposit scheme allowing withdrawal (twice the amount) after a fixed period. The diversified savings take care of seasonalities and ensure food security during emergencies. The flexibility of differential savings enables the poor women to save according to their needs and also on the basis of ability to earn. Many groups during the lean season save differential amount.

Many microfinance organizations do not emphasize on savings. While for DHAN Foundation savings emerges as wherewithal for viability of groups. Savings helps the groups in following ways:

— Own resources for internal rotation

— Savings provide own capital for own development

— Localized product suiting local context

— Peer pressure leads to self-regulation

— Helps in regulating cash flow

— Enables to leverage credit from mainstream institutions

Community banking programme provides range of services to meet different credit needs of the poor including consumption, health, education, income generation, housing and asset creation. Credit for food security and for social security like health education is considered credit for consumption. Usually, during first year, the loan is given eight times of savings while after first year five times of savings is considered for credit. The number and amount of loan of each member increases as the age of group matures.

There is no tangible collateral requirement for availing loan for the women. Indirectly Savings works as collateral as it gets adjusted incase of default of loan. Installment repayments are fixed flexibly on the basis of purpose and quantum of loan. the older federations the individual loan amount has increased to Rs.20000 - Rs.25000. The bigger loans are given for house repairs or construction of house. In these cases it is ensured that asset is created in the name of women only. It will be advisable if these members are encouraged to open individual bank account to avoid handling large cash on one hand and on other to inculcate the habit of direct mainstreaming with the bank. The major impact is noticed in redeeming outside debt that is availed at the rate of 10-15% per month.

Moneylenders refuse loan to very poor unless they pawn their small assets and that also under great humiliation. However, a few women have stated to be saying that flexibility of very small amount like 50 Rs for very short period is available only with moneylenders.

Repayment

The repayment at different levels is presented below:

Member to Group:

Groups below six months - 80% to 94 %

Groups above six months - 100%

SHG Bank Linkage

Groups to Bank - 98% to 100%

Group to Cluster - 88%

Cluster to Federation - 96%

Federation to Apex banks - 100%

It is felt that there is some pressure on the members for regular repayment. Women have stated that sometimes there are conflicts with their husband for repayment during tough time. Usually all women take consent of their husbands before availing the loan in order to enable them to share the joint responsibility of repayment. Rescheduling of repayments during emergency is possible for 2-3 months but after that there is a pressure to repay the installment particularly interest payment.

There is also the pressure of being removed from the group. Penalty for nonpayment of installments can be

Rs.20-50 for each installment. In the older federation the installment comes to Rs.800-1000 per month for those availing large loans. It appears that since the loan is available there is temptation to use the loan but also feel the pressure of the regular repayment. Hence there is need to look at credit size and rationing the credit according to the absorption capacity.

With regular repayment women have become aware that they will get repeat credit. One of the groups found stating: "We are quick in repayment on time, so that federation is giving us loan and bank is also giving loan because of this. So we have the right to access to further loans". This indicates the awareness and the confidence gained due to different processes. There are also cases of individual self-exclusion among the group members mainly because of poverty. The groups have been able to access the finance from banks as well as from apex banks through federations.

Insurance

Insurance services are very vital for the poor because of their vulnerability. Each member is a productive asset and any calamity with any of the member influences the cash flow of the family adversely. The federation provides life insurance, medical insurance and housing insurance however, there are certain conditionalities attached for initiating this product. Before initiating insurance in a federation detailed analysis of death rates over the past 5 years is conducted. Premium of Rs.100/- per year is to be paid by each member, which covers the natural death to the tune of Rs.10000/- and accidental death up to Rs.25000/-.

There is separate insurance fund but most of the federations have also created linkages with insurance companies for giving different products. There is flexibility of providing premium in three installments for very poor female headed and widow families. Dhan is conscious of reducing the premium over a period of time and it is planned to reduce the premium to smaller amount and after five years the premium will be paid out of group common fund. There are also complexities involved and perhaps more clear consensus should be formed.

MIS, Record Keeping and Monitoring

Given that the community-banking programme deals mainly with the money the need for strong financial system is obvious. Record keeping and MIS from the Kalanjiam to cluster level and cluster to federation level allows for the detailed analysis and monitoring. There has been considerable improvement over the years. Group wise and cluster wise computerized data are maintained at federation level.

Each Kalanjiam is viewed as an autonomous financial institution and maintains a standard set of books of accounts and records like cash books, vouchers, member ledger, general ledger, demand collection and balance statement, members pass book, receipt book, minutes book etc. Group accountant appointed by the group maintains all the records updated. The respective executive committee (EC) members monitor the working of the group accountant and cluster accountant. The accounts are discussed in the Kalanjiam meeting and the EC members crosscheck the entries made by the group accountant. Though illiterate, leaders will remember by memory and try to cross check through showing it to the children going to school in the village.

Cluster leaders ensure quality check of groups through spot visit to the meetings. Quality check entails that regular meetings are held with members sitting till end with precise operations of savings and lending and also repayments are monitored. In the process the leaders also revive the defunct groups by solving the conflicts and attending the meetings.

There are clear policy guidelines on accounting system, which ensures effective check and monitoring at each level by multiple crosschecks. The role clarity and accounting policies indicate transparent procedures. In fact, many of the organizations have adopted the procedures from Dhan Foundation. However, in spite of such system there are 15-20% groups who are not regular in submitting the MIS on time.

Internal auditing of the groups and clusters is done once in three months. External audit is conducted once in a year for group, cluster and federation level accounts. Provision of loan loss and bad debt is maintained at group level account itself in order to cover the delinquency. Groups and clusters are not registered bodies but the auditing reflects the problems and mistakes in accounts to be rectified. During the audit, the EC members, group accountant and cluster accountant remains present. Audit, besides, helping the groups and clusters to create direct linkages with the banks also builds up the women's capacity for management and account keeping.

Capacity Building and Training

Training for community-banking programme is vertically integrated through bottom up approach. While the group formation activity is initiated, the co-learning starts in the meeting itself. During the meetings the training is sequenced starting from structure modules for first five months on financial management, record keeping and administrative aspects followed by linkage orientation for one month and two months training on concept of networking. Refresher courses are conducted once in a year.

Thus capacity building at all levels is one of the important strength of the community-banking programme. All staff members are associated in organizing capacity building. The Programme concentrate on capacity buildings of Kalanjiam members, leaders, functionaries by conducting training, organizing exposure trips, exchange visits and also through even celebrations like annual festivals, Annual Mahasabha meetings. Dhan academy organizes many workshops and seminars for developing professionals in order to share the experiences as well as new issues arising across the nation.

There is a separate Kalanjiam Training Centre (KTC) besides Dhan Academy to groom women volunteers from villages as cluster associate to be groomed through 42 days package of training programmes. This is a new experiment in order to support upcoming Kalanjiam foundation. The training programmes have built up the capacity of the members in a financial administration and management. Based on discussion with one of the leaders, it is felt that there is need to create greater awareness of the impact of the inter play of various types of oppressive social structure. Training modules have now taken into account these issues but it needs to be percolated to the member level.

The programme has become a resource centre for micro finance and there is high demand from external agencies to learn from it. The demand has been from other NGOs, Bankers, and Government agencies, training and academic institutions alike. Dhan as a support institution has been conducting the training programmes on micro-finance for different NGOs, for government officials' of 28 districts in Tamil Nadu state, bank officials from different states. The varied structure of training has given Dhan a special niche in terms of a support institution.

Sustainability

The mission statement of Dhan Foundation has cryptic strategy of sustainable approaches, which will enable to build institution and upscale the activities. In order that any initiative introduced has sustainable approach, there is lot of brainstorming and deliberations among Dhan functionaries with experimenting at lower scale. Dhan, of course, has been very successful in maintaining the set quality standard as micronance institution like reaching the scale of one lakh very poor women and achieving operational self sufficiency at group, cluster and federation level. The sustainability can be categorized as follows: -

Financial sustainability

Financial sustainability is generally defined as not only yielding income to cover the cost but also creating sufficient reserves through earning reasonable level of profit. The reserve at different levels group, cluster, federation of the Community Banking Programme, which was just, Rs.5000 at the initiation of the programme in 1991, has moved to Rs.274 lakhs as of March 2001. With savings of Rs 1067 lakhs, own fund of the programme has reached the level of Rs 1341 lakhs. The saving lending ratio has been 1.94% indicating leveraging additional funds available through bank linkages.

Operating cost ratio of a typical rural Kalanjiam is 15% (a good MFI has 13-21%). This has been possible as each Kalanjiam as a basic unit is considered an autonomous financial institution. The Kalanjiam has to cover its cost right from the first day. The Kalanjiam, as a people's institution, considering a basic unit has to cover the entire cost of cluster and federation. Besides this, out of the common fund Kalanjiam sets aside the fund for education, health and village development fund.

Moreover, all the loan loss provision is accounted for fully. Dhan will support for two years to cluster association and federation for first three years but after this period these structures need to be self-sustainable.

At present the source of income for a Kalanjiam is an administrative fees and 12% is spread available on rotation of members money (it pays on 12% on savings and charges 24% from members). The loan available from federation to clusters and clusters to members leaves a spread of 6% for Kalanjiam on account of apex bank linkage or any other funds available. (Federation receives the fund at 12% lends to cluster at 15% and cluster on lends to Kalanjiam at 18%) On the other hand, Kalanjiam has to cover the operational cost (by paying the salary of group accountant, audit charges, share capital to federation and to cluster), other administrative fees (Rs.100 to federation as entry fee, up front 1% cost on loan as risk fund) and also has to pay the service cost to the federation and cluster depending upon the size of loan and period.

In a typical Kalanjiam, when an analysis of income expenditure is made, payment of different costs to cluster comes to about 44% of the total expenditure and this is 40% of the interest income earned. However in spite of all these costs Kalanjiams reflect net profit which speaks about efficiency and capacity of kalanjiam to absorb the costs. It should also be noted that number of women are foregoing their wages for the day they attend to cluster and federation work which is a financial cost to the poor women and this is going to be increased with the formation of women led institution of Kalanjiam foundation. Well, Women have not complained about this.

Under the new policy, no money will be accumulated at cluster level or federation level in order to avoid power related hierarchical structural conflict.

Similarly the federation and Clusters will not retain the interest spread to cover the cost for on lending the loan amount disbursed by apex banks but will transfer to the Kalanjiams. This will help the Kalanjiams to strengthen their position and also higher level of ownership and responsibility and can demand accountability of cluster and federation. This is being experimented and the impact is yet to be seen. Institutional sustainability

Institutional sustainability

Financial sustainability is not an end in itself but the means of reaching a large and growing number of women. The outreach of community banking programme from 20 groups in the beginning to 6051 group and from 286 members to 95000 members as of August 2001 speaks the volume of the programme. The major expansion in the number is evinced from March 1998. This continuing growth is enabled due to financial discipline introduced at Kalanjiam level.

The Kalanjiam level growth, in essence, could well be defined as institutional sustainability having sound management, continuity and growth and its lack of dependence on the leadership of any particular person. At such a point, financial sustainability is an essential but not a sufficient condition. Kalanjiam movement has become conduit to attaining sustainability in expansion and coverage of members. Add on Kalanjiam members will replicate the systems and procedures of older Kalanjiams.

Besides expansion, women members have started managing the operational aspects of the programme through the cadre of the trained leaders at different levels with continuous capacity building. The women have been managing collection, disbursement, default, accounting, appointment of staff, audit, as well as interaction with banks and government agencies. On the basis of needs, these women have also addressed social and civic programmes in the villages. This part of managerial sustainability is closely woven with empowerment processes. These empowering processes are reflected in collectives.

The organizational sustainability at Kalanjiam level has an in built support from clusters as well as from federations. Since the approaches are "bottom up" the systems and procedures setup by Dhan help in making a sound institution. It needs to be taken in to account that such a large expansion cannot happen unless the programme is responding to the needs of the people by offering different products and ensuring financial discipline. The federations are registered bodies and there is technical support through deputation of a Dhan professional as Managing Director of the federation. There is a constant re-building of the issues originating from the village level through interaction with the programme leaders in order to enable them to introduce policy changes. Long term sustainability

Long term sustainability

Long-term sustainability can be achieved when women members respond to changing environment and emerging opportunities and also when the aim of poverty alleviation is achieved. Besides lack of economic opportunities, on the one hand, the vicious circle of poverty is also the result of forces like lack of awareness, education, child labor, early girl marriage, early child birth, social evils like dowry system, girl infanticides, desertion of women and unnecessary expenditure on social ceremonies like puberty, ear piercing.

As long as these systems remain, the programme will always go on adding to the category of the poorest within its ambit. This will work like a vicious circle. The sustainable impact of economic empowerment has to be followed by addressing the social issues systematically in order to have long term sustainable impact on poverty. Broadening and deepening the community-banking programme is another way of achieving the sustainability.

The programme has to move from only providing financial services to livelihood issues through business development support. The livelihood comprises of capability, assets and activity required as a means of earning. Somewhere, there is a need to develop capability and human assets. This, of course, is a wider agenda and needs different strategies which is out of purview of DHAN presently.

Social Mobilization and Empowerment Impact of Micro Finance

The sharp visible impact of the Community Banking Programme is seen in its outreach to the poorest of the poor in backward and remote locations and curbing the moneylenders' activities of up front usurious interest rate. Substantial resource mobilization and more than 98 % repayment pattern with negligible non-performing assets are other quantitative indicators helping to further upscale the programme. Qualitative indicators like cadre of poor women as leaders, strength of collectives as social support structure creating an identity of women in the home as well as in the village, confidence, physical mobility, access to public space and increased control on financial resources are to be observed and believed. The biggest impact is seen in successfully creating Kalanjiam movement led by the poor women and has given the poor women a sense of achievement.

The programme has provided the space and opportunities for the poor women. The saving by poor women facilitated greater control over financial resources and access to cash in need. This has enabled the women feel more secured during emergencies. Women take pride in owning of assets in their name like land and house through loans. Access to productive assets like land lease and tree lease through credit utilization is available to women for undertaking doing business activities. Women do take the consent of men for obtaining the loan and for the purpose for which it is to be utilized. Undertaking self employment activity like petty shops, land cultivation, dairy activity, Small trading activity, flower selling and rope making etc have been initiated by many women but are not seen on large scale.

Most of the time self-employment activities become the collective activity for men and women though there are examples of women taking up the activity solely There are also examples of women like Kartamma saying "I cannot afford to own any asset from loan as I need to spend for my daughter and grand daughter as my daughter is widow at 20 and son in law committed suicide he was in love with other woman." It is also noticed that wherever women are doing independent activity, they have better control in decision making as compared to women doing labor work. Perhaps this is so due to differences in wages of the men and women.

Due to access to resources women's status has enhanced to a small degree and the bargaining position in household has become little better. Repayment of installment becomes joint responsibility. Women have discussed that there are tensions and conflict during tough time and at the first instance men will like to curb on the repayment of loan installment. A Kalanjiam cluster leader stated, "Men allow attending meeting in kalanjiam as suddenly we have become source of money". A feeling of resistance among male for attending the meetings previously has changed. Wherever the male opposition still persists it is noticed that women are ignoring and attending the meeting. Men now support and wait at bus stand with bicycle for the women coming late after attending the meeting.

Graduation of leadership has enabled the women to share larger responsibility and decision making. Many cluster and federation leaders have to spend lot of time for meetings, monitoring, group formation and other managerial work are happy to forgo the wages for the day they are giving for this programme.

Women headed household due to (widowhood, desertions, single women) are perforce taking their own decisions. They are taking greater leadership roles and have greater degree of control over assets and income. It is noted that in such cases when the son grows up he starts controlling on mobility and income of women and tend to load with household work also increases. This indicates gender subordination passing from father to son. Position of women headed households due to male migration is more or less same.

Poor generally eat rice, a regular staple food in this area. Therefore decision making in food preparation does not have much choice. In Mandapam Block women did mention that men demand cooking fish every day while children and women are happy eating rice every day. Women said "We have to cook what they want". Decision to save is influenced due to availability of repeat credit. Rural women are able to contribute from their wages. Women in semi urban areas save by curtailing certain expenses like cutting down on Tea or cutting on tabbaco chewing. Sometimes men help in contribution of savings but they do not seem to be cutting their unnecessary expenses.

Intra household change analysis indicates that in semi urban area women are able to speak and assert their rights. They have become bold and much articulated. Women are able to put up their demand forcefully. Kalanjiam has enabled them to get social and emotional space to shed their tears.

Most poor in rural area cook rice once a day in the evening and manage till next after noon. In such a situation it is difficult to comment on nutritional status & also difficult for them to discriminate between boy and a girl. Access to private resources has given sense of pride and ownership along with increased selfconfidence. Above changes are more reflective in leaders and in those who have availed different cycles of loans.

Educational Opportunities

With the introduction of Kalanjiam Community Banking Programme an effort is made to introduce functional literacy. 70% of the Kalanjiam members are able to write their names and signature while 30% are still using thumb impression. Women do feel the need and importance of education for girls but do not make sustained efforts for girl's education. A few cases are seen at town/SU center that girls are studying up to 12th standard. Education loans are taken for the higher education of son but not for daughter though she is doing well in her studies.

A feeling still exists that "It is waste to educate the girl as she will be married." The general view is that by giving education the person neither remains fit for village life nor for city life. Probably identification of new livelihood sources with vocational or technical training may be considered.

In all the areas visited, women are aware of child care services and do send the children to ICDS centers and also avail the facility of supplemental nutrition for lactating mothers. However women are not aware of the role of these centers. At few places women did complain about the quality of food but never seem to have challenged. A close convergence between the programme and ICDS centers may be advisable for obtaining better services of ICDS.

Women do support the PHCs during polio vaccination campaign but do not seem to be utilizing or challenging the services. First aid training to 59 women in VVK Federation has enhanced the health & hygiene awareness and these first aiders are able to serve 59 villages in their area. TBA (Traditional Birth Attendant) training has helped the women to conduct safe maternity but these developments are area specific.

Access to training on administration and financial management has given the women a sense of sharing responsibility and ownership. Individually women are more aware, have got an ability to analyze, questioning and negotiating, cost conscious and moreover enhanced confidence to deal with tough situation in day to day life. Co-learning and sharing experiences in Kalanjiam gives them ability to understand each other. In urban federation women have accessed to new technology of accessing low cost housing. Women have started building a training center with the support of HUDCO. In rural federation access to new technology is not availed.

In MKVS federation (older) women did mention that we now need skill building training to earn more. Providing vocational training or BDS support is not presently done by DHAN. Women are able to access bank credit and talk boldly with bank officials. With the good repayment record these women are promptly attended. Women feel that over the years attitudinal change is observed towards the poor. Women are telephoning the bank manager demanding the status of their applications.

Apex bank linkages through federation are accessed for asset building and for income generation activities. However women have taken a note, "apex banks do not recognize us individually and are giving loans due to Kalanjiam and Federation". Access to housing loan and apex bank linkage has enabled number of women to own houses in their own name. This facility is available but many women need to utilize this facility.

Labour and Income

In order to understand the nature of waged and non-waged work and also the workload, an exercise of mapping of daily routine was undertaken for men and women in all the three federations visited. Shockingly, despite working for 14 hours a day, women did not admit that they were working more than the men. Most of the men are found not working for more than 7 hours but considerd harder working and bread earner for the home. Income of Women on the other hand is considered supplemental. Non wage work is a household work and there is no autonomy to choose in this unless girl child starts helping the women. No choice is available to women in seasonal agriculture labour work as women only do weeding and transplanting.

The men do object to non wage work of women for instance taking the responsibilities in Kalanjiam and spending time for that. Looking at the benefits men have stopped reacting. According to husband of one of the cluster leaders "my wife is already overworking at home. She should not take additional responsibility still objects her owning responsibility." According to the same cluster leader her husband says, "it is our money and we are getting loan on therefore there is no need to spend so much time for Kalnjiam". This actually reflects the mail ego and jealousy due to that fact that she is much-respected leader and getting recognition. These cases may be sporadic but sensitizing the men on entire issue of the programme may be considered through Kalanjiam foundation. Time spent on different activities

Mapping of daily routine also revealed that as soon as man is free he would take bicycle and go to teashop or in a common place where men assemble. For women leisure is to sleep and now watching TV and nothing beyond that. Now at least women are able to spend time in Kalanjiam, which is generally two times in a month. Women doing self employment activity feel they are putting in more efforts to see that it does not make loss. Men's participation in household work is found in few cases but this seems to be more related to the gender and age composition of the children. Men do help in fetching water and breaking the fuel wood. This remains clearly within home and women were quite reluctant to talk about it. In majority of the cases the men do not share household work.

Wages are unequal for men and women as women feel that men's work require more strength. Wages for men are Rs.40 toRs100 while for women Rs. 25. Men and women are able to work for six months as agriculture laborers. Men try to look for alternate work like construction work or migrate to but women have no work during this period. Therefore women think men's wage contribution is more important.

Self Employed Case in Semi Urban Area

All most all the women with whom discussion took place were married as soon as they attained puberty. They were not even aware about the marriage institution. Even now, the girls are married at the age of 14-17 years. Most of the women in the age group of 45 and above have given birth to 10-12 children. Most of which used to die immediately after the birth due to lack of proper care.

This is one area that needs attention. The issue of child morality and maternity under proper case needs attention. Child deaths either due to lack of proper cares after birth or infanticide need to be addressed by the federations.

The women were aware of family planning. Amazingly the younger lot between the age of 20-30 have undergone family planning operations after 2-3 children. This was something prevalent in all the villages. Therefore, a gradual change is visible but there was no evidence of spacing between the children. Women are also aware of ultrasound test providing sex determination facilities, which is in fact working more as negative factor. Craze for male child is still felt strongly.

In Kadamalai Block female infanticide a practice has been very strong. This has been curbed substantially due to DHAN's intervention. In order to support the women with girl child, federation gives Rs.2000/- to the mother of two daughters. It was very sensitive to talk about the issue of contraception, abortion and sexual relations with partner but it was very clear that men were reluctant to use contraceptives.

The men desert many women. Sometimes, due to giving birth to only girl child, or falling in trap of other women. Most of the men migrated to Kerala will normally not come back and marry someone there. "Still it is noted that wherever man is not involved in alcoholism and woman is little educated, the relationship was found to be congenial." Besides this, there are strong social taboos of different ceremonies particularly puberty ceremony, ear-piercing ceremony involving wasteful expenditure and increases the burden of debt. Dowry is another social evil which keeps the women always under the control of men and indebted through out their life.

Domestic violence as mentioned elsewhere is just accepted by the women. Many women have reported that earlier they used to be beaten for even attending Kalanjiam meetings. There has been moderate change after the association with Kalanjiams and also the realization that role of women has widened in the family. There is scope for DHAN to address some of above issues systematically to curb above practices.

The women have achieved significant control in physical mobility. Physical mobility has been possible due to attending Kalanjiam meetings and acquiring training. This has enabled the exposure to the different villages and cities to the women. Women expressed that earlier going out was possible with men only. Some women had not even visited the next village also. SHG - bank linkage has given access to the banks.

Women are able to visit banks, collector office and also local B.D.O office independently and have established relationship with the local police. Local police also trust Kalanjiam women and have made them member of the village level committee of "Friends of Police". Men do have a feeling of resistance but looking to the benefit emerging due to their mobility gradually they have accepted. Number of places men have been encouraging the women to go out for Kalanjiam's work.

Assuming responsibility for the Kalanjiam at different level essentially makes them mobile as a feeling of responsible behavior. Being mobile has enhanced women's confidence, courage and access to knowledge and information. It has also enabled them to express themselves at various forums. Self-employment activities taken upon by the women solely have also enabled her to be mobile.

The name given to the group - KALANJIAM has become well known in the villages and within the overall community. The success of Kalanjiam in achieving social space, negotiation, building solidarity and confidence in collective action is laudable. Many issues mainly on community infrastructure like access to water, road repair, electricity has been taken up successfully. These issues are non-controversial and benefit all. Existing power structure and gender relationships are not threatened by taking up such issues therefore there are support from men also. However, the collective strength has shown the empowerment processes happening at Kalanjiam level and collective impact is conspicuous.

Women in semi-urban and rural areas are going for electoral voting but decision to vote is influenced on the basis of the political promises or pressures from male members. Many cluster leaders are getting ready to participate in Panchayat Election. Women are looking for their own space to make an impact so that they can be heard and have strength in negotiating with the Government.

Local Government has taken note of Kalanjiams and in recognition has invited the leaders on various committees. It is not clear how much the kalanjiams are able to challenge and assert their own needs. There is need to have facilitation support where poor can demand and exploit in their own favor. These changes are seen more in the leaders. Gradually women are realizing their own importance.

In one of the Gramsabha Meetings the cluster leaders refused to participate in the meeting, as panchayat did not respond to their request earlier. By not participating in the meeting Kalanjiam members have shown their resistance but not challenged therefore facilitation efforts will strengthen the women's position. There has been significant change in the attitude of local government towards women. Panchayat president not only interacts with the cluster leaders but also encourage the women to speak overtly in the villages. During festivals in the village the Kalanjiam members are made the committee members for water and food distribution. In Mandapam Block, Panchayat has allocated space for conducting the functions to the Kalanjiams.

As a Kalanjiam women have been able to bargain and negotiate their own space in the village. As mentioned earlier they also challenged the panchayat members for some of their decisions but they have not shown a collective action against panchayat despite their own resistance. Women have participated successfully in elimination of arrack distillation and opium cultivation. On the complaint of Kalanjiam women in Kadamalai block police raided the village and arrested the men for arrack distillation.

No sooner the men were released, the arrack distillation restarted. Fuming with anger, women took the initiative to break all the mud pots installed beneath the land for arrack distillation and even burned the opium plots. Women thus have. worked for removal of alcoholism amidst the threat of the men. Most of the Kalanjiams are limited in caste composition to scheduled caste, schedule tribes, dalits,and from different religions. The resistance to sit together previously has been replaced by the feeling of solidarity.

The Kalanjiam festival and Mahasabha celebrations are conducive in breaking the class, caste and religion barriers. Thus caste structure has weakened considerably at village level. Numerous examples of initial rift and conflict are there but finally relationship has built up due to being part of Kalanjiam family

Women were quiet upset when the issue of caste hierarchies was discussed. They were very categorical in saying that they had forgotten such differences and did not want to be reminded. In the initial period it was difficult to address this issue but it appears that the common issue of poverty brought them together.

There is an increased awareness generation among women for sending the girls to school but awareness has not made much impact among the women to send the girls to school. Those willing to send the girls for higher secondary school find limitations due to lack of transport, as each village will not have the facility for higher education. Normally going to school up to 4th and 5th standard is found common.

There has been a change in this pattern particularly in urban areas. For e.g. in SPMS Federation in Tirupati, Vidyadeepam programme is initiated. This federation has also started a school for the children of Kalanjiam members. Thus, Though there is a realization that education of girl can bring the social change for the future generation but women are tied with social customs of getting them married at early age.

Similarly MKVS Federation the oldest federation has taken up the health issue. In a regiona family welfare conference organized by district family welfare board 65 Kalanjiams and cluster leaders and barefoot health workers participated. A few awareness camps on reproductive system, video shows for AIDS and waterborne diseases etc. are organised. In Theni region the federation played an active role in the governments sponsored comprehensive health check-up programme for poor in rural areas. In Vaigai federation 59 members have provided training with medical kits that were providing services to 52 villages.

It seems increased awareness generation on health issue is emerging but again a systematic attempt to address the issue has been lacking. In Thoppaiyapuram village of Kadamalai block, A few Kalanjiam women have also started dairy activities with 30 cows with market linked with Kerala milk chilling plant. Women are managing this activity successfully through hiring the men and they have full control on sale proceeds of milk.

Support services like arranging for veterinary doctor's etc are provided by the federation. Such cases are few but have considerable domino impact this appears to be more a collective impact.

The very fact that Gramsabha's are inviting the Kalanjiam groups is an indication of visibility as well as recognition. The kalanjiam have taken up the infrastructure issues like obtaining electricity and electric pole for the street, drinking water facility, roads etc. for the village. For e.g. in Kadamalai Kundu an initiative to provide electricity at lower cost without paying any bribe was undertaken for 45 households in a village. In VVK Federation the chronic drinking water problem in Genguvarpatti village was solved through the efforts of cluster committee leaders and kalanjiam members. The formal recognition by government agencies is definitely visible through inviting the federation in all the meetings.

The women also got recognition in this block as they took up the challenge of constructing 150 toilet buildings, which men could not finish and amount was eschewed. These women have now decided to take up the contract of road construction of village with panchayat.

Moreover awareness on capacity to mobilize own resources is seen as pride of the Kalanjiams. The realization that "We can do the development work through our common fund" speaks of the capability to manage civic issues with their contribution. Federation leaders are able to challenge the decision of MD of federations if not found proper. These achievements as collectives are laudable.

Socio-economic Environmental Changes

A change in approach towards women is distinctly visible at all levels. A positive change in terms of attitude and practices of mainstream financial institutions, government departments, weakening cast and religious barriers is notably conspicuous. There has been substantial reduction in turn over of local moneylenders. In fact this is one of the major achievements of community banking programme. There have been instances where the moneylenders have been challenged by the Kalanjiam members for misappropriation of poor people's money or exorbitant charging of interest rate (10% a month). Money lenders did try to dissuade the women initially but in the process lost their BUSINESS.

Successive smaller loans have enabled the women to come out of debt and ensured them the security of food. At least they are out of negative cash flows. There has been protection of the existing income level but increase in income is felt only when women have taken the loans for business activity. There has been no perceptible change in the consumption pattern of the poor people. Women are aware about obtaining food grains from PDS. Evidences in Mandapam block are seen challenging the PDS shops for lower weights and long uneven queues but the local government ignores this.

The processes of impacting poverty are happening in individual cases and will take time to see drastic changes in reducing poverty profile. On the basis of observation it is noticed that nutrition status of the children appear satisfactory. There is definitely scope for groups to create systematic links with ICDS programme to strengthen health and nutrition impact. But there is general lack of awareness among the women on health aspect as information on reproductive health system is highly desirable.

The impact is also difficult to ascertain in terms of increased participation of girls in formal education. As referred earlier, the women are recognizing the importance of educating young girls. It is a point of concern as girls stop going to school as soon as they attain puberty. Girls are also dropping out of school to take care of younger siblings incase mother is doing self-employment activity. They do get back to school after a break but by this girls have lost the interest in studies. Boys loose interest after 8th or 9th standard and start getting in to labor work.

In semi urban and small town the trend seem to be reversing and illiterate women are keen to send the girls and boys to school. Child labor is the impact of the programme can not be said. On the contrary women take loan to help the son to study. Thus it can well be inferred that in terms of Kalanjiam an alternative women friendly financial institutions has emerged giving space to market leaders from village to district level. The biggest achievement of Dhan is in providing financial services to the poorest women. This however, has yet to make a considerable impact on poverty profile of villages; nonetheless the economic entry approach has made the beginning arresting the income leakages.

9

Rural Micro-finance in India

Credit is sought for basic requirements such as food, as well as for income generation activities. The rationale of micro-finance is based on the hypothesis that the poor can be relied upon to return the money that they borrow. Moreover, the repayment will also be on time. It has been proved that the poor are capable of thrift and savings. It is these existing requirements and conditions that are tapped by micro-finance initiatives.

Micro-finance as a development initiative has been justified on the grounds that it is beneficial to both micro-finance institutions as well as clients. Since the poor can be banked upon to return loans on time, it is believed that micro-finance and profits are not antithetical to each other. In fact this intervention is being hailed as the one method that will address both development and promote market behavior. On the part of the clients, it is believed that it is possible for micro-finance institutions to instill trust in the poor to give up their savings and to avail of micro-credit so that they can pull themselves out of the poverty trap.

The need of the poor for credit is not new. So far, this need has been met largely by informal sources such as moneylenders, support by kith and kin, friends, employers and landlords. Borrowing from these informal sources often involves exploitative rates of interest and results in strengthening of systems of oppression. The formal sources of credit in India have been banks and poverty alleviation programs promoted by the government.

The track record of these formal sources has not been positive. Micro- finance, in the form in which it is being promoted currently, circumvents the drawbacks of both the formal and the informal systems of credit delivery. Among the real and potential clients of micro-finance, women are seen as the most reliable in terms of repayment and utilisation of loans. The gender dimension of micro-finance is based on the understanding that the entire household benefits when the loans are given to women. Further, it is argued that micro-finance can empower women since it instills a perception of strength and confidence when the poverty trap is broken.

Most micro-credit initiatives require the formation of small 'selfhelp groups' (SHGs) of 10-20 persons, who come together with the intention of saving and rotating loans amongst the members. Once these groups stabilize, they are accorded formal support so as to widen their lending capacities. The entire process of forming a group, of functioning in a sustained manner, of regulating finances, and being mutually accountable, is in itself, empowering.

An important dimension of SHGs is the peer pressure, which the members of a group exert amongst themselves, which acts as a substitute for formal collateral in that it is taken as the guarantee for loan repayment. The initiative of providing credit to the poor is not a new one in India. In the mid-sixties, the Government set up cooperative societies to meet the credit needs of people. Unfortunately, for a variety of reasons, this initiative did not meet the purposes that it was supposed to fulfill.

Following this, 1969 saw the nationalisation of banks in the hope that the credit requirements of the poor could be addressed in a more meaningful manner. These efforts were supplemented with poverty alleviation programmes like the Integrated Rural Development Programme (IRDP), Jawahar Rozgar Yojana (JRY) and Pradhan Mantri Rozgar Yojana (PMRY), the results of which have also proved unsatisfactory.

Over the past three decades, women and their credit needs have been explicitly addressed by women's organisations like Self Employed Women's Association (SEWA) in Ahmedabad, Gujarat, Working Women's Forum (WWF) in Chennai, Tamil Nadu, and Annapurna Mahila Mandal in Mumbai, Maharashtra. Their efforts have resulted in far-reaching changes in the lives of their women clients. Even so, today, micro-finance is perceived as a paradigm shift in the quality of micro-finance delivery. Further, the push has come internationally, from donor agencies, UN organizations, and the World Bank, all of whom are advocating micro-finance as the banner under which development can be achieved and poverty can be eradicated worldwide.

Officially, the intervention of microfinance has been heralded world-wide as the best cure for poverty. There have been a series of meetings and summits that have been held over the last few years, to design an approach that can been be followed by all countries across the globe. The meetings worked towards contributing inputs for the World Micro-Credit Summit Campaign held in February 1997.

The South Indian Consultation was held in Hyderabad, India on, 23-24 August 1996. A meeting of 20 practitioner NGOs, development financial institutions and development professionals arrived at a common position and action plan. The Dhaka Declaration of the South Asian Coalition for the Micro-credit Summit articulates the collective consensus among 21 networks and agencies delivering financial services to over 4.5 million poor people across Bangladesh, India, Nepal and Pakistan.

It endorsed the importance of micro-credit and emphasised that microcredit should be approached as a socially responsible business. Prior to the Washington Summit, a group of NGOs and development finance institutions met in New Delhi on 23, January, 1997. The objective was to review the progress made and to discuss modifications to the draft documents released by the Summit Secretariat in November 1996.

World Micro Credit Summit

The World Micro Credit Summit was held in Washington DC in February 1997. More than 2,900 people representing 1,500 institutions from 137 countries participated in the Summit. The Summit announced a global target of supporting 100 million of the world's poorest families, especially women, with micro credit for self-employment and other financial and business services by the year 2005. This Summit received impetus in the mid-1990s after the World Summit for Social Development in Copenhagen in March 1995. Four core themes were stressed as part of a 55- page Declaration and Plan of Action.

— *Reaching the poorest*: 1.2 billion people some 240 million families - in the world are living in absolute poverty. This is the group that is targeted by the Microcredit Summit. The Summit promotes the use of quality poverty measurements to identify the poorest.

— *Reaching and empowering women*: Since women are supposed to be good credit risks, and women-run enterprises yield benefits for their families, micro credit is seen as a tool to empower women.

— *Building financially self-sufficient institutions*: This theme is based on the experience of developing countries which have shown that micro credit programs can improve their efficiency and structure their interest rates and fees to eventually cover their operating and financial costs. The Campaign offered daylong courses at global and regional meetings held from 1999 through 2001, which trained practitioners in this regard.

— *Ensuring a positive, measurable impact on the lives of clients and their families*: Two impact evaluation studies conducted by an NGO, Freedom From Hunger, showed that current clients of its affiliate institutions in Honduras and Mali had experienced positive program impact at the individual, household and community levels. The studies showed the higher levels of empowerment of client households as compared to non-client households in terms of larger enterprises, increases in personal income and household food consumption, savings and a feeling of self-esteem.

These four core themes of the Summit Campaign help to focus on both the targeted poor households as well as on the quality of the practitioner's work. Papers prepared for the Summit, substantiated these themes and have since been updated and used widely as guidelines by practitioners in this sector. After the 1997 Washington Summit, by December 1999 more than 1600 micro credit institutions joined the Summit's Council of practitioners.

In doing so each institution had endorsed the Summit goals and agreed to submit an Action Plan within one year of joining the council. In November 1999, Institutional Action Plan grids were mailed for the year 2000 to the 1,600 institutions. In India the All India Women's Conference was designated to collect data for this survey. All practitioner-Action Plans submitted were reviewed by the Summit staff. In an effort to verify the data, the fifty largest institutions in Africa, Asia, and Latin America were asked to identify donor agencies, research organizations and networks that could take up this task.

Issues Regarding Data

The data generated by various micro-finance initiatives are both quantitative and qualitative in nature. Data can be scrutinized on the basis of two factors:-

— Availability and

— Requirements

Available data is the end product of an exercise of generation, collection and tabulation. Access to available data is mediated by the following factors:

— *Genesis*: The purpose behind the exercise throws light on how the data has been generated and collected.

— *Method*: A variety of methods and a combination of them can be used to collect the data that is pertinent to the purpose of the exercise. Data formats in particular are important in understanding the method.

— *Adequacy*: While methods can be evaluated individually for their consistency and correctness, their relevance to the genesis is also important. Data formats can be studied in order to assess whether the method/s used are adequate for the original purpose or not.

— *Gaps*: Ascertaining of the level of relevance and adequacy of data available automatically leads to identifying gaps that exist in the available data. These gaps could emerge at any of the above levels, and could be due to a lack of clarity about the purpose of data collection, methodological shortcomings or inadequacies in data format/s.

The requirement(s) of generating data links closely to the ethos of micro-finance per se. In as much as there are gaps in the available data and inadequacies in the existing exercises, the data will fall short of enhancing an understanding of the intervention and its dimensions. This understanding is absolutely vital if the initiative of micro-finance is to be harnessed for poverty eradication.

Wherever there are gaps, there is also scope for improvement both in the methods of data collection as well as in the way the micro-finance initiative can be carried forward. Requirements could include extensions of existing efforts, new methods of data generation and collection for the existing purposes, and new methods / new kinds of data for new purposes. These issues will be highlighted with explicit examples and references from available data efforts.

Data issues with respect to micro-finance emerge in as many ways as purposes for which data is collected. Both quantitative and qualitative data should be examined for their availability and their relevance to the requirements of a specific micro-finance initiative. This can be approached through either of two methods. The first method traces data through the institutional mapping in the credit delivery system and is called the 'vertical approach' to data issues. This approach illustrates how the initiative of micro-finance is carried out.

The data points to the socio-economic health and performance of the various participants within the institutional mapping. The second method is to trace data through the contextual mapping of the conceptual rationale of micro-finance, through the intervention, to the impact that this effort has had on the lives of clients. This method is called the 'horizontal approach' to data issues. This approach matches impact evaluation studies with the philosophy behind micro-finance and helps to ascertain whether the ends have justified the means.

Institutional Mapping

Availability of Data

The available data can be scrutinized using the vertical approach. In such case, one finds that the data emerges in six different dimensions. Data throws light on the following aspects of each of the participants in the institutional mapping:

— Status of the participant (nature, composition, socio-economic profiles)

— Organizational working (democratic nature, nature and turnover of staff members, laws, bye-laws)

— Operational functions of the participant (availing of funds, disbursement of loans, mobilization of savings, saving- investment-credit products available, repayment rules).

— Performance of participant (financial health, sustainability, quantitative data about intermediaries, judgmental data regarding standardization, rating, regulation and monitoring of participants, especially MFIs)

— Operational dynamics (inter-participant, intra-participant, both in relation to conflict resolution in the formation of groups and their relationships with other participants)

— Resultant best practice norms relating to 2-5

Structure of the Micro-finance Sector in India

The rural financial system in India has evolved through two sets of financial institutions - formal and informal. The formal system consists of a multiagency approach, comprising co-operatives, public sector commercial banks (CB) and regional rural banks (RRB), private sector banks. The public sector banks and RRBs constitute the government sector. The cooperative sector comprises of district cooperative banks (within which are primary societies and urban banks) and primary land development banks.

Private commercial banks constitute the third channel. Since existing private banks do not do much rural lending, the Reserve Bank of India has provided for the setting up of Local Area Banks in the private sector to promote savings in the rural sector and to provide credit locally. The rules and regulations within the financial sector govern these institutions. The informal system consists of rotating savings and credit associations (ROSCAS), traders, merchants, contractors, commission agents, moneylender's etc. Each of these are governed by norms and rules that have been formulated by the concerned instituion/person.

The major objective of the nationalization of banks in 1969 and 1980 was to improve the flow of institutional credit into rural households, especially the poor. Commercial Banks play a dominant role in rural financial markets in contemporary India. Priority sector lending was one of the most important tenets whereby the RBI stipulated commercial banks to ear mark 40 per cent of their advances for priority sector lending.

Of this 18 per cent was for agriculture and 10 per cent for weaker sections. The rural credit market expanded significantly in the post- nationalization phase. There has been a significant improvement in outreach due to nationalization and social banking. Between mid 1970s and mid 1990s bank credit in the rural sector increased by nearly 240,000 million and rural deposits increased by about 410,000 million. Therefore, the share of both rural credit and deposits almost doubled during this period.

The poverty eradication programs of the government also played important roles in addressing the credit needs of the poor. The Integrated Rural Development Program (IRDP) was the largest ever anti-poverty program launched during the Sixth Plan. It used the banking channel to direct assistance, which was a combination of credit and subsidy to those below the poverty line.

However, trends also show that the accent on development banking of commercial banks weakened considerably in the 1980s and 1990s. There has been deterioration in the pace of increase in outreach of commercial agencies and a decline in non-institutional sources in the 1980s. There is also a deceleration in the growth of commercial bank credit to rural areas in terms of both disbursal and outstandings in the late 1980s and early 1990s.

Further there has been relative fall in the proportion of bank credit flowing to the priority sectors, especially agriculture, since the mid-1980s. There is a close connection between the commercial banks outreach to the rural economy and the government's commitment to anti-poverty programs. It may be argued that the so-called development outlook of the banking sector is in fact a reflected one and does not by itself signify its belief in the bankability of the poor.

The IRDP targets were achieved because the banks were compelled to do so. Several relaxations were made with respect to eligibility criteria, procedures, rate of interest, collateral security and guarantee for the loan etc. However, the viability of loans is open to question and the recovery performance has also not been satisfactory. A dilemma seems to exist between developing a sound banking system and simultaneously dealing with poverty.

There appears to be a mismatch between development goals and what is expected of economic/ financial prudence. Banks have generally shown disinclination to service the poor who are distanced spatially and metaphorically from them and hence whose risk profile is difficult to assess. In the recent years, economic factors eventually took precedence over the social agenda. Regional Rural Banks which were set up with the primary objective of meeting the credit needs of the weaker sections, were advised to lend 60 per cent of their incremental credit to the target population in the early 1990s. This was later brought down to 40 per cent and by end 1990s it was 10 per cent.

Further, frequent loan waivers and write-offs, which were steps taken in political interests, hastened the process of the erosion of the rural credit delivery system. Now there seems to be a general agreement among the banking authorities and development professionals that development agencies in the non-governmental sector should be called upon to act as intermediaries in the delivery and management of rural credit.

The formal sector consequently took the initiative to develop a supplementary credit delivery mechanism by encouraging non-governmental organizations (NGOs) to act as facilitators and intermediaries. Currently, the rural micro-finance sector is dualistic in nature. The formal structure has a legal and regulated component, which provides credit and other services to the non-formal sector. The non-formal structure largely comprising

NGOs, SHGs, clusters and federations of groups operate outside the legalized structure and have demonstrated considerable organizational flexibility and dynamism in responding to the demands at the grass roots.

The institutional mapping of the participants involved in micro- finance interventions spans from regulatory bodies (like the Reserve Bank of India and NABARD), to apex bodies that disburse bulk credit for onlending to intermediaries that are involved in providing financial services to clients, and finally to the clients themselves who are the beneficiaries of the initiative.

Institutional Mapping

Within the institutional mapping of micro- finance participants in India, the players constituting the regulatory bodies, apex bodies, and intermediaries, comprise those responsible for the supply side of the intervention. The clients constitute the demand side of the intervention. The regulatory body is primarily the Reserve Bank of India. NABARD also performs a regulatory role, although this bank features among the suppliers of bulk credit too.

The apex bodies, also called the wholesalers, are those who supply bulk credit for onlending purposes. Some of the major institutional sources of bulk credit to the Indian micro-finance sector consist of

- — NABARD, Mumbai;
- — Small Industrial Development Bank of India (SIDBI), Lucknow;
- — Rashtriya Mahila Kosh RMK, a government initiated NGO under the department of Women and Child Development;

— Housing and Urban Development Corporation (HUDCO), New Delhi;

— Housing Development Finance Corporation (HDFC), Mumbai;

— Friends of Women's World Banking (FWWB), Ahmedabad

The next components of the institutional mapping are the intermediary agencies, which comprise of banks of various kinds-scheduled, regional rural and co-operative, micro-finance institutions and facilitating NGOs.

Regulatory Bodies

Regulatory bodies like the Reserve Bank of India and NABARD, perform the role of officially regulating micro-finance interventions and providing directions for policy. The RBI sees the provision of micro credit by banks as an important instrument for poverty alleviation, particularly in the rural areas, as it raises the productive capacities of the beneficiaries. In keeping with this philosophy, in February 2000, banks were advised to make micro credit an integral part of their corporate credit plan.

Since then micro credit is reckoned as part of the banks' priority sector lending. Separate data about credit flow to women is to be generated by the banks and quarterly reports submitted to the RBI, which will create a separate database for women. Data are to be collected separately for micro credit, for credit to the small scale, medium scale and large scale industries. Already, most banks have started collecting data, as required, from the branches, on a periodic basis. The data is consolidated at the head offices.

A 14-Point Action Plan, which concerns credit for women, was outlined for implementation by banks. By the end of the first year of the implementation of this

Plan, factual data would be available on the number of women financed, the amount of credit flow extended to women as also the percentage to net bank credit. It is recommended that the RBI should prescribe a special format for data collection from the banks so that the data is available separately for amounts advanced to women entrepreneurs for micro credit, for small/medium/large scale industries.

NABARD is the primary agency for coordinating and facilitating the extension of rural credit. Commercial banks supplement the efforts of NABARD and co-operative banks, in meeting the credit requirements of rural India. In the year 2000, the RBI set up a special cell to liaise with NABARD and other institutions for augmenting the flow of credit. A Task Force was instituted by the Bank to evolve an organizational and regulatory framework for mainstreaming micro-finance operations.

Prior to that, the SHG - Bank linkage was introduced by NABARD in February 1992, as a Pilot Project to cover 500 SHGs with policy back-up from the RBI. NABARD brought together the SHGs already promoted by NGOs, and the banking system, to provide various financial services. The launch was tried in Karnataka and Tamil Nadu. The pilot phase was followed by the setting up of the Working Group on NGOs and SHGs by the RBI in 1994. This came up with wideranging recommendations on the internalization of the SHG concept as a potential intervention tool in the area of micro-finance.

Totally, under the linkage program, 81,780 SHGs were provided micro credit by banks during 1999-2000 bringing the cumulative number of SHGs credit linked to 114,775 as on 31March 2000. NABARD has also introduced the concept of bulk lending to NGOs in the form of revolving fund assistance to be provided on a selective basis to NGOs who find it difficult to secure loans from banks for on-lending to SHGs.

The amount of such assistance, cumulative upto September 1999 is Rs.110.7 million. NABARD provides 100 per cent refinance assistance to banks at an interest rate of 6.4 per cent per annum for financing SHGs. Cumulatively till March 31, 2000, the bank loans disbursed to the SHGs aggregated Rs.1929.8 million while NABARD's refinance availed of by the banks aggregated Rs.1501.3 million. NABARD has also been providing grants on a selective basis for the capacity building of the NGOs that are involved in microfinance activities.

The cumulative grant assistance sanctioned till March 31, 2000, for promotion and linkage of SHGs, aggregated to Rs.24.8 million, covering 72 NGOs and 16,911 SHGs. Additionally, NABARD also provides other types of support, such as, for training of bank staff, NGOs, and government agencies involved in the area of micro-finance. As on 31 March 2001, the regional spread of SHGs was as follows the cumulative number of SHGs credit linked in the northern region was 3222, in the north-eastern region was 196, in the eastern region was 9298, in the central region was 15256, in the western region was 7983 and in the southern region was 78720.

Totally in India 114,775 SHGs were credit linked as on 31 March 2001. NABARD's credit schemes are gender neutral. Focussed attention to gender issues in credit and support services, is given through the women's cell set up by NABARD where credit is provided in the form of refinance assistance to the banking system in respect of their advances for agricultural, allied sectoral rural cottage and village industries activities.

NABARD has brought out a number of schemes exclusively for the benefit of women- entrepreneurs. These are

— Assistance to Rural Women in Nonfarm Development (ARWIND)

— Support for setting up women development cells (WDC)

— Assistance for Marketing of Nonfarm Products of Rural Women (MAHIMA)

— Gender Sensitization Programs NABARD has also sanctioned a number of credit-linked promotional programs in the form of Rural Entrepreneurship Development Programs (REDPs), Artisan guilds, and Training-cum Production Centres (TPCs), with the intention of enhancing women's entrepreneurial capabilities and settling them into selfemployment and wage employment.

The research study 'Micro-finance Regulation in India', unravels the features of a self-regulatory mechanism in micro-finance in India. The sequel to the report of the National Task Force on Supportive Policy and Regulatory Framework for Micro-finance, had suggested the need to encourage the development of a self-regulatory mechanism and had also defined some of the broad parameters under which such a regulatory mechanism could be given shape.

The role of the government is seen as one that provides an enabling environment and does not proactively direct and control the activities of the participants. The potential objectives and benefits of self-regulation lie in

— Protecting the depositors,

— Offering saving services,

— Gaining access to refinance facilities

— Lower refinance costs,

— Enhancing the image of the sector,

— Helping MFIs build capacity and improve performance,

— Pre-empting regressive governmentintervention.

The report lists the participants that should come under self-regulation as - the SHGs; the Federations of the SHGs; NGO MFIs; NGO facilitators; Co-operatives; other formal MFIs like banks, NBFCs, and LABs. The Self-Regulatory Authority (SRA) is expected to verify if the MFIs are really serving the poor, set accountancy rules, reporting and disclosure requirements, establish prudential norms and performance standards, and accredit the complying MFIs. It is also expected to give credit ratings and provide deposit insurance financed from contributions of members. The study recommends that even if regulation norms and standards are established by the MFIs themselves, supervision must be done by an independent institution.

Wholesalers

Apex bodies are responsible for the disbursement of bulk credit for on lending purposes. Following are some of the major apex bodies operating in the Indian micro-finance sector. It must be noted here that NABARD is also an apex body along with being a regulatory one. As examples, below are outlined the operations of SIDBI and Rashtriya Mahila Kosh (RMK).

SIDBI Foundation for Micro Credit (SFMC), in November 1998. It is a fully functional separate department of SIDBI since January 1999. The Foundation is supposed to assist NGOs and voluntary organizations on soft terms, which would in turn extend micro credit to poor people. As of March 31 2001, the SFMC has 49 MFI clients. It has an outstanding loan portfolio of Rs. 332

million. 150,000 are ultimate clients, out of which 80 per cent are poor and 70 per cent are women.

SIDBI has designed a number of schemes and programs to support women entrepreneurs with financial assistance as well as providing training and extension services. These schemes are, Mahila Udhyam Nidhi, Mahila Vikas Nidhi, Micro Credit Schemes (MCS). Under the MCS fund, support is provided to well managed NGOs to on-lend to rural poor women to set up their own micro enterprises. Wherever SHGs exist, the NGO lends to them, and they in turn advance the credit to their members.

The cumulative assistance under MCS for the period March 1999, aggregated Rs. 307.1 million, channelised through 142 NGOs/ MFIs across 24 states/union territories benefiting over 112,000 rural poor, of which more than 90% were women. In all, 97 programs have been supported with the assistance of Rs. 6.7 million for providing training to 1550 NGOs in the areas of credit usage, management, monitoring and administration on credit programs.

The Government of India established the Rashtriya Mahila Kosh (National Credit Fund for Women), in 1993, with a corpus fund of Rs. 310 million. This initiative was taken since there was a need for a quasi-formal credit delivery mechanism which was client friendly, had simple and minimal procedures, disbursed credit quickly and repeatedly, had flexible repayment schedules, linked credit to thrift and savings, and had low transaction costs.

The Main Loan Scheme of the Kosh aims to provide credit to poor women both in the urban and rural areas for income generation activities (unless specifically sanctioned for other purposes). Specifically, women below the poverty line are eligible for support. The credit facility is channeled through eligible organizations to needy women without the insistence of collateral. During the year 2000-2001, totally in the country, RMK attended to 46,559 borrowers. The cumulative number of borrowers since inception upto 31, March 2001, was 406,942. During the same period, 861 new NGOs availed of RMK assistance and 354 repeated previous experience. In all, the amount sanctioned by RMK was Rs.1034.73 million and the amount disbursed was Rs. 765.53 million for the same period.

Intermediaries

The intermediaries consist of institutions that act as the link between the apex bodies and the clients. Public sector banks are currently extending credit facilities to women entrepreneurs both under Government sponsored schemes and under other schemes designed especially for women. The credit extended by Scheduled Commercial Banks (SCBs) primarily cover priority sector lending and the sponsoring of Regional Rural Banks (RRBs).

As reported in March 2000, the total priority sector lending of PSBs constituted 43.6% of net bank credit. The total priority sector lending of private sector banks as of the same date was 38.7 % of net bank credit. The Lead Bank Scheme (LBS) of the RBI is supposed to enhance the proportion of bank finance to the priority sector. This scheme co-ordinates the activities of banks and other developmental agencies.

As on 31, March 2000 the LBS have covered 575 districts. The co-operative banking system in India is structured along the following lines - the urban areas are served by the Primary (Urban) Co-operative Banks, whereas the rural areas have two sets of institutions dispensing short term and long term credit respectively. The former group consists of the State Co-operative

Banks at the apex levels, the District Central Co-operative Banks at the intermediary level, and the Primary Agricultural Credit Societies at the grass root level.

Under the long-term credit structure, the State Cooperative Agriculture and Rural Development Banks are at the apex level, the Primary Co-operative Agriculture and Rural Development Banks are at the base levels. NABARD has been working towards linking more self-help groups to the banking system also through the co-operative banking system. Further, in a significant move, since April 2000, micro credit/rural credit has been included in the list of eligible nonbanking financial companies' (NFBC) activity for being considered for FDI/OCB/NRI investment. This would cover extension of credit facilities at the micro level to small producers and small enterprises in the rural and urban areas.

Besides the data that is available with the RBI, NABARD and SIDBI, there are individual case studies of banks and their efforts to promote micro-finance among the rural poor. For example, the Cauvery Grameena Bank (CGB), a Regional Rural Bank (RRB) sponsored by the State Bank of Mysore, was launched on October 2, 1976. It now operates in three districts in Karnataka with a network of 118 branches. CGB has been actively financing SHGs prompted by NGOs since the launch of NABARD's pilot project during 1992-93.

In 1995- 96 CGB was identified as the first RRB in the country to participate in NABARD's project of promoting RRBs as Self-help Promoting Institutions (SHPI). By March 1998, the bank had formed 143 SHGs of which 92 are women's groups with a total membership of 2,135. The groups were able to generate savings of Rs.1,320,000 upto March 1998.

NGOs are the most preferred MFIs as they are particularly good providers of socially oriented financial services. Many of the NGOs have completely changed their strategies of social intermediation - from issue based activities to financial intermediation. Some of them are on their way to becoming formally established, self-sustaining commercial banks. The transition is not a simple switching from one activity to another. There is a radical transformation in the way NGOs have to function. These require dramatic changes in approach (from intensive area-centric planning to extensive target oriented planning); in the language of communication within the organization; in the language of communication between the organization and the people; the skills of functionaries in the organizational culture and in administrative practices.

The Government of India has initiated schemes that are directed towards extending micro credit towards rural poor households. Some schemes are exclusively directed towards women. Intermediaries are instrumental at various levels and in different capacities, in implementing these schemes. The SIDBI Best Practices Handbook in Micro-finance describes three types of NGO-MFIs depending upon the amount of savings they have mobilised. The first type are without deposit taking or have mobilised savings of less than Rs.0.2 million.

The second type are those with mobilised savings more than Rs. 0.2 million and less than Rs. 2.5 million. The third type of NGO-MFIs are those with mobilised savings more than Rs. 2.5 million. NGO-MFIs are functioning in diverse manners thereby generating different models of micro-finance interventions. The SIDBI Handbook has outlined fourteen different types of generic approaches that have evolved in India. These are

The basic SHG model and minor variations thereof: Examples of these are PRADHAN (Professional Assistance for Development Action), DHAN (Development of Human Action) Foundation, MYRADA

(The Mysore Rehabilitation and Development Agency), CARE (Co-operative for Assistance and Relief Everywhere) India, NBJK (Nav Bharat Jagriti). This type mobilises clients into self-help groups, which are mostly of women.

Shared problems of poverty, oppression and gender-based discrimination are used as entry points after which credit and savings are introduced. The SHG is not too large or too small and functions on a democratic basis. Savings are a compulsory feature of the SHG activity. Only those SHGs which have performed well and have sustained, are assisted with linkages with banks and other financial intermediaries like federations and clusters. Hence the NGO acts as a catalyst and performs the role of social intermediation. It plans, builds capacity, creates linkages to donors, and MFI wholesalers.

The Federated SHG Approach: Examples of these are PRADHAN, DHAN, MYRADA, Chaitanya, SEWA (Self Employed Women's Association), etc. NGO-MFIs such as these have federated several SHGs so as to overcome the limitations of individual SHGs. Federations when registered, usually come under the Societies Registration Act. They have between 1000-3000 members. In a three-tiered structure, the groups form SHGs after which clusters are formed and then Federations. In the two-tiered structure, the SHGs are directly federated.

The Rural Industries Promotion (SHG) Framework: MYRADA is an illustration of this kind of an approach, which attempts to facilitate delivery of a total package to women. The structure is so established that it manages itself like a private limited company for, by and of women.

The Pure/Adapted Grameen Replicator Approach: These undertake essentially, individual lending, but all borrowers are members of groups within which peer pressure is the key factor in ensuring repayment. Each borrower's credit-worthiness is determined by the overall credit worthiness of the group. Savings are a compulsory component of the loan repayment schedule, but do not determine the magnitude and timing of the loan. SHARE (Self Help Association for Rural Education and Employment), ASA (Association for Social Advancement), NBJK (Nav Bharat Jagrati Kendra) are examples of this approach.

The Urban Co-operative Banking Model: SEWA is an example of this kind of a model which primarily lends to the urban sector but has also extended its services to rural women. Savings groups consist of 10-15 members whose deposits range from Rs. 10-25 per month. These are collected from the women's homes by bank staff. The ability and motivation to save is an important pre-condition for a woman to be able to obtain credit.

The Co-operative Solidarity Model: ICNW (The Indian Co-operative Network For Women) is an illustration of this model where women organise themselves into neigbourhood-loan groups of 5-15 members. The women are residents of the same area and have lived there for a period of more than 5 years.

The Enabling Co-operative Networking Framework: The CDF (Co-operative Development Foundation) is an example of this approach. The CDF is a Not-for-Profit institution involved in promoting and supporting MFIs. This co-operative system consists of bringing together women's and men's thrift co-operatives which consist of 300 members usually from the same village.

The Co-operative-Grameen Hybrid Model: Mahila Vikasa is an example of this kind of an approach wherein it is registered as a Mutually Aided Co-operative Society (MACS), and covers clients in five different districts, three rural and two urban. The Society uses joint liability groups of five members each to provide loans.

The Ecelectic NBFC Approach: BASIX, a group company, is an example of this model of micro-finance. The mission of BASIX is to promote a large number of sustainable livelihoods through the provision of financial services and technical assistance in an integrated manner. The entire community is viewed as an interconnected whole, hence this institution involves the poor as well as the notso- poor.

Credit is seen as a necessary but not a sufficient condition for generating and sustaining livelihoods. BASIX consists of - a for-profit NBFC, Bharatiya Samriddhi Finance Ltd. which provides the financial services and a not-for-profit company, Indian Grameen Services, that provides the technical assistance.

— *The Training cum Production Centre Approach*: This approach is unique, since it provides for loans of raw materials rather than real money. Poor women are organised into groups of 5-10, which are then provided extensive training in the specific processes involved in any production activity. The members are then issued the raw material required for the particular production process that they are trained in. The value of the raw material is credited to their name as the loan amount.

— *The Kosh NBFC Model*: Sarva Jana Seva Kosh Ltd. (Kosh) is a non-banking financial company and is an example of this kind of approach. It is owned by the members of village communities, which provides a variety of financial services to a group of people, otherwise untouched by formal financial institutions. This insitution provides support to the Gram Sabha Nidhi foundations in managing the rural communities' financial resources.

— *The SHG Co-operative Model*: Youth Charitable Organisation (YCO), is a non-profit rural development agency based in Andhra Pradesh. This NGO works with the poorest marginalised rural families and promotes self-reliance and self-help. Programmes include micro-finance, housing, income- generation, water, sanitation, agriculture, health, education, agroforestry and waste-land management.

— *The Federated Society Model*: SIFFS is a large network of fishermen's organisations and currently operates in the states of Kerala and Tamil Nadu and the Union Territory of Pondicherry. It is to establish its operations in Andhra Pradesh too. The NGO has three core business areasfish marketing, technology intervention and credit delivery/facilitation (linkages with banks). SIFFS establishes bank linkages, enables fishermen to tap external funds and directly lends to members.

— *The SECTION 25 NBFC (Sanghamitra) Model*: This is a new model of micro-finance that attempts to cater mainly to the needs in mature SHGs. It is related to aspects of scaling-up and sustainability. It lends to mature SHGs with a good savings and credit background. Loans are disbursed in the form of cheques only and repayment is also collected in the form of cheques only. Consequently SHGs and its members understand and utilise banking mechanisms.

Data is available about the status, organizational working, operational functions, performance and operational dynamics of various MFIs in the country in different forms. One is through the institutions self-reporting to various evaluatory and rating organizations. Two is through the documentation and annual reports that the institutions maintain for their own records. Three is through the presentation of case studies of the institutions and their successes for different audiences. In addition MFIs/NGOs who are working with SHGs necessarily collect information about the groups that they are working with. As part of the operationalising of

SHGs and as a requirement of their functioning, the following documentation is carried out:

Accounting Systems which generally include

- *Cash Books*: Meant to record each cash transaction as it occurs in a meeting;
- *Member Ledger Book*: A document that is derived from the cash book which may be used to keep track of the current balance of each individual member in the group-her savings, loans taken and repayments;
- *Pass Books*: These are given to individual members to record their individual savings and loan status. In new groups, introducing pass books often encourages members to save more as they have a personalised document of their net savings amount;
- *The Minutes Book cum Attendance Register*: Used to record the proceedings of each meeting and the names of members present.
- *Loan and Repayment Forms*: To be filled each time a member takes a loan. Each form has details of the loan amount, the purpose for which the loan has been taken, the frequency of repayment and the amount of each installment.
- *General Ledger*: To be maintained along with the member ledger for receipt and payment transactions, common to the whole group.

The performance of the SHG is also documented using indicators that are seen as relevant to the situation and region. For example, the Cooperative Development Foundation (CDF) in Hyderabad, records performance with the help of the following indicators:

- Number of members;
- Number of Thrift Cooperatives;

— Association of Thrift Cooperatives (number);
— Regular Thrift (Rs.);
— Thrift Defaulters (number);
— Thrift Default Amount(Rs.);
— Members with recurring deposits (no.);
— Recurring Deposits (Rs.);
— Members with savings accounts (no.);
— Savings (Rs.);
— Members with fixed deposits (Rs.);
— Fixed deposits (Rs.);
— Members in DRAS(no.);
— DRAS deposits (Rs.);
— Other funds (Rs.);
— Total own funds;
— Borrowings (Rs.);
— Borrowers (no.);
— Loan outstanding (Rs.);
— Loan defaulters (no.);
— Loan default amount (Rs.);
— Average membership in a cooperative (no.);
— Average thrift per member (Rs.);
— Average loan outstanding (Rs.);
— Loans disbursed during the year (Rs.);
— Number of loans given during the year (Rs.);
— Average loan size during the year (Rs.)

What must be noticed here is that the variables documented and tracked are those which constitute the operational requirements of the intervention of micro credit. The process of empowerment that the intervention unleashes is not documented by the MFI/NGO. It is only later when outside agencies are entrusted with the task of assessment and evaluation that indicators of empowerment are looked into. The performance indicators that NGOs use in order to indicate that SHGs are performing well are more in the nature of meeting targets and proving financial sustainability.

While the importance of these indicators cannot be understated, it has to be noted that the purpose of the entire intervention is lost sight of. The changes in the lives of the clients on account of the generation of livelihoods in the form of enhanced economic and social status, alterations within households of structures of decision- making, etc. can be captured if change is monitored through qualitative variables as are used in impact evaluation studies.

Empowerment is a process and not a goal or target to be reached. Hence impact evaluation studies are not well equipped to document change. They can capture perceptions of respondents at one point in time. The NGOs/MFIs themselves can build in variables that allow for the processes of empowerment and change to be recorded. Changes in the standard of living, in household structures and roles, in mobility, in confidence and sense of self-worth can be part of the documentation carried out. Both the perceptions of field staff and of the clients themselves should be tracked.

Clients within the institutional mapping consist of the poor who are reached by micro-finance interventions. They are reached through SHGs. Certain intermediaries are involved in not just the formation and nurturing of

SHGs, but also in organizing them to form clusters and federations. The DHAN Foundation in Tamil Nadu and the FWWB in Gujarat are such institutions. The data on this account is largely available with the institutions and is both qualitative and quantitative in nature.

Data on individuals as participants in the institutional mapping is usually collected through impact evaluation studies. However, case studies of MFIs, of facilitating NGOs, and of the intervention of micro-finance per se, also include case studies of individual clients, which have benefited from the use of micro credit. In the process, the socioeconomic profiles of the individuals are documented and their experiences about availing of, using and repaying loans are documented. It must be noted here that the documentation is largely of 'success' stories, and cases that have failed to benefit from the intervention of micro-finance are rarely recorded.

Data related to the vertical approach also takes the form of being judgmental in nature. In fact these are the most significant types of data that exist in the intervention of micro-finance. Data which 'judges' is necessary to the intervention because, on the one hand there is no one model that can be deemed as 'ideal', and on the other hand, there is a need for some kind of consistency in the effort because the core needs of the poor are similar. Consequently, there are efforts to gather data that will throw light on the need for standardization, for regulation, for monitoring, etc. The most important of these kinds of data, is the rating that is undertaken on the basis of the financial performance of the MFI.

Over the past two and a half years, Micro-Credit Ratings India Limited (M-CRIL) a limited company established to facilitate the flow of commercial funds to the micro-finance sector has undertaken credit ratings of about 70 MFIs in South Asia. M-CRIL has compiled the information from its rating studies into a database and used it to analyze the performance of the microfinance sector in the region. This analysis of data from the 51 MFIs rated until end - November is contained in the M-CRIL Report 2000. Over the period September 1998 to November 2000, M-CRIL had completed 53 rating assignments, covering India, Nepal, and Bangladesh. MFIs are disaggregated by the methodology they adopt to function and by their age. They are classified by virtue of their methodology into

— Self-Help Group;

— Individual Banking model;

— Grameen model

According to their age they are classified into

— New institutions, which are less than three years old;

— Maturing Institutions, which are between 3-7 years old and;

— Mature Institutions that have undertaken micro-finance programs for more than 7 years.

The MFIs in the database have also been classified by the size of their outstanding portfolios at the time of the rating field visit. The sample by portfolio size shows that there are a few large MFIs and many small ones. As per the regional distribution of MFIs in India the south predominates but the west is also significantly important. M-CRIL awards grades to reflect the credistworthiness of the MFI. The data shows that relatively few MFIs are creditworthy enough to borrow money in excess of Rs. 2.3 million.

Based on indicators of 'best practices', data includes client outreach, productivity, efficiency, portfolio management of the MFI and financial performance. The top ten averages indicate that best practices are being followed in the concerned region. M-CRIL's ratings are intended as a direct service to lenders by providing them with an informed opinion of the credit worthiness of the MFIs. All ratings undertaken use a rating instrument that has been especially developed for the assessment of MFIs.

The instrument consists of a series of indicators that measures organizational and governance aspects, managerial and resource strengths, and financial performance. The indicators and standards for scoring on each indicator have been arrived at after an intensive process involving field-testing of the instrument, discussions with the experts and MFI leaders, literature survey and consultative meetings with the MFI support institutions that have made pioneering efforts in the area. Each indicator has a weight attached to it and is measured on a 0-10 scale.

The weights are used to compute the rating score for each indicator to arrive at a percentage score that determines the overall risk profile of the rated MFI. In addition, the rating instrument also evaluates the performance of the MFIs against minimum conditions. These conditions have been developed after an extensive analysis of M-CRIL's MFI data base and constitute some of the most crucial performance indicators.

Meeting these conditions is essential for the MFI to achieve a given rating grade. An important component of the methodology is to construct appropriate financial statements for the micro-finance operations of the MFI. This involves making detailed calculations of the various financial account heads.

The non-financial standards include governance, management practices, human resource management, track record of borrowing, relationship with community, local agencies, etc, outreach and impact, program design and external program. The financial standards include the track record in terms of repayment, financial performance, financial control system and accounting and reporting. Each of these factors listed above is linked to appropriate parameters, which have to be traced in order to set the best practices standards.

The MicroBanking Bulletin is one of the principal outputs of the MicroBanking Standards Project, which is funded by the Consultative Group to Assist the Poorest (CGAP). The purpose of this project is to

— Collect financial and portfolio data provided voluntarily by leading MFIs;
— Organize the data by peer groups;
— Report this information;
— Help through this database MFI managers and board members understand their performance in comparison with other MFIs;
— Establish industry performance standards;
— Enhance the transparency of financial reporting;
— Improve the performance of MFIs.

The Project seeks to provide customized financial performance reports; the MicroBanking Bulletin; and network services.

The available data points to areas in which improvements can take place. "Best Practices" have been outlined with respect to each of the above facets of the participants of micro-finance. In the context of SHGs and their functioning, BASIX has formulated a method of awarding scores while assessing SHGs. The interviewer has the choice of awarding the score within a range depending on the answer given.

SHGs are hence rated as very good, good, satisfactory, and not good. Generally, Best Practices are in the areas of SHG formation, nurturing, organization, financial management of the participants, especially the MFIs and SHGs, training of members vis-à-vis financial management, etc. There do not seem to be any outlined "Best Practices" to capture gender dimensions within micro credit interventions. Perhaps this is so because by and large the SHGs comprise of all women groups and it is assumed that issues related to them will automatically surface in the enumeration of other parameters.

In reality however, this assumption subsumes gender-related problems. Even if the groups are allwomen, the lives of women are not limited to their identities as members of SHGs. Household dynamics spillover and affect functioning within and of groups. Further, as a class, women suffer from discrimination in the community. The lapse on the part of Best Practices is, however understandable. Since available data does not squarely address gender biases, data formats are not equipped to capture variables that can track change in gender biases. Consequently Best Practices which draw their roots from available data also do not include gender dimensions.

As per the vertical approach, data that is generated points to the supply-side factors involved in the intervention of micro-finance. There is however a need also to document the factors that determine demand within micro-finance. Only when the supply and demand factors are studied together, an evaluation can be made of whether the intervention has been successful.

In as much as there is a mismatch between demand and supply, the primary goals of the intervention per se in terms of poverty reduction and empowerment of women will be at stake. In such a case, there will be a need for modifications, improvements and changes in the methods of micro-finance. The demand factors need to be observed from the perspective of all the participants since each of them has requirements that have to be correspondingly matched with the supply. The data on supply reflects information about products, services, capacity building, asset building, and training.

The demand factors will similarly reflect the needs of participants in the context of these parameters. The second and equally important data requirement of the vertical approach is to have data formats that are gendersensitive. As has been suggested in Will succeed in recording gender biases and also track changes both positive and negative in them. Since the second purpose outlined by the Summit is to empower women, it is necessary for data collection efforts to build-in variables that address change in women's lives from disempowerment to empowerment.

It is not enough to leave the task of tracking change to impact evaluation studies since their assessments are made after a lapse of time during which gender related change has not been documented. Similarly, the vertical approach needs to include qualitative and more detailed indicators of poverty. Micro credit has been primarily aimed at economic poverty. However, social poverty and gender discrimination are intimately connected with economic poverty, which is why development initiatives that address only economic poverty do not succeed in pulling the poor out of the poverty trap. This is not to underestimate the capacity of livelihoods, income and assets in improving the quality of lives.

If one goes back to the fourth purpose mentioned in the Summit of having a measureable impact in the lives of clients, such an impact is seen by existing data in the narrow sense of increase in livelihoods and incomes, which in turn are responsible for increases in self esteem. It is however, important to ascertain whether an initiatve that is narrow in scope as is micro credit, also has an effect in shifting positively, social poverty and gender discrimination indicators.

Conceptual Mapping

The second approach to data issues within micro-finance is through what has been called the 'horizontal approach'. This approach focuses upon the linkages between the conceptualization of micro- finance, the intervention and the impact of that intervention and is called the 'conceptual mapping'. The linkages are studied so as to determine whether the impact has justified the intervention and has ratified the conceptual premises on which the intervention is based.

The conceptual premises are given by the four core themes of the Micro credit Summit:

— Reaching the poorest;

— Reaching and empowering women;

— Building financially self-sufficient institutions; and

— Ensuring a positive and measurable impact upon the lives of clients and their families.

The 'intervention' has been highlighted by the institutional mapping and the corresponding data that has been generated in that context. The impact of the intervention cannot be understood unless one focuses upon many Impact Evaluation Studies that have been conducted by various organizations. The IES constitute the judgemental data relevant to the horizontal approach. The recommendations also dovetail towards contributing to resultant best practices about the functioning of NGOs and MFIs.

For any IES, the first question to be answered is the purpose of the study. Most often the study is conducted by an NGO/ funding organization, or academic/research institution. The reasons for undertaking an IES can vary from the need for policy formulation/modification within the organization, to wanting to assess the changes in the lives of the clients, to influencing policy makers, practitioners and researchers on the basis of the findings, or a combination of these. Again IES may be conducted by the staff of the concerned organization, or by an external consultancy firm/consultant.

Particularly important are the methods used in IES. It is seen that almost all the studies definitely have a combination of methods and do not rely on one method only. This combination is mostly one of purposive sampling, where the respondents are administered structured questionnaires; selective sampling of beneficiaries whose case studies are documented, and focus group discussions where issues are brought out into the open. These methods are in stark contrast to the Participatory Rural Appraisal (PRA) methods that recruit local persons to appraise.

While the value of PRAs cannot be denied, it is not always possible for institutions that require IES to find suitable local persons to conduct PRAs. This is especially true if the study is being conducted by an 'outside' agency which does not have an intimate rapport with the village(s) under scrutiny. Whatever be the method, it is important for researchers to be focussed about hypotheses and variables that are being sought as reflections of 'impact'. The difference between variable, parameter, and indicator should not be blurred over.

Bibliography

Acton, D.F and L.J. Gregorish (eds). "The health of our soils : toward sustainable agriculture in Canada. Ottawa: Agriculture and Agri-Food Canada", 1995. 120 p.

Agarwal, Anil and Sunita Narain, *Towards green villages : a strategy for environmentally sound and participatory rural development*, New Delhi: The India Centre for Science and Environment, 1989. 51 p. : ill.

Alders, Carine and others (eds). *Linking with farmers : networking for low-external-input and sustainable agriculture,* London: Intermediate Technology Publications, 1993. 298 p.

Barbier, Edward B. (ed). *Economics and ecology: new frontiers and sustainable development*. London: Chapman & Hall, 1993. 205 p.

Baudry, Jacques. "Interactions between agricultural and ecological systems at the landscape level." *Agriculture Ecosystems and Environment* 27 (1989) : 119-130. Amsterdam: Elsevier Science, 1989. 12 p.

Beets, Willem Cornelis. Raising and sustaining the productivity of smallholder farming systems in the Tropics : a handbook of sustainable agricultural development. Alkmarr, NL: AgBe Publishing, 1990. 738 p. : ill.

Bollman, Ray D. and Richard C. Rounds. "Employment trends in rural Manitoba : the role of manufacturing". *RDI report series*. No.1993-6. Brandon: Brandon University Rural Development Institute, 1993. 73 p.

Brklacich, Michael and others. "Forum: review and appraisal of concept of sustainable food production systems."

Environmental Management 15(1) : 1-14. New York: Springer-Verlag, 14 p.

Brown, Lester R., "The changing world food prospect: the nineties and beyond" *Worldwatch paper no.85*. Washington, DC: Worldwatch Institute, 1988.

Burke, Stan., *People first : a guide to self-reliant participatory rural development*. London: Zed Books, 1993. 256 p.

Edwards, Clive A. "The importance of integration in sustainable agricultural systems." *Agriculture Ecosystems and Environment* 27(1989) : 25-35.

Engelman, Robert and Pamela LeRoy. *Conserving land : population and sustainable food production*. Washington, D.C.: Population Action International, 1995. 48 p.

Feath, Paul, "Evaluating agricultural policy and the sustainability of production systems: an economic framework ". *Journal of Soil and Water* (March/April, 1993): 94-99. 1993.

Gates, Jane Potter, *Educational and training opportunities in sustainable agriculture*. (6th ed.) Beltsville, MD: United States National Agricultural Library, 1993. 31 p.

Gold, Mary V., *Sustainable agriculture : definitions and terms*. Special reference briefs no.SRB 94-05. Beltsville, MD: United States National Agricultural Library, 1994. 10 p.

Izac, A-M.N. and M.J. Swift. "On agricultural sustainability and its measurement in small-scale farmining in sub-Saharan Africa." *Ecological Economics 11* (1994): 105-125. New York: Elsevier, 1994. 20 p.

Jahn, Laurence R. and Eric W. Schenck. "What sustainable agriculture means for fish and wildlife." *Journal of Soil and Water Conservation* (July-August 1991): 251-255.

Postel, Sandra, "Water for agriculture: facing the limits". *Worldwatch paper no.93*. Washington, DC: Worldwatch Institute, 1989.

Scruggs, Patricia and Angela Park (ed)., *Guidelines for state level sustainable development*. Washington, D.C.: Center for Policy Alternatives, 1993. 75 p.

Index